# in defense of PARTISAN CRITICISM

FRONTIERS IN POLITICAL COMMUNICATION

Lynda Lee Kaid and Bruce Gronbeck
*General Editors*

Vol. 7

PETER LANG
New York • Washington, D.C./Baltimore • Bern
Frankfurt am Main • Berlin • Brussels • Vienna • Oxford

OMAR SWARTZ

# in defense of PARTISAN CRITICISM

## communication studies, law, & social analysis

PETER LANG
New York • Washington, D.C./Baltimore • Bern
Frankfurt am Main • Berlin • Brussels • Vienna • Oxford

**Library of Congress Cataloging-in-Publication Data**

Swartz, Omar.
In defense of partisan criticism: communication studies,
law, and social analysis / Omar Swartz.
p. cm. — (Frontiers in political communication; v. 7)
Includes bibliographical references and index.
1. Communication in politics. 2. Communication in social action.
3. Rhetoric—Political aspects. I. Title. II. Series.
JA85.S85 302.2'24—dc22 2005015698
ISBN 0-8204-6940-8
ISSN 1525-9730

Bibliographic information published by **Die Deutsche Bibliothek**.
**Die Deutsche Bibliothek** lists this publication in the "Deutsche
Nationalbibliografie"; detailed bibliographic data is available
on the Internet at http://dnb.ddb.de/.

Cover design by Sophie Boorsch Appel

For my wife, Rui Zhao, and son, Avi Zhao Swartz

— *Without love, there is no justice.*

*All universities worthy of the name have always been centers of social protest. If American universities ever cease to be such centers, they will lose both their self-respect and the respect of the learned world. It is doubtful whether the current critics of the universities who are called "conservative intellectuals" deserve this description. For intellectuals are supposed to be aware of, and speak to, issues of social justice.*

(Richard Rorty, 1998a, 82)

# CONTENTS

*Acknowledgments* ........ xiii
*Foreword: In Support of Partisan Criticism by Phillip K. Tompkins* ........ xv

Introduction ........ 1

PART I: AIM AND SCOPE OF PARTISAN CRITICISM

Chapter 1: Animating the Communicative Imagination ........ 19

Chapter 2: Endorsing Critical Education as a Corrective for Alienation ........ 27

Chapter 3: Confronting the Barrier of the US Constitution for Change and Social Justice ........ 37

Chapter 4: Offering a Radical Critique of the Problem of the Present ........ 55

Chapter 5: Outlining a New Vision of Law, Social Justice, and Power ........ 63
Toward a Critical Legal Perspective ........ 65
A Theory of Power: Duality and Community ........ 69
Power as Constitutive of Community ........ 73

PART II: INTELLECTUAL AND CRITICAL ASSUMPTIONS OF THE PARTISAN CRITIC

Chapter 6: Academic Scholarship Is Often a Constraint to Social Justice ........ 81
The Example of "Sextext" ........ 82
The Traditional Disciplinary Persona ........ 85

Chapter 7: Materiality Is an Important Challenge for Professional Criticism ... 101
Rorty on Cruelty and Struggle ... 111

Chapter 8: Partisan Criticism Has a Commitment to Labor and the Poor ... 119
Definition of "Working Class" ... 120
The Importance of Equity in Labor Relations ... 121
Labor's Role in Communicating Hope ... 127

PART III: LAW, LABOR, DEMOCRACY, RACISM AND COMMUNITY: CASE STUDIES IN PARTISAN CRITICISM

Chapter 9: Defending Labor in *Commonwealth v. Pullis*: Contemporary Implications for Rethinking Community ... 139
The Economic and Social Context Behind Labor Unrest in the United States ... 139
The First Labor Case ... 142
Context for the Conspiracy Charge ... 143
Analysis of *Pullis* and the Construction of Community ... 145

Chapter 10: The Challenge of Anarchism and Its Lessons for Partisan Criticism ... 159
Haymarket Bombing and Trial of Prominent Anarchists ... 167

Chapter 11: Eugene Debs, Reformist-Socialism, and the Pullman Strike of 1894 ... 177
Comparing Reformist-Socialism and Anarchism ... 178
The Pullman Strike and Its Effects ... 181

Chapter 12: Law, Community, Racism, and Slavery ... 195
The Term "Racial Tension" Is Misleading ... 196
The Judiciary and the Power of Discourse ... 203

Natural Law, Positive Law, and Slavery ................ 205

Chapter 13: Definitional Assumptions and Differential Arguments in the Construction of the Law of Slavery in North Carolina ................ 215
Richard Weaver and the Politics of Definition ...... 216
Disciplining White Violence ................ 220
Debating the Integrity of the Slave's Self ................ 232

Chapter 14: In Search of Political Transcendence ................ 245
Transcending to the Human Community ................ 246
Ethnic Conflict and National Identity ................ 248
Elite Control and Its Effect on the Quality of Life ................ 252
The Kropotkin Solution ................ 255

*Bibliography* ................ 261
*Index* ................ 289

# ACKNOWLEDGMENTS

All writers grow from the dialectical experience of sharing their developing ideas with others. In the case of this book, my thinking was greatly enhanced by the careful (and critical) readings and suggestions offered by Ryan Bloom, Kimberly Elliott, Professor Lawrence Frey, Professor Bruce Gronbeck, Heidi Roat, and Professor Phillip K. Tompkins. I particularly want to thank Professor Gronbeck for his commitment to this project. His editorial feedback on previous drafts of this book was both generous and compassionate. He may not agree with everything I wrote, but he believed in me and in my vision. His support made all the difference in the world. I am immensely grateful for his help.

The book was professionally formatted by Dee Morgenthaler, a graduate student of mine. I appreciate the time and energy she put into her task. I thank my wife, son, and mother for their love, patience, and understanding of my life as a scholar. I want to thank Professor Michael Monsour, my colleague at University of Colorado at Denver and Health Sciences Center, who embodies a dignity rare in the academy. Finally, I want to thank Professor Philip C. Wander, the intellectual grandfather of all my writing, for having inspired me with his path-breaking scholarship on ideological criticism. From him I learned that scholarship can have a soul.

Portions of this book have appeared, in slightly different forms, in the following: *Bad Subjects: Political Education for Everyday Life; E Law: Murdoch University Electronic Journal of Law; Ethical Space: The International Journal of Communication Ethics; Human Nature Review; In Motion Magazine; Mississippi Review; Nature, Society, Thought; Reconstruction: Studies in Contemporary Culture; Shout!; Secular Nation; Socialism & Democracy;* and the *Thurgood Marshall Law Review.* I thank each of these publishers for their permission to reprint the material here.

# FOREWORD

*Phillip K. Tompkins*

## IN SUPPORT OF PARTISAN CRITICISM

It was my great intellectual pleasure to read *In Defense of Partisan Criticism*, by Omar Swartz, in manuscript form. My initial response, rather reflex, was that he had chosen the wrong phrase for his title and program. Partisan criticism sounded too much like Republicans screaming at Democrats and Democrats yelling back. Since Newt Gingrich's election to the position of Speaker of the House of Representatives, partisan rhetoric has reached a degree of polarization that is destructive to the country and its people. I came to be convinced, however, that Swartz did not get to choose the terms of the debate. The phrase was already in the conversation when he joined it.

My own education in criticism led me to accept the idea of a neutral analysis of rhetorical artifacts; as a professor of comparative literature, I came also to accept that field's objective, known in English as the explication of the text. Reading Swartz's manuscript, however, I was moved by his use of Richard Rorty's work, particularly the idea that all intellectual work ought to be "aware of, and speak to, issues of social justice."

I was also reminded of the first lecture I heard Kenneth Burke deliver—it had this rather awkward title, as I recall: "On the Suasive Nature of Even the Most Ordinary Nomenclatures." After revisions, it was published under the more familiar title: "Terministic Screens." Revisiting Burke's lecture in 1962, I recalled how he showed us that the basic terms of a discipline, its nomenclature, had a suasive effect on the field's work. No general theory of human action, for example, could emanate from one of the specific social sciences for the reason that each justified its own existence by a distinct nomenclature, a set of terms that screened in certain types of action and screened out others. Our nomenclature determined what we looked at and what we ignored. At that time, our field was known by a single word: *Speech*. This term placed suasive blinders on us, forcing us to concentrate on orality. Many of us fought to change the name of our departments and associations with terms such as *rhetoric* and *communication*—so that we could work on nonoratorical forms and study how different media work together to produce effects. That lecture by Burke forty some years ago taught that academic discourse is by its nature suasive; and that includes criticism.

Swartz would have us imitate his critical method, would have us become partisan critics who abandon ethnic and nationalist provincialisms in favor of pursuing social justice for all the people of the planet. He wants us to criticize the maldistribution of wealth and power and justice. I was so taken by this notion of criticism as a medium of achieving social justice that I imitated his approach in my keynote address to the Rocky Mountain Communication Association in 2003. In that address, I drew on my background in organizational communication to criticize corporate power, and its abuse, in contemporary America. The corporate scandals were widely reported in the press, ranging from antisocial actions in organizations and institutions ranging from Enron to the US Catholic Church. A member of the audience peppered me, at my conclusion, with hostile questions about my practice of drawing on sources in the liberal media. She was clearly unhappy about my application of partisan criticism to what was being reported on a daily basis. Later I revised the speech into a chapter of a book that I was writing on the decline of the US space program. In one of the prepublication reviews an angry critic singled out that chapter for some partisan criticism, branding the chapter as the mere expression of Phil Tompkins's opinions, despite the documentation of facts and analyses of them.

I like to think my two critics were in the minority. I mention the two incidents to demonstrate the possible costs of partisan criticism. One can be labeled a dupe of the press and the promulgator of mere opinion. Partisan criticism will be heard and read as ideological diatribe. It will evoke ideological rebuttals. Some of these will come from outside the ivy-covered walls of the academic world. The Governor of Colorado, the state where Omar Swartz teaches, recently attacked the ideological commitments of the faculty employed in the state's colleges and universities. Specifically, he said he wanted to see more Republicans in Political Science departments.

Regardless of the risks associated with partisan criticism, I must agree with Swartz that what we say and write is connected to our "political, social, moral, philosophical and aesthetic commitments." Partisan criticism will fail, however, unless it embraces more than ideology. It must also be *just* in the discovery and presentation of the evidence, scholarly in its critical analyses and, of course, have the highest regard for telling the truth.

I now move from the abstract to the concrete in supporting partisan criticism. Swartz takes partisan criticism in a turn only he could make. Perhaps there are others in the field who could have done it, but I do not know where to look for them. Who else has his training in rhetorical criticism and legal studies, layered over his distinct set of political commitments? The turn taken by Swartz is what he calls a "Critical Legal Perspective."

His chapter on the limitations of the US Constitution had something approaching a profound effect on me. In this, and in another book-length manuscript by Swartz I have read (*The Rule of Law, Property, and the Violation of Human Rights: A Plea for Social Justice*), he rekindled the fury I felt in my undergraduate course in Constitutional History. I eagerly pointed out to him, in response, a study I had seen by an Israeli scholar who concluded that the only democracy in the world that could elect an executive president with fewer votes than his principal opponent is the United States of America. Only in America, and it happened several years ago because of an archaic, obsolete provision in our Constitution—the Electoral College.

The labor chapters also reminded me of a graduate class in Economics and Labor Law. They also reminded me of Burke's fascinating analysis of the concept of *property*. Burke said, in a lecture at University of Colorado at Boulder in 1987, that the settlement of the US West transformed the lands of the Native Americans into *real estate*. Swartz shows how the notion of property has skewed court decisions and laws into a sad state of injustice.

Swartz turns his critical-legal perspective on the law of community, slavery, and racism; the result is a withering, yet persuasive, criticism of our past and present. His chapter titled "Definitional Assumptions and Differational Arguments in the Construction of the Law of Slavery in North Carolina" is a *tour de force*.

I present myself, therefore, as a supporter of partisan criticism. Those who have not yet read this good book have a delightful moment of finality to look forward to when they read Swartz's treatment and recommendation of the Kropotkin solution. I endorse it in its idealism and with what I hope will become an increasing sense of solidarity.

# INTRODUCTION

This book is about my passion for *partisan criticism*, defined here, in part, as the integration of scholars' lives and values with their scholarship to enact a profound commitment to social justice. Because the ideal of social justice is such an important construct animating this book, it must be defined. In general, social justice is a commitment that scholars have to reducing the suffering of the poor. It envisions a redemptive, progressive social change in the form of a movement toward *social democracy* or *democratic socialism*—a society grounded in equitable social, economic, and political relationships. An implicit assumption of a social justice perspective is that the integrity of any community is violated when some of its members are systematically deprived of their dignity or equality through poverty or class oppression.

This book seeks two ways of understanding social justice, based on unorthodox notions of rhetoric. The first is to understand how *rhetoric*—defined broadly as the sustained social manipulations by cultural elites—affects society in ways that lead to a limiting of thought and to the lessening of cultural and economic opportunity for a large sector of society. The second is to understand *rhetoric*—defined broadly as a liberating counter-discourse, the act of speaking truth to power—as a method for the flowering of new potentials for thought and experience. Scholars can understand these limitations and potentials to attain a degree of power over them. This power is not a selfish or self-serving power but a healing power—a power of peace, balance, and reconstruction. This power can be used as a means of correcting the many wrongs of the world. Scholars lack the sword and should reject the sword if it were offered to them. The power we covet is the power of ideas, the power to see swords as arguments lost.

The phrase "speaking truth to power" is not original; it is an inspiring slogan animating much intellectual resistance throughout the twentieth century. In using it, this book honors the intellectual tradition it represents. Such language is problematic, however, in light of an assumption grounding this book that truth is relative. Although many scholars in the humanities and social sciences reject traditional notions of truth, this does not obligate them to give up practical distinctions between right and wrong or just and unjust. These distinctions "must be argued, constructed; they do not simply present themselves to the discerning eye" (Agger, 1990, 57). As will be developed later, the truth animating this book is that which helps the poor and powerless resist an overwhelming political and military power intent on perpetuating their poverty.

This book's goal is to help redescribe US society so as to enable inclusive and fair communities to emerge. Its representations seek to construct communities that protect individual freedom and ensure everyone equality and dignity. Thus, an important objective is to critique the practices of hierarchy, elitism, racism, and inequality in the United States. There is no reason why this critique cannot be offered from the position of the university professor or through the literature produced by scholars. A scholarship of social justice is not incompatible with more traditional research. It is merely different:

> The social justice sensibility does not even pretend to be objective, neutral, or dispassionate, even though these are among the most important virtues identified by the dominant discourse in research methodology texts. Rather, social justice research makes an explicit "preferential option" for those who are disadvantaged by prevalent social structures or extraordinary social acts; it emerges from and channels the emotions of the researcher. (Frey, Pearce, Pollock, Artz, and Murphy, 1996, 115)

Embracing this description does not require that scholars cast aside their professional persona; rather, it means that scholars may assume an academic world in which they take none of their assumptions for granted but, instead, evaluate the relative worth of their work in terms of its social utility. The most fundamental assumption of this book is that there is no worthier end for measuring social utility than the abolishment of social injustice. Thus, it is important to critique what appears to be the concrete nature of the social, political, and economic worlds, as well as the histories concerning those worlds to suggest new options for establishing social, economic, and political relationships.

## II

The word "partisan" has roots in French, Italian, and Latin. The Italian *partisano* (*parte* means "part") comes from the Latin, *participatio*, meaning "participation" or "participant" (Pinkerton, 1982). In Latin, *participium* means "that which takes part" (Pinkerton, 1982). In 1658, the French word *partifan* was defined as "a partaker or partner" (Phillips, 1969). In context, partisan was a descriptive term for a person who stood for some ideal, party, or value related to the good of a community; to be partisan was to make common cause with others to fight, resist, and transform an inequitable status quo. In the nineteenth century, Noah Webster (1970) defined the English word *partisan* as "a person able in commanding a party, or dexterous in obtaining intelligence, intercepting convoys or otherwise annoying an enemy." Exemplifying Webster's definition is the partisan resistance movement to the Nazis throughout occupied Europe during the Second World War (Simpson and Weiner, 1989). In short, to be partisan has come to mean being oppositional, joining with others with a deep commitment to be a part of a counterforce to normative power (Ayto, 1990). The following passage from Michael Chowaniec (1998), Chair of the Burlington Republican Town Committee, illustrates this point:

> It is important to recognize that being "partisan" in its original definition is valuable, even (or especially) at the local level. Burlington, like most Connecticut towns, has a history of being under the influence of one party for long periods of time. Our current Democratic First Selectman, Mr. Scheidel, has been in office for the last 18 years. Before him, Mr. Spielman, a Republican, served our town for many years. In these circumstances, an active "opposition" party is necessary to ensure a healthy debate on issues. This loyal opposition party serves to avoid the inevitable paralysis and stagnation that occurs when any party, Democratic or Republican, is in power for too long.

The term "partisan," however, is commonly understood as denoting a person who speaks on behalf of a political machine and carries connotations of a person being imbalanced, unreasonable, zealot, pathological, or biased (*Oxford American Dictionary of Current English*, 1999). This book rejects this sense of the term and embraces the heroic tradition of partisanship that suggests political resistance and redescription, particularly as directed toward change in US culture. In the context of this book, partisan criticism is an *attitude*—a will to create solutions to reduce the suffering caused by political, legal, and economic alienation. Partisan scholarship embraces a deep commitment to a cause and the championing of an ideal—social justice.

Fundamental to this book's notion of social justice is the assumption that the human condition is articulated by humans and is *not* the result of a metaphysical source. As Richard Rorty notes, human beings are a work in progress—unfinished texts—and are incapable of completion "because there is nothing to complete, there is only a web of relations to be rewoven, a web which time lengthens every day" (1989a, 43). In other words, the human world is radically contingent in that morality, truth, and our sense of other foundations are subject to periodic reevaluation (as in Nietzsche, 1997). Progressive people should take pleasure in this thought, for it suggests that society can be *different* and, hopefully, *better* (defined as a world in which social hope and progressive transformation flourishes).

An assumption this book makes is that the exemplification of social justice between individuals should be fundamental to organized human society. Without a profound commitment to social justice, a society may be well organized, hierarchally situated, and possess a well-developed legal system, but it would likely be one in which oppression is legitimated and human dignity sacrificed. The United States, in some respects, is one such society.[1]

A social justice perspective works to free society from the bonds of tradition, superstition, entrenched privilege, and faith in the superiority of the present over the potentials of the future. Yet changing the social, political, and economic orders is difficult. People often resist change because they benefit greatly from the current structured relations. Others, those who do not benefit from the social order but think that they should, often remain committed to the status quo, clinging to the hope that they will benefit in the future. Still others resist change because they believe that human beings require an anchor, a standard, or a foundation to determine what is uniquely special about them; they mistakenly view the current economic system, for instance, as such an anchor. Such fear, although genuine, is misplaced. The real terror lies not in the absence of faith but in the cruel practices of the material present (many of which are critiqued in this book). The current preeminence of neoliberalism results not from the correspondence of the capitalist vision with truth, but from the collapse of socialist and communist alternatives. Logically, the collapse of these alternatives does not justify neoliberalism nor attest to its supposed foundational qualities. Change from the current order is inevitable: The question is not whether society will change, but when will it change and how can we ensure that such change will be progressive?

This book is both personal and public. As far back as Aristotle, the public persona was recognized as being intimately tied to private selfhood, such that people gain influence with others through who they are as individuals. Aristotle called this influence *ethos* and argued that it was more important than the emotions appealed to by a rhetor or to the reasoning used in an argument. In other words, we are the message; we are what we speak and write and our messages are processed in relation to how others perceive us. Some scholars (what this book defines as *critical intellectuals*) engage in research because they identify with a certain academic persona and need the tools provided by that persona. These people can be known as "life scholars"; they do not pursue truth but, instead, pursue their life through their work, inventing themselves and their communities as they proceed through their inquiry. For them, each publication becomes a building block in their subjective knowledge and community identity—a bridge simultaneously *to* and *from* themselves and their social worlds.

## III

As noted above, this book assumes a view of truth that is contingent and impermanent. It critiques what US society often assumes to be true—what the founding documents of the United States consider to be "self-evident" and impervious to change. In challenging the status of these truths, this book's narrative seeks to replace them with other truths, other visions of the good. These new truths are ways of discussing important political and moral preferences and, at the same time, recognizing the partiality and temporality of these commitments. The terms "truth" and "real" as implied in this book are—in spite of their limitations—convenient terms for championing the book's narrative. When these terms appear or are implied, they should not be understood as metaphysical claims, but rather to be shorthand for statements that I find useful, particularly those that help create substantive and ameliorative changes in the lives of those who suffer from poverty and oppression.

As children, people are given truths about the world and their place in that world. They are taught not to see, not to feel, and not to understand the larger macroinfluences in their lives. Specifically, they are taught not to question the forces of their society that cause so much suffering and destruction in the world. Instead, they are taught to focus on the microelements of their lives, emphasizing comfort and security at the expense of a critical awareness of the larger society (Slater, 1970, 2). This practice contributes to the profound alienation of the nation, in which the excessive pursuit of "comfort" and "security" results in neither. As Anthony M. Platt observes, the United States "has the largest, most complex, most expensive, and most punitive system of justice in the world" and, yet, public safety "is an illusion" (2001, 140). Since September 11, 2001, this insecurity has become increasingly globalized.

When world problems are ignored, they become chronic, and their causes are further mystified and obfuscated. As discomfort and insecurity creep in, what appears to be the richness of people's lives turns out to be little more than crass, cultural scripts, written by others, in which most people have been given bit parts. At this junction, it becomes possible to appreciate how language has been divorced from experience and how the world created for us does not have to be the world in which we live. In his reflections on the holocaust, Bert Lang discusses this power of language:

> [The] language of genocide, even in its many complex facets, reveals the singular intention to turn language itself into an instrument of domination and deceit, enabling in practice and principle an act that controverts the most basic ideals of moral life as it denies the social reality of language and then the reality of human experience beyond that. (1988, 357)

As people struggle to find ways to articulate their discontent, they often face the realization that few others can understand them; their existential pain is often as incomprehensible to others as others' pain is to them; this is the condition of alienation, which occurs when people forget how to relate to each other and to themselves as human beings:

> Alienation reduces us to objects. It dehumanizes us. It erases the complexity of our humanity. It stops us from questioning and acting on our questions. Its

> most potent effect, however, is the undermining of our faith in a better tomorrow. With that our ability and willingness to fight are diminished. The result is fatalism and nihilism. It is for these reasons that alienation poses such a pernicious threat to our well-being. (Rodriguez, 2001, 63)

Alienation is a powerful condition that makes people susceptible to manipulation, coercion, hierarchy, and oppression. Alienation is most severe when people internalize the limitations imposed on them by society, so that they come to see manipulation, coercion, and hierarchy as natural and the existence of such phenomena in the world as inevitable. In this state, people are degraded; they become servants to a master—the advertiser, the company, the official, the teacher, the preacher, everyone and everything that screams at them to be "normal," to conform.[2] The master is the monster that demands silence and obedience—that which makes the insane appear as sane and illness appear as health.

In a fundamental sense, an understanding of alienation cannot be taught; it must be experienced, and that experience must be translated into a vocabulary. For example, the way I learned about alienation was through books that opened my mind to ways of thinking and knowing that contrasted with what the dominant culture advances as truth. Writers such as Kenneth Burke, Noam Chomsky, Michel Foucault, Emma Goldman, Russell Jacoby, Martin Luther King, Jr., Karl Marx, Friedrich Nietzsche, Michael Parenti, Neil Postman, Richard Rorty, Bertrand Russell, Lu Xun, and Howard Zinn convinced me that humanity is at war with itself and that conscientious people must choose sides. Since realizing this, there has been no doubt in my mind where my sympathies lie—in Albert Camus's terms, I side with the victims against their persecutors.

Many people attend college with the expectation that an education will help them to alleviate the suffering of people in the world, naively believing that the function of the university is to educate students to improve society. Yet, similar to the experience of Kent A. Ono, they are often "disheartened to learn over and over again just how often the University speaks on behalf of the United States . . . or on behalf of the US armed forces" (1997, 123; also see Sciffrin, 1997). Moreover, the apparent openness of the university is "tempered by a tacit valuing process wherein some questions are considered more laudable or interesting than others, the lives of some individuals are likely to receive our attention to the exclusion of others, and some approaches to research are praised while others are ignored, distorted, or disparaged" (Spitzack and Carter, 1989, 12). Realizing this, many students and scholars become disillusioned:

> My life in the academy has not turned out the way I had anticipated when I so eagerly pursued the career as a graduate student. I entered the profession because I believed it offered me the opportunity to do politically meaningful work, to use my scholarship and my teaching in support of an agenda for social change and progressive values. I was inspired by the idea of the transformative intellectual who might serve as a catalyst for initiating real change in the classroom and, ultimately, in the world beyond that classroom. (Boyd, 1999, 379)

Once we understand that progressive truth is not the inevitable end of a college education, we can learn to appreciate that for such truth to exist, it must be created from the fragments of ideas that circulate throughout the academy, embodied in the hopes and the despairs of human beings. Furthermore, we can see that all the things that define our society—notions of freedom, justice, and equality—are not what they suggest; instead, they often serve as rhetoric for manipulation and control. Since no one "owns" this rhetoric, the same language and the same economy of thought that mystify can also be used to edify. Thus, we should take seriously Robert L. Scott and Donald K. Smith's call for a study of communication that takes "into account the charge that civility and decorum serve as masks for the preservation of injustice, that they condemn the dispossessed to non-being, and that as transmitted in a technological society they become the instrumentalities of power for those who 'have'" (1969, 8).

Humans are free to define for themselves the world anew, but given that the weight of the status quo is heavy, humans frequently need inspiration. Such inspiration can be drawn from the thought that change is always possible; that dullness, boredom, poverty, cruelty, excessive wealth, and violent institutions are impermanent; and that they are all symptoms of the same disease—the stultification of power. Power and freedom need to flow and be shared to be healthy. Power, in other words, can be approached as diffuse and collective. People are truly free when their communities are free and they are only healthy when power flows through them—affirming and sustaining them. Within the United States, however, power has not flowed diffusely and communities are often unhealthy (many are gated and many are decayed). In spite of this, there is an unquenchable human will that rises frequently in the most unlikely of places, like a flower at Auschwitz—hope in the face of hopelessness. In theory, this will is limitless; in practice, however, this will is often constrained.

The view of the human will championed in this book is grounded in a species wide solidarity. For example, when I contemplate my son, a boy barely past his toddler years, I feel an immense love for him. Yet, I am painfully aware that all my love for him is shallow if I do not feel as much love for someone else's child. To love my son is to love *the* child, not my *possession* of him. For me to love my own offspring, but not to care as much about other children, suggests that the love I have for my son is a selfish love. As Martha C. Nussbaum warns, "Compassion for our own children can so easily slip over into a desire to promote the well-being of our children at the expense of other people's children" (2003, 13). Following the Israeli invasion of Palestine in 2002, I had a conversation with an Israeli in which I criticized Israel for, among other things, killing Palestinian babies. After cursing the Palestinians, the Israeli responded that she did not "give a damn" about Palestinian babies and wished for the Palestinian people to "disappear." This response was paradigmatic, for most people are guilty of hating others at some point in time. When we express this hate, however, we become unable to see how *all* children are special, including the children of those we define as our enemies. Yet, by being insensitive to the suffering of other people's children, we cheapen the love we have for our own, and we lose respect for the adults that children become. In this way, the common good suffers and hope for a better future grows more dim.

Most nations and ethnicities, at some point in time, have used hate to gain or protect a material or psychological advantage over another group. When this practice becomes a frenzy, human communities perpetrate immense tragedies. The more extreme the tragedy, the more people strive to dissociate themselves from the tragedy so as not to feel polluted. This perceived distance, however, is itself a mystification—a way of coping with our guilt for not really caring enough to intervene.

## IV

Selfishness creates the conditions that invite tragedy. This argument can be illustrated by highlighting our relationship to the Nazis, perhaps the most extreme example of what this book is against. Although defining ourselves as being in some essential way different from the Nazis is tempting, this tendency should be tempered. In demonizing the Nazis—as much as they deserve to be demonized—we must be careful not to use such tactics as a way to purify ourselves or to misrepresent our own immoral actions. To do so would be to invoke the scapegoat, an important Nazi method—as revealed in 1938 by Kenneth Burke's (1973) review of Adolph Hitler's *Mein Kampf.* We must reject such methods to defeat the aspects of ourselves that resembles this part of Germany's past. To reject Nazism in *all* of its forms, US Americans (indeed, all people) must first condemn the logic of greed and the practice of selfishness.

Millions of Germans during the Nazi era were enthusiastic about Nazism (Goldhagen, 1997). Although we can condemn these people, more important for our current society is to understand how many of the practices of the United States have been Nazi like and enthusiastically supported by many citizens. The popular participation of average Germans in the extermination of the Jews makes sense when we learn to appreciate that anti-Semitism was a respectable position, just as racism and anticommunism have been in the United States. From the experience of Nazism, there are important lessons to learn about US politics. In particular, a small class of people in the United States (and throughout the world) practice a greed that is unparalleled in history (Robinson and Harris, 2000). Furthermore, these people control a nation that is many times more powerful and destructive than was Nazi Germany, reifying US elite privilege as an unquestionable foundation of the social order.[3]

We can recognize our sanctioning of terror and learn to reject selfishness and greed where we can. To do this, we can challenge our foreign policy and our economic system so as to treat all people on this earth—without exception—with dignity and respect. The normative goals of civilization can be to reduce poverty, disease, homelessness, and hopelessness. However, these clearly are not the goals of what President George H. Bush christened the New World Order in the early 1990s. If the Nazi past means anything today, it means that selfishness anywhere is a threat to people everywhere. Selfishness and greed make people cruel. To be anti-Nazi means to be able to reject the part of ourselves that longs to be cruel.

The issue, therefore, is how to accomplish this self-mastery over greed and selfishness and continue to remain a member of US society. To be both a part of US society and to remain at a critical distance from this society is difficult. The mere fact of our residency in the US causes us to become complacent with the injustices of the system. Arguably, cruelty and greed—particularly in the economic realm—are the oils that keep US culture running smoothly. This becomes increasingly true as globalization accelerates:

> Globalization and militarism should be seen as two sides of the same coin. On one side, globalization promotes the conditions that lead to unrest, inequality, conflict, and, ultimately, war. On the other side, globalization fuels the means to wage war by protecting and promoting the military industries needed to produce sophisticated weaponry. This weaponry, in turn, is used—or its use is threatened—to protect the investments of transnational corporations and their shareholders. (Staples, 2000, 18)

Although voluntary exile is one option, leaving would do little to change the system, a change that is urgently needed. People can, in short, learn to resist empire and the "Americanization" of the world. US Americans have a moral responsibility to recognize the immorality of much Americanization—how it rubs against the grain of what the United States ideally represents—and to rechannel their energies toward the creation of a just and equitable world.

Unfortunately, many US Americans are slow in realizing that their cultural practices are often selfish and cruel. This obliviousness is accentuated when the victims of US selfishness are far away—when the people affected are different from themselves. Further complicating matters is the fact that the US system is not entirely cruel or corrupt (Said, 1994, 12, addresses this point). Given this situation, how do we distinguish between US virtues and vice? In short, how do we become aware of what should be done so that social justice may prevail?

Answers to these questions are not easy, particularly when considering the political economy of the mass media. The mass media are owned by a handful of powerful people (less than two dozen) who control most of the information to which average US citizens are exposed (McChesney, 2000). The practical meaning of free speech and freedom of the press lies with these corporate media elites: They alone decide what to cover and the tone in which a story is expressed. These select few—nonelected and largely beyond legal or political accountability—produce and "spin" the news to meet their needs and to reflect their own values. Media consumers are presented daily with digested and fabricated news, information, advertisements, and entertainment that have been designed to placate and control them. Given the pervasiveness of this propaganda system, the fact that most US Americans accept complacency in an unjust system is not surprising. An effect of such manipulation is to relieve "a peace-loving people of guilt they might otherwise feel" (Ivie, 1980, 292). Because US Americans do not want to believe that their nation is often extremely cruel, they refuse to question the information they do have and, consequently, retain an unwarranted faith about the integrity of their government and its policies.

## V

Scholars of communication can play an important role in helping to usher the progressive change encouraged by this book. As Lee Artz explains, "Our discipline's ongoing concern with democracy, justice, and ethics compels continued reasoned attempts to put communication at the service of humanity" (2001, 243). In addition, Judith S. Trent urges us to "link our work as scholars to the most fundamental problems of our communities in new and more forceful ways, and that we are uniquely positioned to do so" (2000, 190). Since communicative practices, from the mass media down to interpersonal relationships, are important means by which society reproduces itself, communication scholars study essential mechanisms of power in modern society. Our discipline, notes Trent, "offers a wider range of possibilities for the scholar as citizen than perhaps any other of the social sciences because it includes areas such as media, family, politics, health, and the environment, any one of which offers unparalleled opportunity for the engaged scholar" (2000, 191). Unfortunately, scholars in our discipline often "stop short of serious consideration of the fundamental systemic practices and relations that give rise to the injustice they experience at the interpersonal level" (Artz, 2001, 240). As a result, we often teach our students how to be good corporate citizens and good workers and, by doing so, we trick ourselves into thinking that that we have made a difference in the world. W. Charles Redding (1985), who recommended that communication professors become "consciousness-raisers," once warned that disciplinary education in communication encourages a "Don't-Rock-the-Boat" mentality, reinforcing the negative aspects of corporate culture.

Because critical scholars live daily with the contradictions between their informed visions and the structural limitations of the academy, they often experience what Richard Boyd calls a "sulky gloom" (1999, 378). Boyd's gloom results from his difficult and unsuccessful struggles to enact his political and ethical ideals within an academic environment that is structurally antithetical to such ideals. Boyd writes, as other critical scholars do, to help academics "overcome those deep contradictions I so keenly feel between the reality of my professional life and my convictions about what that reality should be" (1999, 378).

Over time, this gloom can turn into intense rage. Reflecting on her maturation and reception as an intellectual, bell hooks writes, "I felt as though I were a marked woman . . . [I] had no real place in the existing social structure. I felt like an exile" (1995, 16). Although hooks is discussing the alienation of being African American, female, and poor in the United States, her rage is a rage against *all* injustice. There comes a point at which individuals refuse to suffer further; when this occurs, their collective rage grows. At the beginning of the twenty-first century, critical intellectuals in the United States may be approaching this threshold:

> Despair can no longer be contained in a gloomy or perverse individualism. Regarding the "future," despair finds common ground. It finds it in the threat of global annihilation made possible by modern weapons technology, in the terrible slaughter and increasing dangers brought on by a policy of empire, in the rise of authoritarian efforts to increase weapons production and protect spheres of influence. (Wander, 1990, 280)

We must harness this rage, for if we do not, it will consume us before our influence can be felt. This does not mean that we must deny our rage. We should not close our eyes and pretend that the world's diseases do not exist; to do so is to abdicate a critical consciousness and to practice an unreflective selfishness, which bell hooks and others are unwilling to do. Thus, their hostility is a controlled anguish—a productive channeling of rage:

> [A] politics of despair begins with a loss of hope and acts in ways consistent with bringing hope back into the world. This is the point at which political activity transcends expression of rage, the point at which feelings of intimacy with and trust in the other becomes possible and desirable. . . This is where free and open

> exchange between people lives, where the line between persuasion and coercion, consent and force, voluntary and involuntary activity becomes meaningful. (Wander, 1990, 285)

Intellectuals and scholars who feel they have a voice and who recognize and lament the inequalities in US society should feel safe to speak out with moral indignation. Such moral indignation can be seen as a sign of creativity. In Ono's words, "When we do speak, it is so often a voice of desperation: a last act. However, it may be the first one to change things. By speaking, we hope to voice something that does not necessarily exist prior to its having been spoken; we hope to utter a unique thought" (1997, 122). When the oppressed, no longer able to live under the conditions of denigration, stand their ground and call for justice against the oppressor, they are not being foolish. In their voice, stance, and expression of anguish, they cultivate a power that is, in some significant ways, greater than the force that is used to repress them. Maya Angelou explains why the caged bird sings: "His wings are clipped and his feet are tied, so he opens his throat to sing" (1994, 194). Angelou reminds us that sometimes the power of our voice is the only thing we have from which to draw strength. This is rhetorical strength, the strength of persuasion, the strength cultivated by Martin Luther King, Jr. and by Mahatma Gandhi—the power of our ideas that become expressed in human speech. This is the power behind all national liberation movements and the power behind the yearnings of all people to be free. The expression of freedom, even in the face of brutal repression, is itself an act of liberation.

Critical scholars deny that the United States is great because of its excessive wealth and power; a wealth and power, which, in the words of Susan Sontag, is "indecent in its scale" and "an insult to the possibilities of human growth" (1967, 51). Critical scholars remind people not to be comfortable with their excessive privileges, lest they forget that others pay the price for their comfort. However, others should not uncritically accept the argument advanced by critical scholars. The articulations in this book are not intended to be the "final word" on what constitutes social justice or how to achieve a better world. Rather, they revisit definitive critical themes in Western social theory in the hopes of reanimating our professional and social commitments toward making the current social reality less cruel.

## ✶ NOTES ✶

1. Dmitry Shlapentokh (2002, 269) notes that Europeans, who once needed the United States to protect them from the Soviet Union, are now fearing an overreaching United States that seeks to transform Europe into another version of itself.

2. In the mid-1920s, Everett Lee Hunt (1961, 70) noted that the study of rhetoric was important for much the same reasons as suggested in this book.

3. G. John Ikenberry characterizes US hegemony this way: "The United States makes its power safe for the world and in return the world agrees to live within the American system" (2001, 22).

# PART I

## AIM AND SCOPE OF PARTISAN CRITICISM

The five chapters of Part I delineate framing devices or critical perspectives to situate the aim and scope of partisan criticism exemplified in this book. These include: the communication imagination; the importance of critical education as a corrective for alienation; the barrier of the US Constitution; the importance of radical critique for engaging the problem of the present; and my new vision for law and social justice. Fundamental to each device or perspective is the notion that democracy, education, and criticism can all be understood in communication terms; the practice of each is constructed through discourse. More specifically, meaningful democracy is difficult without critical education and robust criticism; civil society is most healthy when democracy, education, and criticism are infused with a commitment to progressive change and to providing localized communities with the political vocabulary to enact such change.

# CHAPTER 1

## Animating the Communicative Imagination

The first framing device is the *communicative imagination*. Because people are bombarded by communication influences, receive stru-cture and guidance from them, and thus become indistinguishable from these influences, they fail to notice that they are what they communicate as well as constrained by the communication of others. By heightening a sensitivity to the manner in which communication positions people in the world, the important intersections can be identified more easily among history, ideology, language, gender, politics, and law contextualizing their life choices. As described by David E. Engen, the communicative imagination is a worldview in which individuals "possess a *state of mind* making them especially attuned to both the significance and complexities of the meaning production process in general and human social interaction in particular" (2002, 42). A sensitivity to the communicative imagination and to social justice scholarship "identifies and foregrounds the grammars that oppress or underwrite relationships of domination and then reconstructs those grammars" (Frey, Pearce, Pollock, Artz, and Murphy, 1996, 112).

Adopting a communicative imagination, critical scholars assume that individuals cannot escape their historical context and its associated restraints and emphases; people only become what their place in history allows them to become, and this becoming is expressed through communication and in the construction of community life. Simply, individual human choice is constrained (although not precluded) by material conditions. Although it is not possible to deny that what people think is real for them (individuals construct their own meanings), this construction should not be mistaken for "free will." When people's belief in freedom helps them to be happy, productive, and healthy, then their metaphysical belief in free will may in fact be useful, but they should not mistake that usefulness for an unchanging reality; people change when the historical narratives that belie their beliefs change.

In a practical sense, any option that exists for human identification is dependent on communication within the context of the material world and, thus, the communicative imagination is an empowering and strategic resource. As my work is largely concerned with the constraints of law as a communication practice, I focus on how attention to the communicative imagination encourages a questioning of the reification process behind legal reasoning. Normative legal reasoning conceals the implicit politics of the system, negating the *what can be* by asserting the *a priori* of the present and is "an inherently repressive form of interpretive thought which limits our comprehension of the social world and its possibilities" (Gabel, 1980, 25). Most people are unaware that the social order creates pacified individuals who are unconnected, impotent, and isolated, as this "felt reality is *denied* by the socially communicated reality" (Gabel, 1980, 28). Our suffering often goes unrecognized because the social and linguistic space for conceptualizing our discontent is denied. The dismay that cannot find expression with our voice often becomes reinterpreted as a condition of social existence.

The rhetoric of "rights" and "ordered liberty" is part of the mystification process, as it often overstates its importance for the organization of a just society. "Rights," and other legal concepts, no matter how important they may be in certain instances, constitute only a selective part of the moral order. Although necessary for a certain stage of the moral evolution of a just society, at other stages they can limit social progress. Courts, for example, routinely nullify contracts derived from the threat of force. The "doctrine of duress" is exemplified graphically in the motion picture *The Godfather*. Early in the film, Michael Corleone tells his girlfriend Kate that his father helped a family friend to break into show business by threatening an influential producer; a gun and a contract were held to the producer's head, and he was told that either his signature or his brains would be on the contract. If the producer were later to breach the contract, he would have a perfect defense in court. In the law of contract, the government holds people responsible only for those obligations that they voluntarily assume; in this example the prerequisite agreement to be bound was coerced.

Few people would disagree with the doctrine of duress. However, the doctrine is not applied when the duress is the result of poverty, as when a worker is forced by hunger to contract to unhealthy or inhumane working conditions. Physiological need is considered a normal motivation for labor. Freedom to contract is not really freedom when the conditions of labor are mandated by necessity for life and health. In this way, the "conceptual system of the law recognizes physical coercion but not economic coercion" (Boyle, 1992, xviii). Although both phenomena have the same effect on an individual, society does not recognize the violence of the second example. Social freedom derives not from the law, which only recognizes specific negative freedoms from government coercion, but from the community when society articulates a more inclusive view of social relationships. An example is provided by Rorty:

> The *Brown v. Board of Education* decision was not a discovery of a hitherto unnoticed constitutional right, or of the hitherto unnoticed intentions of the authors of constitutional amendments. Rather, it was the result of our society's long-delayed willingness to admit that the behavior of white Americans toward the descendants of black slaves was, and continued to be, incredibly cruel—that it was intolerable that American citizens should be subjected to the humiliation of segregation. (1996, 16)

Society progresses when crucial historical, ideological, linguistic, political, and legal influences coalesce in ways that encourage people to expand their notion of community. Community is, therefore, performative; through social conflict a group of people articulate "the divisions within a community by constructing, maintaining, reinforcing, or renegotiating the relationship among a community's members" (Fuoss, 1995, 94). The law, in many cases, will follow from this expanded notion of community.

As of yet, US society does not recognize economic violence in the same manner as it does the physical violence epitomized in films such as *The Godfather*. This may change as people become increasingly able to understand the potency of historical, ideological, linguistic, political, and legal influences. For this to occur, however, people must be willing to consider the moral implications of the way society is currently constructed. Yet, normative legal reasoning, along with "the help of such overpowering psychological symbols as robed judges, quasi-ecclesiastical schools, the Professions, and the Tribunal [institutionalizes] the boundaries of a legitimate rationality," helps divorce moral inquiry from the practice of law (Gabel, 1980, 28).

The ability to think in terms of greater possibilities in law, politics, economics, and society can be accentuated through the development of a person's communicative imagination. The terminology for the communicative imagination is derived from C. Wright Mills (1959), who articulated the "sociological imagination." Mills argued that the individualizing of social pathologies mystifies the systemic roots of cultural disorder. Individuals, therefore, must learn to question their internalized discomfort in light of the larger social, political, and historical positioning of their subjectivities:

> Know that many personal troubles cannot be solved merely as troubles, but must be understood in terms of public issues—and in terms of the problems of history making. Know that the human meaning of public issues must be revealed by relating them to personal troubles—and to the problems of the individual life. Know that the problems of social science, when adequately formulated, must include both troubles and issues, both biography and history, and the range of their intricate relations. Within that range the life of the individual and the making of society occur; and within that range the sociological imagination has its chance to make a difference in the quality of human life in our time. (Mills, 1959, 226)

By comprehending the influences constructing social maladies, the root causes of systemic trouble affecting large numbers of people can be identified and appropriate interventions and redescriptions applied (Mills, 1963, 303). Such reflexivity helps people to appreciate the complexity of human social life and to avoid the fallacy of individualization—the belief that social ills are caused primarily through individual agency.

An exchange I had with Sonja K. Foss (a colleague whose work on "invitational rhetoric" is critiqued and contrasted with partisan criticism in Chapter 7) illustrates the contrast between individualized and systemic agency and what happens when a communicative imagination is neglected. Sonja and I had both listened to a report on National Public Radio describing the street culture of a community of homeless people in New York City. The report glowingly described the entrepreneurial spirit of this subgroup, in which they created a street market for the products that they scavenged or produced from rubbish. This society developed a highly structured economy, with rules, methods of enforcement, separation of labor, and significant salary differentials. In short, these homeless people replicated a market economy, with competition, rank, hierarchy, privilege, status, and deprivation.

This report angered me for two reasons. First, I felt ire against US society for allowing a lumpen proletariat (ie, the severely disfranchised) to exist. Second, I was angry that this lumpen class embraced the political and market ideology that is responsible for the poverty of its members, denying them adequate food, health care, and shelter. In contrast, Sonja argued that these street people were exercising power over their lives and were choosing a different lifestyle, one which they desired. Rather than fearing their condition and blaming society for it, as I did, Sonja applauded the ingenuity of these street people and respected their choice and their efforts to create their own community.

From the perspective of partisan criticism, Sonja's response is unsatisfactory. For the vast majority of the homeless, their condition is *not* a lifestyle choice; rather, their condition is an avoidable personal and social tragedy. These people need help and medical, psychological, and occupational services, not distant admiration. The apparent compliancy of members of this homeless community, as well as the radio report and Sonja's response, illustrate how people are often unaware of the manner by which history, language, and law (among other phenomena) mold their subjectivities and ability to respond strategically to material conditions. Simply, homelessness should not exist. The resources of the media, as well as those of individuals (not to mention the government), should be directed at eliminating homelessness rather than making excuses for its existence.

Homelessness is only accepted by US society—and by the homeless themselves who do not organize and engage in mass civil disobedience—because of communal assumptions and influences, reified by language, downplaying or naturalizing the horror that homeless people are made to suffer (in Denver, in 2003, over sixty homeless men and women died or were murdered on the street). Such assumptions and influences affect people much in the same manner as the air that they breathe. People, however, usually do not notice the air that they breathe until breathing becomes a problem (such as experiencing a respiratory disease), at which point breathing becomes the focus of their lives. The same can be said of the powerful influences of communication. Although communication affects us constantly, people do not pay attention to it until there is a tangible problem. When such disruption occurs, an exigency is created and the affected community faces the challenge of adjusting its vocabularies and its thoughts to reestablish a sense of order. Since the problem of homelessness has not reached this level in our social awareness, society does not recognize it as an exigency and the larger social order remains unaffected.

This order is not necessarily bad, as the larger community must think in common ways to fulfill important tasks (the good of everyone in a community is dependent on internalized understandings of social value). Thus, there is always a sense in which authority and tradition have an important role to play in guiding the structure of people's lives. However, authority and tradition are often used as excuses for not changing. Moreover, social order is often "a thinly coded representation about race and class, an 'ideological conductor' for both popular discontents and the state's inability to manage racial [or class] antagonisms" (Platt, 2001, 141). Awareness of this fact means that we have the responsibility to question the demands of others so that authority and tradition do not become calcified and reify, in this case, a lumpen proletariat.

Utilizing a communicative imagination, scholars can understand and educate others about how language contributes to the unhealthy social and economic relationships that plague our society and the world. A pioneering scholar in this regard is Philip C. Wander, whose most important essays appeared in the early 1980s, a period in which the US government was intensifying a cruel war against the people of El Salvador and Nicaragua. The people of Central America were struggling against the United States to obtain food, health care, decent housing, and for the right to plan their own destiny. Wander argued that this context constituted "a real crisis involving actual alternatives" and urged a "reconsideration of the purposes of criticism and the study of rhetoric" so as to invest our scholarship with meaning (1983, 18). Wander was careful to note that, in the struggles of others for social justice, our lives are affected as well. The fortunes of most US Americans are interdependent with those of the majority of people living in Central America. The US government, which created the suffering in Central America, has the power to create similar suffering at home. Indeed, this is occurring in the United States, as "the welfare-state buffers that once softened the market's disciplines are dismantled, we're being returned to the savage rule of pure nineteenth century capitalism" (Henwood, 1987, 29).

Communication scholars comprehend how many of the problems of the world stem from or are grounded in the strategic use of language to mystify, identify, justify, reify, or demonize. Two classic examples of studies documenting this phenomenon are worth noting. The first explored how the cancer metaphor was used to make acceptable the extreme violence used by the United States against left-wing political movements

(Black, 1970). The second explored how the mystification of language was used to deflect critical attention from a criminally unethical and racist research project that existed for four decades and was part of public culture (Solomon, 1985). These examples illustrate how communication scholars are strategically placed to intervene in the larger cultural politics of society and to accentuate alternative courses of action for those disrespectful of human dignity. Wander explicitly lays out this position (which he calls an "ideological turn"), situating academic scholarship within the larger context of the world in which we live:

> Criticism takes an ideological turn when it recognizes the existence of powerful vested interests benefiting from and consistently urging policies and technology that threaten life on this planet, when it realizes that we search for alternatives. The situation is being constructed: it will not be averted either by ignoring it or placing it beyond our province. An ideological turn in modern criticism reflects the existence of crisis, acknowledges the influence of established interests and the reality of alternative world-views, and commends rhetorical analyses not only of the actions implied but also of the interests represented. More than "informed talk about matters of importance," criticism carries us to the point of recognizing good reasons and engaging in right action. What an ideological view does is to situate "good" and "right" in an historical context, the efforts of real people to create a better world. (Wander, 1983, 18)

Much of the intervention that Wander advocates takes place through education and teachers' daily interactions with their students and with people in their communities. Such intervention, however, does not preclude direct action in the political realms when the opportunity presents itself. This approach to scholarship "frames its research program and its conceptual framework with an eye to the aims and activities of those oppositional social movements with which it has a partisan though not uncritical identification" (Fraser, 1985, 97).

# CHAPTER 2

## ENDORSING CRITICAL EDUCATION AS A CORRECTIVE FOR ALIENATION

The second framing device involves alienation and critical education. Because human beings are works in progress, their needs, desires, thoughts, and understandings are not "givens," not inevitable; rather, they are "takens"—phenomena constructed to meet political and social needs (Dewey, 1929, 178). Humans are educated to meet certain goals which define and reify their self-images. Through this process, humans assume their place in the social hierarchy. What education creates, a critical education can challenge. A critical education can, therefore, be a corrective for the alienated condition that many experience living in the United States.

A critical education challenges many of the values and beliefs that US Americans hold dear, cutting deeply into national assumptions of law, history, and economics. It questions the relationship between the US people and their society, for this relationship is generative of much discomfort throughout the world. Admittedly, developing a critical appreciation of the status quo is itself painful and, thus, critical ideas may be unacceptable to some because those ideas refuse to reinforce common, comfortable myths of US society.

Critical scholars reject orthodoxy and the comfort that comes from accepting the intoxicants of the status quo—power, wealth, drugs and alcohol, pornography, entertainment, propaganda, and religion. These stimuli distract US Americans, define them, limit them in fundamental ways, and give them the impression that they are, above all else, content (see Frug, 1980, 1069). Yet, the social world exists to meet the conditions of a past world, a world that is only ours by default; we are born into a specific *episteme*. Rather than live life in default mode and to accept the conditions of the present as justified, as many Americans do, a critical perspective urges people to realize that the present has different needs than did the past—which is why the communicative imagination is important. In seeing how the past was constructed for us and how, to a large extent, the past controls us, people can free themselves from ideas that no longer serve contemporary needs.

The notion of human need highlights the importance of consciousness and alienation. Central to a critical education is the imperative to address the sense of disconnectedness people feel from the nurturing and creative energy of social life:

> When an individual is no longer a true participant, when he no longer feels a sense of responsibility to his society, the context of democracy is emptied. When culture is degraded and vulgarity enthroned, when the social system does not build security but induces peril, inexorably, the individual is impelled to pull away from a soulless society. (King, 1987b, 19)

Under such circumstances, human beings become malleable and intellectually flabby, leading to the pronounced immaturity of substantial numbers of the American public:

> No one is normally aware of his or her sense of unconnectedness, passivity, impotence, and isolation, because this felt reality is *denied* by the socially communicated reality. Each person denies to the other that he or she is suffering, because this collective denial has been made a condition of what social connection there is. One cannot assert that the Pledge of Allegiance is insane and still remain "with" one's friends and family—so we forget that this pledging is insane and reinforce the collective coercion. (Gabel, 1980, 28)

In such a world, people are dispersed, isolated, and alienated.

Alienation is the condition we experience when we allow ourselves to be placed in the world by other people who serve their agendas at the expense of our own. To be alienated is to be influenced by events and processes that one cannot perceive. Alienation involves the manner in which language and society interfere with our self-creativity and our own sense of agency, reducing our capacity to resist manipulation. Alienation is the opposite of human freedom, severing the human will from human consciousness and power. When alientated, people become:

> . . . impotently linked through the cycle of production and consumption that determines their social existence. We find the mechanical functioning that most people call work, the packaged emptiness of fast food, the obsessive manipulation of appliances that occupies the boredom of leisure time, and the sort of "love" that attempts to realize desire through ambivalent dependency and pornographic fantasy. The unhappiness and sense of hopelessness embedded in these processes are not simply the consequence of "psychological problems," as

> popular culture keeps insisting in despair; these concrete processes constitute the social totality within which the psyche is formed and finds itself in difficulty. And it is the effects of these processes that express the true morality of our political institutions. (Gabel, 1977, 312)

Fortunately, alienation can be combated through education, although education by itself is not a panacea. In fact, education, as largely experienced in the United States, is often a dangerous form of alienation (see Burke, 1935, 89, discussing what he calls "adult education" in "capitalist America"). If society takes solely a corporate or technocratic view of education, it runs the risk of losing important moral and human visions, as illustrated by the following note circulated to faculty each year by a school principal:

> Dear Teacher:
>
> I am a survivor of a concentration camp. My eyes saw what no man should witness:
>
> Gas chambers built by learned engineers. Children poisoned by educated physicians. Infants killed by trained nurses. Women and babies shot and burned by high school and college graduates.
>
> So I am suspicious of education.
>
> My request is: Help your students become human. Your efforts must never produce learned monsters, skilled psychopaths, educated Eichmanns.
>
> Reading, writing, and arithmetic are important only if they serve to make our children more humane. (cited in Shapiro, 1994, 18)

This principal knows the difference between education and edification because, in Roderick Hart's terms, "teachers are good at remembering" (1993, 99). The more teachers experience life critically, the more they understand that their most important task is to help their students become critical thinkers. Unfortunately, education is often not about such criticism. In the communication discipline, for example, resistance to such criticism can be traced back to the inception of our field:

> The passage of speech instruction from the elocutionary period into the academic professionalism of the national association put in place a legitimized system not only for the study and teaching of "better speech," but for the correction and exclusion of unfit, unpleasant, and deviant speech. (Macke, 1991, 133)

A critical education, in contrast, emphasizes that education is a realizing, a way of turning people into something that they never were before, something edifying and inspiring. Such critical education gives people power to reinvent their lives and to control the way in which they are asked to think. This becoming, this change, involves a more complete freedom than the limited "market" freedom celebrated in the United States. Such freedom involves an awareness of the limits of our thoughts and social opportunities, as well as an understanding of how to challenge these limits.

To achieve this type of education, teachers need to set their own agendas, "putting their individual, lovingly prepared specialties on display in the curricular cafeteria, without regard to any larger end, much less any institutional play" (Rorty, 1989b). This, for Rorty, "is what non-vocational higher education is all about" (1989b, 204). As Rorty elaborates, an important goal of nonvocational education is "to help students realize that they can reshape themselves—that they can rework the self-image foisted on them by their past, the self-image that makes them competent citizens, into a new self-image, one that they themselves have helped to create" (1989b).

Rorty recognizes that the practice of a critical education is politically unacceptable in our current environment, forcing the humanities scholar to live a double life between the social expectation of the scholar as responsible for the systemic transference of knowledge across generations, on the one hand, and the vision of the humanities scholar as being directly subversive of such knowledge, on the other. This confused identity often muddles scholarship and promotes professional alienation, institutional insecurity, a culture of gamesmanship, a show business mentality, puffery, and possessiveness. This does us and our students a disservice.

The ritualistic danger of scholarship resembles that of show business in that the practice of both, as all communication generally, requires an *audience* that must identify, in some sense, with the source before that audience is willing to embrace any message. The success of any presentation depends on this identification; thus, rhetors always exist for and at the suffrage of their audience. The basic appeals of any rhetor should reflect the biases, psychologies, desires, and understandings of his or her audience. In other words, scholars can only enunciate that which is acceptable to their audience. Without the audience, there is no presentation; classrooms are empty, and library books gather dust. Scholars, therefore, ought not take themselves too seriously. As a class, scholars are no better and no worse than any other productive worker. The importance of scholars lies solely in their utility—the ability to inspire others and to suggest new possibilities for enriching the human condition—not in their status as "knower." With regard to human culture, there is nothing to be known—there is only experience, the critique of experience, and the articulated vision of a new experience.

Furthermore, scholarly disciplines often internalize a sense of self-importance.[1] Given that academic departments are created on college and university campuses, political justification is required to support their existence.[2] This justification is particularly true when institutions face tight budgetary constraints, as they have steadily since the 1960s (see Deetz and Putnam, 2001, 23).[3] Each academic unit, therefore, has a discrete and perilous status in the academy in that its existence is contingent on the value of its perceived unique contribution. Above all else, scholars must argue constantly for their discipline's importance. Disciplines that are not perceived as being important are often relegated to a precarious existence on the fringes of academic culture. Most vulnerable are disciplines serving minority populations, such as women's studies, African American studies, Latino/a studies, queer studies, and critical legal studies.[4] In addition, other departments prosper or falter on political or cultural conditions outside their control. For example, the demise of the Soviet Union has reduced the importance of Slavic studies in the United States, whereas the rise of modern China since the early 1980s has led to an increased demand for programs in sinology.

Because the academic fortunes of scholars are largely dependent on the perceived uniqueness and importance of their departments (exceptions exist for instances of favoritism, campus politics, and other abuses of administrative power), scholars often repress what they understand professionally—that their uniqueness is illusionary. All humanities scholars—broadly defined to include the social sciences—study essentially the same phenomena: the moral, spiritual, epistemological, and social construction of the human being. Thus, we should heed Rorty's call to de-emphasize disciplinary boundaries: "When some government body needs advice on something, it should not ask, do we need a historian, or a philosopher, or a classicist, but rather, who has read a lot of books? And it will find those people pretty much throughout the humanities departments" (1983, 44). In short, the substantive difference among the humanities disciplines is their vocabulary.[5] Perhaps, therefore, we should accept Rorty's redefinition of the academy:

> We should not try to define "the humanities" by asking what the humanities departments are which distinguishes them from the rest of the university. The interesting dividing line is, instead, one that cuts across departments and disciplinary matrices. It divides people busy conforming to well-understood criteria for making contributions to knowledge from people trying to expand their own moral imaginations. These latter people read books in order to enlarge their sense of what is possible and important—either for themselves as individuals or for their society. (1989c, 9)

One way to avoid the alienation that often results from disciplinary behavior and to enact some form of Rorty's vision is through the widespread acceptance of a supradisciplinary perspective.[6] This perspective would supplement, not supplant, the traditional disciplinary persona and would empower scholars to speak back to the academic bureaucracy. As this bureaucracy attempts to manage the humanities, scholars who embrace a supradisciplinary perspective respond to bureaucratization by changing "fast enough so that they remain indefinable and unmanageable" (1989c, 12). For this, scholars need academic freedom, so they can "shrug off the heresy hunters and their cries of 'politicization,' as well as freedom for each new batch of assistant professors to despise and repudiate the departmental Old Guard to whom they owe their jobs" (1989c, 12). Change, under this Kuhnian model of academic freedom, derives from discontinuities in thought and assumptions rather than from an allegiance to invested icons and their defenders.

The development of a supradisciplinary perspective is particularly necessary for scholars who are committed to wide-ranging social critique. Society is complex and, therefore, requires a plurality of approaches and perspectives. Disciplines, by definition, have limits to what they can contribute. What different disciplines produce is useful but localized. A supradisciplinary perspective is needed to bring the diverse pieces together—to humanize and to socialize knowledge.

This notion of a supradisciplinary perspective, however, is controversial. The controversy arises from the current practice of situating the political foundations of all knowledge in a disciplinary bureaucracy. In other words, knowledge only "makes sense" when judged by scholars under disciplinary norms and expectations, and the supradisciplinary perspective is adverse to such constraints. To the traditional disciplinary persona, the supradisciplinary perspective does not produce knowledge; at best, it leads to a suspect knowledge. Such knowledge is suspect because the disciplinary bureaucracy cannot control the accreditation process.

In the knowledge industry, bureaucracy is tremendously important for sanctioning and rewarding scholarship. This importance is grounded in a powerful and foundational myth pervading academic culture—one embraced by students, faculty, administrators, and legislators. This myth maintains that essential differences exist between disciplines; that the social world can be broken down into discrete and self-contained categories, such as English, communication, philosophy, or law. Each discipline is considered unique and is often kept insulated from influence by other disciplines: sociology is divorced from psychology, literature from philosophy, political science from anthropology, and communication from English. Apparent differences between these disciplines, however, are superficial. The subject matter of the humanities are human beings—what they think and how they become—as well as the human expressions of, for instance, friendship, hope, love, fear, hate, and despair.

More specifically, to master any humanistic field, scholars must draw on the resources of all the other fields. Literary experts, for instance, must also be fluent in philosophy and history, philosophers must be fluent in literary criticism, historians must understand both philosophy and literature, and sociologists must understand anthropology as well as rhetorical theory. Systemic scholars downplay these connections in their work, whereas edifying scholars highlight in their work as many connections among these fields as is possible.[7]

This book is offered as an example of what Rorty calls edifying scholarship—it is abnormal. Its purpose is "to take us out of our old selves by the power of strangeness, to aid us in becoming new beings" (1979, 360). Although this book is grounded in disciplinary scholarship in communication, contemporary law, continental philosophy, critical rhetorical studies, legal history, political science, postmodern literary criticism, and sociology, it was not written exclusively for scholars in any of these particular fields. It seeks a wider intellectual audience and represents an amalgamization of knowledge. Furthermore, as this text performs practical, political, and social criticism, it intends to generate social controversy. Such controversy is not negative, for to be controversial is to speak against the accepted notions of what is "true," and these notions change all the time. Thus, all scholarship should strive to be controversial, or else how can people feel comfortable with what they think they know? Furthermore, controversy is often heuristic. As Kuhn (1970) has argued, controversial claims often lead to the widening and transformation of disciplinary thought. In Raymie McKerrow's terms, "The act of performing, within the context of our expertise as critics/readers of the social condition, moves the focus from criticism as method to critique as practice" (1989, 108). The aim of this book parallels McKerrow's function for critical rhetoric: "To understand the integration of power/knowledge in society—what possibilities for change the integration invites or inhibits and what intervention strategies might be considered appropriate to effect social change" (1989, 91). Such criticism has a unique value—a value distinct from the disciplinary knowledge contributing to the conceptualization of this book.

## ✶ NOTES ✶

1. Throughout this book I frequently evoke such terms as "disciplines," "scholars," and "public intellectuals." Although I define these words in context, more clarification is helpful. By discipline, I mean normative discourse controlled by a professional community with clear boundaries and identifications. Scholars are often members of a professional community, although they do not necessarily have to be members. Public intellectuals may or may not be members of a discipline. Scholars may or may not be public intellectuals and public intellectuals may or may not be scholars. What matters is not the terminology, but the commitment by individuals to use all of their resources–professional, literary, academic, etc., to further the ends of social justice. Discourse communities that strive for this goal are, in my view, laudable.

2. For a particularly vivid example of this in the communication discipline, see Burgoon (1989). A more global statement of this phenomena appears in Readings (1997) in which he argues that the university has become corporate and that the humanities are being marginalized because they lack a perceived economic benefit. For a response to this condition, see Katz (2002).

3. As I was writing an earlier draft of this book in the Fall of 2002, severe state deficits and an increased Republican hegemony at the state and national levels was accentuating the problems discussed in this section.

4. Currently, scholars are discussing the institutionalization of women's studies, in which some scholars claim that portrayals such as mine are deleterious to these programs. See Messer-Davidow (2002).

5. I recognize that this statement is reductionist. Yet it is in line with the neopragmatist vocabulary of this book. My point is that by utilizing different "terministic screens," each discipline brings with it different ways of knowing and varying descriptions of the human being. While each discipline is replicating similar knowledge, the poetry of each field lies in its stylized nuance.

6. Rorty himself declared his discipline (philosophy) "dead" and moved from Princeton University to the University of Virginia where he joined a humanities program. More recently, Rorty has moved to a comparative literature program at Stanford University. See Rorty (2002, 54-56) for his rejection of academic philosophy and his switch to departments of literature.

7. For an elaboration on the distinction between systemic and edifying scholarship, see Rorty (1979). Here Rorty notes that the "cultural role of the edifying philosopher is to help us avoid the self-deception which comes from believing that we know ourselves by knowing a set of objective facts" (373).

# CHAPTER 3

## CONFRONTING THE BARRIER OF THE US CONSTITUTION FOR CHANGE AND SOCIAL JUSTICE

The third framing device for understanding the arguments in this book is the need to deflate respect for the Constitution of the United States and for the law in general. Specifically, an important barrier to a national commitment to economic justice (on which social justice depends) is the Federal Constitution. This claim does not repudiate the virtues of a constitutional state, as constitutions play an essential role in helping to stabilize many societies and, thereby, enabling them to flourish. Societies without such constitutions are often unable to actualize their collective aspirations. Constitutions represent order and structure, and much of this book is an extended argument for an increased order and structure—particularly in the economic realm—to improve the quality of community life. A constitution is a way to enact and to normalize such relationships. Constitutions, in short, can be extremely useful. A text, however, is only as valuable as that text is drafted, interpreted, and applied. As James Boyd White notes, "What matters is always what place, if any, such an instrument will have in the lives of those it is intended to regulate" (1984, 245).

There is a tendency in the United States to overemphasize the importance of the Federal Constitution. This is a mistake. The Constitution is nothing more than language and is no more important than the importance people invest in the narrative provided by the text. As White explains, "Despite its tone, and despite the way we often talk about it, the Constitution has no force except to the extent that it is invoked and used by individual Americans pursuing actual goals" (1984, 244). Because of the Constitution's legal preeminence in the United States, this investment demands the most stringent critical inquiry. To passively accept society's dominant portrayal of the Constitution, to be swayed by the mysticism of the Supreme Court, and to defer uncritically to what the nation's leaders claim as truth is to mistake the Constitution for a sacred text, elevating nationalist pride to the status of dogmatic religion. Democracy and liberty are ill-served by such devotion.

The Constitution can generally (but not exclusively) be seen to serve interests that are fundamentally at odds with social justice. Although US case law contains examples of meaningful constitutional victories that have brought relief, hope, and opportunity to millions of people (*Brown v. Board of Education of Topeka* [1955], is a paradigmatic example), this social progress has come at the price of an unjust bargain. The terms of this bargain can be stated as follows: Poor, average citizens of the United States were granted specific (and often limited) fundamental liberties such as freedom of speech and religion; in return, the concentration of massive wealth in the United States was granted insulation from political accountability and moral responsibility. In other words, the poor received protection for *symbolic* resources, whereas the wealthy received protection for their *material* resources (Lewis, 1999, 256). Furthermore, the protection for speech and prayer pales in comparison to the protection of private property. This latter protection is perhaps the essential concern of the Constitution.

As wealth is power, extreme constitutional protection for property is terrifying. Although citizens have been granted protections from certain forms of *state* action, they received few protections from *private* action. As power in the United States is largely private, many citizens—particularly the laboring classes—live under a *de facto* tyranny. As argued by Boyle, "The language of rights focuses attention on excesses of public power, state power. In a world where enormous concentrations of power are in private hands—Exxon, AT&T, IBM, and the rest—to accept a vision of social justice which worries only about the dangers posed by the state is to condemn oneself to willful blindness" (1992, xli). Arguably, therefore, the fundamental bargain at the heart of the Constitution is no longer tenable and the legal relationship between the wealthy and the poor must be renegotiated.

Private power in the United States is undaunted by the right of citizens to engage in free speech and religious expression, a small cost for the protection of great wealth. Furthermore, the wealthy are unconcerned that the poor are free to embrace, for example, Catholicism, Lutheranism, Southern Baptistism, or Pentecostalism. These distinctions among Christian religions only had a political importance to the ruling elite when the Church of England (an economic monopoly buttressed by the British Empire) declared itself to be the only true church and, for centuries, waged war across Europe against the rest of Christianity.

Because the framers of the Constitution sought to avoid the religious warfare that plagued Europe for many centuries, the notion of "free religion" originally was conceptualized as applying only to the different Christian faiths. This notion is reflected in an influential nineteenth century commentary on the US Constitution, written by Supreme Court Justice Joseph Story. Story wrote that the "real object of the [first] amendment was not to countenance, much less to advance, Mahometanism, or Judaism, or infidelity, by prostrating Christianity; but to exclude all rivalry among Christian sects, and to prevent any national ecclesiastical establishment which should give to a hierarchy the exclusive patronage of the national government" (cited in Van Alstyne, 1995, 856).

As almost no political or economic power exists outside of the control of the two mainstream political parties in the United States, both of which represent the interests of the wealthy, social elites do not fear isolated pockets of dissent, such as sparsely attended public protests at ignored rallies or the publishing of marginally placed books and newspapers. In other words, although freedom of speech and religion are valuable and should be championed, they are, in practice, largely inconsequential. For this reason, the power elites allow such liberties to exist as long as those liberties do not infringe on their interest. For example, until the mid-1960s, members of the US Communist Party risked summary arrest and imprisonment for nothing more than the fact of their party membership. Prior to the mid-1960s, the Soviet Union, to which the US Communist Party was aligned, was considered such a threat to the United States that, on balance, the liberty of free speech and association granted to US citizens—who happened to be members of the Communist Party—was outweighed by the interest of the state (*Whitney v. California* [1927]; *Dennis v. United States* [1951]. When the perceived threat dissipated, there was less motivation for persecuting US Communists. In other words, free speech is afforded only to those dissidents whose causes are not seen as consequential. To the extent that influential speech can have an effect, that speech is often suppressed. In addition to the Constitution, the US system of federalism creates difficulties for the working classes to develop, collectively, political power (Forbath, 1991, 27). Federalism reflects the principle that political authority in the United States is constituted by individual sovereign states. Each of these states surrendered a portion of its sovereignty to create federal authority. Unlike the states, the federal government can only exercise specifically delineated power; the limits of this delineation constitute the limits of federal existence. In other words, the US government is not a centralist power. As the Tenth Amendment states, "The powers not delegated to the United States by the Constitution, nor prohibited by it to the States, are reserved to the States respectively, or to the people." By allocating sovereignty to discrete state legislatures, the drafters of the Constitution rejected the organization of state power and the civil law tradition, as found throughout most of Europe (Forbath, 1991). The federal frame, in turn, was a document intended to disperse the power of different governmental institutions, as well as to resist social factionalism:

> The framers were haunted by the specter of enduring political "factions" based on economic condition—above all factions based on propertylessness. A poor or propertyless faction could well constitute a voting majority and seek to use the state to despoil the propertied or shirk its own economic obligations. . . . Partly to avert such politics, they created a constitutional scheme that treated the sphere of common law rights of contract and property as a suprapolitical realm of private right. As far as market and property and, therefore, class relations were concerned, the rules of the game were presumptively matters of law and not politics, matters for courts, not legislatures. (Forbath, 1991, 27)

Under a federalist system, no single political unit exists for a worker collective to cultivate influence; in other words, there is no critically independent mechanism that can be targeted to institutionalize political labor gains. As a result, the political struggle of the working classes must proceed piecemeal—state by state—with the approval of the administrative, legislative, and judicial branches of the state and federal governments. This fragmentation provides the enemies of labor many opportunities to frustrate labor's progressive objectives (discussed more fully in Chapters 9 and 11).

In addition, the fragmented nature of national authority creates difficulties for willing state and community governments to enact prolabor legislation (assuming approval by the state judiciary). Given the manner in which the economy is currently organized, the more an industry invests in the well-being of its workers, the less competitive that industry becomes against similar industries that do not provide comparable labor benefits.[1] Political difficulties, therefore, arise when a sympathetic legislature mandates improved working conditions and other states do not require such conditions; this leads to capital flight and to home-state unemployment (Ingram, 2002, 5). Federalism pits states against each other (just as globalism pits nations against each other) and encourages a "race to the bottom" (Broad, 1998, 8-10). The "bottom" is an investment climate attractive to commerce and industry at the expense of labor and environmental concerns.

Structurally, the United States has an extremely conservative government.[2] This statement has nothing to do with political parties in the sense that a party may be either "conservative" or "liberal." Fear of the propertyless majority seizing political control is one of the primary reasons why the federal Constitution was drafted. As Erin Rahne Kidwell explains, "The overriding fear of the Framers . . . was of majoritarian tyranny through the representative branches. This fear was present from the very beginning of the constitutional process" (1998, 131). One Framer, Edmund Randolph, argued that "the 'chief danger' the country faced was from too much democracy in some state constitutions, which placed too much power in the hands of the people, thus producing a legislative tyranny" (quoted in Kidwell, 1998, 131). Another Framer, Alexander Hamilton, argued that "the people are gradually ripening in their opinions of government—they begin to be tired of an excess of democracy" (quoted in Kidwell, 1998, 131; see also Chomsky, 1996).[3] Regardless of whether or not Randolph or Hamilton's views were determinative of this point, it is clear that, as the United States industrialized, the protection of the common law rights of contract and property increasingly came to constitute the mainstay of US constitutional law.

The emergence of this judicial ideology is traced to a dissent in the *Slaughter-House Cases* (1872), as well as to an influential treatise by the Chief Justice of the Michigan Supreme Court, Thomas Cooley (1871). Cooley argued that substantive limitations were imposed on state governments by the "due process" clauses of the federal Constitution. Cooley defined the right to private property as "sacred" and held that this right predated the federal Constitution. Therefore, popular sovereignty of the states was limited, with local governments precluded from creating any liberty interest that infringed on the property interest of others. Under this logic, a state would be precluded from creating a "liberty interest" in a worker's "right to health." Unless the state was willing to fund improved working conditions in the workplace or improved access to insurance, such a "right" would exist at the expense of an unwilling industry. To force industry to assume responsibility for its workers would be considered an erosion of an owner's property right, as well as an affront to the dignity of the worker.[4] With a few exceptions for the maintenance of government (such as the power of eminent domain), a person's vested property rights cannot be hindered by an act of positive law.[5]

In the courts, this view of due process (which evolved to protect any "fundamental liberty," such as property or the right to contract) first was expressed in *re Jacobs* (1885). In *Jacobs*, the New York Court of Appeals struck down a state statute that sought to prohibit sweatshops in the cigar industry by prohibiting the manufacturing of cigars in tenement buildings. The court reasoned that the "law interferes with the profitable and free use of his property by the owner or lessee of a tenement-house who is a cigar-maker, and trammels him in the application of his industry and the disposition of his labor, and thus, in a strictly legitimate sense, it arbitrarily deprives him of his property and of some portion of his personal liberty" (1885, 105). This reasoning was elevated to constitutional preeminence in the paradigmatic *Lochner v. New York* (1905), which held invalid a New York state statute limiting bakers to a sixty-hour workweek and to a ten-hour workday.[6] The court reasoned that the statute interfered with the "right of contract" between employer and employee.

With tools such as substantive due process (and with strong ties to the financial elite), the judiciary—a largely nonelected body—appointed for itself the role of protecting private property against popular demands for accountability. The popular legislature was considered by the framers of the Constitution to be too susceptible to "class legislation." Ironically, legislation intended to help the wealthy classes—perhaps the most dominant legislation in the United States—is seldom denigrated as "class legislation." To protect against class legislation on behalf of the poor, federal judges are appointed by the President and confirmed by the Senate (the more popular House of Representatives is altogether bypassed). Judges are appointed for life and achieve their positions through political criteria. For example, Erwin

Chemerinsky notes that the "Reagan and Bush administrations openly used ideology as a key criterion and by all accounts succeeded in moving the Court dramatically to the right" (1993, 912).[7] As elaborated by Christopher E. Smith and Avis Alexandria Jones:

> The underlying purpose of Presidents Reagan and Bush and their political supporters, in seeking to appoint conservative justices to the Supreme Court, was to undo the objectionable decisions by the Warren and Burger-era Courts that established and protected such liberal judicial policies as abortion, affirmative action, school desegregation, and criminal defendants' rights. (1993, 54)

Through such efforts, the social progress of the Warren era is "now threatened by an ardently ideological majority that is willing to engage in pedantic readings of the Constitution which devalue established civil rights and liberties" (Filippatos, 1991, 345). As documented by Peter Irons (1999), the liberal judicial policies alluded to in the Smith and Jones, quotation were themselves anomalies in constitutional jurisprudence. Progressive judicial actions are democratic *deviations* from a judiciary that was conceived of, and functions as, the guarantor of private rights against what the authors of the *Federalist Papers* called the "gusty passions" of "turbulent majorities" (quoted in Forbath, 1991, 35).

To recognize the existence of anomalies that constitute the jurisprudential evolution of a legal morality is to embrace the notion that the law is not monolithic. Nevertheless, US law has a distinct theme or ethos, which is toward the protection of the upper class or elite privilege. This is a particularly important point when considering the history of labor relations in the United States. According to William Forbath:

> The great majority of federal judges in the late nineteenth and early twentieth centuries were Republicans, and the proportion grew ever greater. Their pre-judicial occupations, wealth, as well as their ties of family and friendship placed 98 percent of these Republican gentlemen in positions at the very top of the nation's class and status hierarchies. Small wonder that one finds no great diversity in their opinions affecting labor. (1991, 33)[8]

In the words of Benjamin Cardozo, "In the life of the mind as in life elsewhere, there is a tendency toward the reproduction of kind. Every judgment has a generative power. It begets in its own image" (1921, 21).

As a result of the above structural conditions, many of the evils perpetuated by the United States have been codified by law. Specifically, Native American genocide, African slavery, the bloody colonization of the Philippines, the domestic povertization of women and minorities, neoliberal economics causing the starvation of many millions in the developing world, and major foreign wars of aggression—particularly against Korea and Vietnam—are all the result of legal or permissible policies. For instance, during the Korean War, the United States killed approximately 2 million Koreans and more than 1,000,000 Chinese defenders of the North (Zinn, 1980, 419). In addition, Stanley Karnow estimates that 10% (more than 4,000,000 people) of the entire population of Vietnam was either killed or wounded as a result of the French and, later, US invasion of that country (1991, 11).[9]

Progressive human beings often experience a profound pain for what the United States has done. This feeling is not dissimilar from the feeling expressed by Vaclav Havel, as he reflected on the Jewish Holocaust:

> I am ashamed, if I may put it this way, of the human race. I feel that this is man's crime and man's disgrace, and therefore it is my crime and my disgrace, too. That paralysis allows me to perceive human guilt, and my own co-responsibility for human actions and the condition of our world, from the bottom up. As a human being, I feel responsibility for humanity as such and, staring uncomprehendingly at this cruelty [the Holocaust], I cease to understand myself—for I, too, am human. (1997, 75)

Although supporters of the United States often excuse the suffering caused by the United States by appealing to the transgressions of the Communists, this reasoning is faulty. By such reasoning, the Soviet Union would be culpable for some of the 24 million Soviet deaths caused by the Nazi invasion of the USSR. (a ludicrous notion). Similarly, the United States (along with its allies—in particular, the French) bear full responsibility for the mass destruction the West caused in Asia.

That which is most admirable about the United States—the relative inclusion of diverse people within the normative legal and social structure of mainstream society—most often has occurred in opposition to the Federal Constitution, in a direct assault on the normative legal, social, and economic systems of the nation. Without the history of turbulent social agitation in the United States—specifically, without the challenge of anarchism, socialism, and communism—US society would be a less tolerant and more repressive nation. This point has been emphasized by Havel, who notes that the challenge of communism forced the Western world to actualize its underdeveloped commitment to freedom and equality. Thus, "the communist world was instrumental in the West's own self-affirmation" (1997, 75).

Moral change and social development in the United States have only arisen as the result of extralegal social agitation and discord, even the threat of revolution. Only with great personal sacrifice and tremendous collective suffering have US Americans forced their government to improve. This sacrifice and suffering highlight the fact that admirable traits that have emerged in the United States were not inevitable; rather, they were difficult to attain and can easily be lost.

In comparison to the wretched conditions of two thirds of the world that is utterly dispossessed, life in the United States is privileged even though not everyone living here shares in this privilege, as millions live in pockets of poverty reminiscent of the developing world. In light of the gross wrongness of this privilege (the privilege of the few is the flip side of deprivation of the many), US Americans would do well to contemplate that there is nothing to guarantee that they will enjoy such comfort tomorrow. Contemporary wealth is no guarantee of future wealth (the height presumes the fall). More important, we no longer can justify such privileges—the world will not allow us this luxury. The socialist movement was only one expression of the world's discontent. This movement, no matter how imperfect, was fundamentally just. Destroying socialism did nothing to alleviate the fundamental discontent that the majority of the world feels. From the ashes of the socialist movement has grown a new worldwide expression of revolt—religious fundamentalism. Although the anguish animating this new movement is understandable, the cause is unjust because the end of fundamentalist struggle is not equality. Where socialism sought to move humanity forward, fundamentalist religion of all stripes seeks to return the world to the inhumane intolerance of mystical hierarchy—condemning both freedom and criticism.

As indicated above, an important thesis of this book is that social progress and justice come to the United States slowly, against the backdrop of great injustice and strife, as part of a haphazard thrust toward social inclusion. US Americans must remember, as they are often apt to forget, that every landmark decision that has expanded US liberty stemmed from a "case or controversy"—a legal context in which some representative of a larger class was suffering who embodied the collective anguish of the group in an individual act of disobedience to authority. In other words, our freedoms expanded when ordinary US Americans began asserting claims to constitutional protection that were being denied to them. Contrary to social expectation, social "justice in America has owed much more to civil disobedience than to the use of the ballot" (Rorty, 1999, 257).

As noted by Peter Irons (1999), the history of social progress in this country is the history of people such as Dred Scott Homer Plessy, Lillian Gobitas, Fred Korematsu, Harry Briggs, Norma McCorvey, and Michael Hardwick. These were people whose lives became, for a time, the subject of serious debate about what the Constitution means. In the lives of these people and millions of others who struggled alongside them, we find important connections among life, suffering, and the law. Irons illustrates this point when he discusses the 1987 bicentennial birthday celebration of the Constitution. He contrasts Ronald Reagan's ideological view of the Constitution (eg, "the triumph of human freedom under God") with that of Justice Thurgood Marshall (1999, 462). Marshall, who was the most important lawyer in the fight for civil rights before he became a judge and a Justice, contested Reagan's vision and urged US Americans to "commemorate the suffering, struggle, and sacrifice that triumphed over much that was wrong" with the Constitution (1999, 463). According to Marshall, the credit for our current constitutional liberties "does not belong to the Framers. It belongs to those who refused to acquiesce to outdated notions of liberty, justice, and equality, and who strived to better them" (1999, 463).

As Irons argues, compared with Reagan's, Marshall's perspective is the better way to approach our relationship to the Constitution if society is to remain committed to the Supreme Court's unanimous (and often ignored) decision in *Ex parte Milligan* (1866). As the Court stated, "The Constitution of the United States is a law for rulers and people, equally in war and in peace, and covers with the shield of its protection all classes of men, at all times, and under all circumstances" (cited in Irons, 1999, 271). *Milligan* was written in the months following the Civil War—101 years before Marshall ascended to the Supreme Court as the first African American Justice. As such, Marshall embodies the struggle he encourages US Americans to commemorate. His substantial achievements, and the judicial philosophy he represents, rests squarely on the social struggles that have helped refigure the Constitution.

Marshall's view, however, is a minority view in this country. The achievements of Marshall's moral example cannot compete with the ideology that Reagan represented. Most US Americans, largely because they have not been exposed to the history of our Constitutional past, assume that the Constitution "does something" for them for which they should be grateful and patriotic. On the contrary, that which is most admirable in US culture exists only because regular US Americans helped themselves and helped their communities in the face of Constitutional roadblocks.

The US Constitution best deserves the respect of all US Americans when the document is made to work on behalf of progressive change. Simply, the Constitution does not have any magical qualities or any inherent greatness for which the US people owe an unquestioning allegiance. This is a point explicit in *West Virginia State Board of Education v. Barnette* (1943), holding that the First Amendment forbids the government from punishing students for refusing to pledge allegiance to the US flag. In what was perhaps the Court's most elegantly written landmark First Amendment decision, the Court reasoned:

> We can have intellectual individualism and the rich cultural diversities that we owe to exceptional minds only at the price of occasional eccentricity and abnormal attitudes. When they are so harmless to others or to the State as those we deal with here, the price is not too great. But the freedom to differ is not limited to things that do not matter much. That would be a mere shadow of freedom. The test of its substance is the right to differ as to things that touch the heart of the existing order.

Then, in an oft-quoted and justly celebrated metaphor, the Court articulated why the state is proscribed from promoting any orthodoxy:

> If there is any fixed star in our constitutional constellation, it is that no official, high or petty, can prescribe what shall be orthodox in politics, nationalism, religion, or other matters of opinion or force citizens to confess by word or act their faith therein. If there are any circumstances which permit an exception, they do not now occur to us.

Although we cannot go back to 1787 to make things different for the tens of millions of people who suffered due to the Constitution—most notably, African Americans, Native Americans, the working classes, women, Asians, homosexuals, and immigrants—the imperative remains to remember (and regret) our past and use this memory to remake the future. To the extent that US Americans can remake the future by reconfiguring the Constitution, the Constitution becomes something to inspire pride. Only then can we overcome the shame of Justices such as Roger Taney, author of *Dred Scott v. Sandford* (1857), holding that slaves were property, that they could not be considered citizens, and that Congress was precluded from depriving white citizens of their slave property without due process of law.

Along with Irons, many critical scholars may agree that we must "speak ill of the dead when they committed acts of infamy" (1999, 184). For committing the United States to the proposition that the word *citizen*, as it appears in the Constitution, was not intended to include the class of African slaves, Taney is no less despicable a human being than was Hitler for his racial commitments.[10] According to Taney's ruling, black people were not entitled to the "rights and privileges" that the Constitution granted people of other races who became citizens and this ruling was intended to reinforce the legal status of slaves as property. Taney's decision meant that slave owners were protected from any act of Congress intended to deprive Southern masters of their slaves in the absence of "due process" of law.

As people remake the future against the conservative structure of the Constitution, the Constitution expands. These challenges, however, are themselves extraconstitutional, making the present Constitution unrecognizable to those who signed the original document in 1787. This is a good thing, although we have much further to go, but this "expansive" view of the Constitution is a politically explosive point of contention in this country, fueling much conservative rhetoric and action intended to curtail the Bill of Rights. "Culture wars" in the United States are often fought on this point.

The pervasive cultural conservatism that exists in this country creates difficulties for scholars to argue that the law—as social and historical force—is fluid and potentially liberating because constitutional jurisprudence often denies the social and historical context of the law. A clear example of this can be found in *McCleskey v. Kemp* (1987) where the Court upheld the death sentence of an African American man, even as the Court acknowledged the systemic racial unfairness of capital punishment.[11]

The self-denial of the law's historical nature is most clear when the words of the judiciary become localized by scholars. From slavery to labor, from sex to abortion, and from welfare to corporate privilege, judges and Justices often shut moral factors out of their legal calculus, instead choosing to focus on a foundation of positive law. Such positive law is found in the governing ideology of wealth, power, and privilege that was codified in the original Constitution and that is often referred to as the *intent* of the Framers. Thus, many individuals who construct our legal commitments find nonsensical the proposition that the law is historical and social. To them, the law is structural and is deduced from the first principles of the framework established by the Framers—white rich men who had no awareness of the concerns or issues found in modern US society.

The Framers enacted their own agendas and compromises that we, in only a vague sense, should regard as our own. Beneath their often inspiring rhetoric, the Framers had many practices that we would find repugnant and morally reprehensible today. Many of these practices (eg, genocide, slavery, torture, widespread executions, misogyny, and class elitism) *were* repugnant, even by the standards of their time. Rather than seeing the Framers as doing the best they could, we may regard them as moral failures and despicable human beings, for it took nearly 200 years to undo many of the systemic cruelties they initiated, and much work still needs to be done.

In terms of their sentiments, values, norms, and beliefs, the Framers of the Constitution are as alien to US culture today as is Jim Crow or Lochnerism.[12] To deny this is to succumb to the narratives proposed by Reagan when he attributed divine influence to the foundation of the US Republic. Unfortunately, the US people largely ignore this historical point and, thus, ignore that the law was intended to be a conservative stabilizing force, "protecting" against popular democratic sentiments, as the Framers intended. To recognize this, we must acknowledge that the law is "historical" and "social," and that a tension exists between the conservative function of the law and the democratic potential of the United States. On the one hand, we have an admirable national *rhetorical* commitment to democracy, equality, and justice. On the other hand, the United States is burdened with a history of fear that its leaders have consistently had of a more inclusive (and, hence, less constitutional but more humane) form of economy and society.

Much faith should be placed in the ability of progressive society to rethink the Constitution. Since World War II, the Constitution, as interpreted by the Warren Court, in particular, has been an important means by which US society has become "less constitutional" and more democratically inclusive (from the point of view of "strict constructionism," which elevates to contemporary preeminence the constitutional standards of 1787). Historically, liberty of contract and liberty of property have been the primary ways by which the Constitution worked against minorities and the working classes. Thus, the belated repudiation of Lochnerism in the 1930s was a crucial step in the direction of democracy. Another important step in the movement away from the Constitution as a weapon of class and racial warfare occurred when the people most excluded from the Constitution took to the streets in a collective stand—as they did in the 1960s—to remind people that the protections of the Constitution are uneven and that the privileges of the elite are well entrenched.

Many people do not suspect or do not care that the US Constitution and the US Supreme Court have tended to stand, during most of this country's history, for all the things that the United States rightly claims today to reject: social evils such as intolerance, racism, terrorism, and classism (see Zinn, 1980). Therefore, a historical understanding of the painful past United States and an acknowledgment of the continual struggle in the United States for community and justice are important today in our continuing effort to take US democracy to the next level—social democracy. These promises are significant, even in light of the structural shortcomings of the Constitution. The fact remains that the Constitution exists whether or not that text hurts us or helps us to be happy and healthy. US Americans deserve an accountable Constitution, one meeting the needs of a people the Framers never intended to protect.

This book's condemnation of the law should not be taken as advocating illegal activity; rather, the condemnation acknowledges that *obeying* the law and *respecting* the law are different activities. Obeying the law is necessary because the entire coercive force of the United States stands behind the law; in other words, the legal order is growing increasingly invincible to a frontal attack. Respecting the law, however, is unnecessary, as the *Barnette* decision made clear.[13] What this book advocates is a fundamental rethinking of many legal norms, such as those that protect the interests of the rich against the needs of the poor or those that allow the United States to abuse most of the world economically and militarily. Those laws and norms should be rendered obsolete, anachronisms of a morally impoverished time, just as, in the United States, slavery is now recognized as repugnant. The way to fight legal injustice is not through lawlessness, but through the restructuring of our moral lives. As Victor Wallis notes, "You don't unravel a deeply institutionalized system of oppression by carrying out acts that reinforce the legitimacy of those who stand at its head" (2002, 158).

Clearly, some laws are socially prudent because violating them hurts people, and the fundamental assumption behind this book's notion of social justice is that hurting people is wrong. Thus, injunctions against murder, rape, and assault are necessary, but accepting this principle should not blind people to the fact that other laws do not, in fact, prevent people from getting hurt but, instead, legitimize the power of some people to hurt others. A foundational assumption in my thinking is that society should be structured so as to maximize the health, potential, and social security of all citizens, as well as to coordinate efforts with other nations to create a world culture grounded in this security. The well-being of all is best derived from a system of social and economic justice that has not been actualized under a system of Constitutional rights and the sanctity of private property.

# ✱ NOTES ✱

1. I recognize that some corporations, such as *Ben & Jerry's* and *The Body Shop*, have created the public image of themselves as being exceptions to my claim. These corporations, however, are not always what they claim to represent. For a critique of "socially responsible business," see Jennings and Entine (1999). These authors provide a scathing critique of so-called "caring capitalism," which markets its products with claims of being socially conscious (*Celestial Seasonings* and *Esprit de Corp* are two further examples of such companies). According to these authors, these companies offer misinformation and other ploys to mislead customers. These authors do not suggest that no company is truly caring, but that many are exploiting what the authors call "rain-forest chic" the "corporate branding strategy of capitalizing on consumer use of environmental issues as a screen for buying decisions." See also Entine (2001). Entine's Website (http://www.jonethine.com) is a distribution center for his many newspaper articles on business, media, and ethics. I do not mean to suggest that no company can ever be socially responsible, only that such efforts are increasingly difficult under a free market and globalized economy.

2. This changed slightly when Franklin Roosevelt was forced by the critical exigency of the Great Depression to save the constitutional system by forcing industry to accept fundamental improvements in working conditions for labor. In Germany, in contrast, the effort to achieve political recognition for labor was easier (although also violent); labor activists had only to convince the German leadership in the nineteenth century that the working classes would no longer tolerate political marginalization. Germany was one of the earliest European nations to create a social-welfare state, and other European nations soon followed–in some cases, seventy years before comparable developments occurred in the United States. A similar phenomenon occurred with the issue of African American civil rights in the United States. For 100 years after the abolishment of slavery, the descendents of slaves were systematically denied their civil and human rights. The federal government made negligible effort to alleviate the profound suffering of the African American community. This changed under the exigence created by the mass civil disobedience of the civil rights movement. Goaded by massive protest, and shamed by international criticism, the federal government expanded constitutional protection to the African American community.

3. Hamilton's fear of an "excess of democracy" is symptomatic of the general distrust that many Framers had of the average US American. Specifically, the Framers were afraid that the mass of poor people would seek redress through the political channels. The phrase "excess of democracy" was also evoked by social elites during the 1960s and early 1970s when popular expressions of alternative values and economics were commonly expressed. Such "street democracy," often with leveling tendencies, was a threat that the Constitution was partly designed to prevent.

4. Nineteenth and early twentieth century common law held that workers assumed the risk of employment on accepting employment. The classical expression of substantive due process was rejected in *Nebbia v. New York* (1934).

5. However, as a result of the post-Reagan dismantling of Roosevelt era reform, modern constitutional jurisprudence on property has largely resurrected classical substantive due process. See Nollan v. California Coastal Commission (1987) and Dolan v. City of Tigard (1994); both cases limited government power to condition land-use permits on land- owner "extractions" in the public interest. This movement suffered a recent set-back in Tahoe-Sierra Preservation Council, Inc. v. Tahoe Regional Planning Agency (2002), holding that landowners are not entitled to compensation for economic loss as the result of a temporary moratorium on the development of their land by an environmental regulatory agency.

6. An important exception to this principle was grounded in sexist assumptions about the inherent frailty of women and their importance in bearing offspring. See *Muller v. Oregon* (1908), upholding a state law limiting women in manual factory labor to a ten-hour workday.

7. Less objectionable presidents, such as Franklin Roosevelt, engaged in similar political behavior vis-à-vis their own party ideology.

8. Although there are exceptions to this analysis in terms of state judges, who are often popularly elected, an extraordinary amount of normative power in the United States lies with an unaccountable and ideologically motivated federal judiciary.

9. It is too early to tell the long-term consequences and Iraqi casualties of the unprovoked US invasion and occupation of Iraq.

10. My position that society must be respectful of all people does not prevent me from condemning those individuals who perpetuate suffering. Such individuals need to be incapacitated; Taney and Hitler were, in my opinion, both guilty of perpetuating immense suffering.

11. McClesky features a strong dissent by Thurgood Marshall, who accentuates the lasting legacy of racism in the United States and chastises the majority for its flagrant anti-historicism and for its blindness in failing to recognize the limitations of the Constitution.

12. "Lochnerism" was a judicial policy governing the Court's reasoning about law and society, holding that laissez-faire capitalism was enshrined by the Constitution, and that the legislature had no business passing social welfare legislation that would impede on the prerogatives of capital and property. Lochnerism died with the victory of Franklin Roosevelt's New Deal, but has been resurrected in recent years by Reaganism and its effects.

13. Although the government can draft a person's body (*Arver v. United States*, 1918, holding that compulsory military service is not precluded by the antislavery provisions of the Thirteenth Amendment to the Federal Constitution), the government cannot draft that person's conscience. Individuals can be forced, under the threat of imprisonment, to kill in the service of the government while, at the same time, that person is free (according to the law) to denounce that killing and to indict the government for its aggression.

# CHAPTER 4

## OFFERING A RADICAL CRITIQUE OF THE PROBLEM OF THE PRESENT

The fourth framing device is a radical critique of the present. Such critique is necessary—indeed, essential—to increase popular resistance to the many deleterious policies of the United States. Since September 11, 2001, an increased cultural current of passive acceptance and quietism has emerged in the United States, companions to the outpouring of patriotism incurred in the wake of the September 11 attacks. Such patriotism is not a virtue, especially when it is used to silence those who would criticize the government. In his keynote address presented on February 16, 2002, to the Rocky Mountain Communication Association, for example, Professor Lance Strate argued that, post-9/11, intellectuals should not be overly critical of the government. In contrast to the ideal of passive acceptance and quietism in the face of "national adversity," this book argues that there are few better times for progressive US Americans to stand up and do their utmost to condemn the actions of the US government that promote an unjust global society.[1] This book distances itself from the negative connotations attached to the label *radical*. To speak "truth to power" should not be considered negative; to hold a mirror to society, even a mirror that embodies the biases and anguish of its creator, is not a negative act. There should be more mirrors, biases, and expressed anguish—more outrage. Such outrage, nurtured by a deep sense of morality, is essential to the concern of the partisan critic. Even through the expression of this concern makes members of society uncomfortable, this is necessary; a society too content with itself, conceited, and oblivious to the pain caused by its excesses, is a society whose moral voice has been silenced.

Most would agree that change is potentially good and that stasis often leads to decay. Life forms or communities that do not change, adapt, or transform to meet new challenges and new conditions perish. Human life would become unbearably boring if 5,000 years from now human society remained the same as it is today. Although many people respect the accomplishments of ancient Greek culture, most would agree that, if Western culture were exclusively the experience of ancient Greece, most of what makes Western culture interesting would disappear. Most people, therefore, do not fear the development of the world that can come about through progressive change; rather, they fear what they have to relinquish in the present to effectuate such change. Thomas Jefferson, for example, envisioned a United States without slavery, yet he was unwilling to free his own slaves during his lifetime. More recently, as noted by Martin N. Marger, "Although whites today seem to generally accept the appropriateness of compensatory polices for racial minorities in principle, their support is not as unambiguous when efforts at applying those principles, in the form of concrete measures and programs, are made" (1997, 364). The radical, therefore, is the person who not only accepts the idea of progressive change, but who also argues for its immediacy:

> What makes one a radical . . . is not that one is against hierarchy, since we all sometimes accept it, nor that one is against "illegitimate" hierarchy, since we're all against that. Nor is the radical the person with the theory that "goes to the root." None of us has such a theory. The radical is the person who wants to go further, right now, practically, to dismantle existing structures of hierarchy that look evil, and wants to go further, right now, practically, in confronting or subverting the forces that keep them in place. (Kennedy, 1983, 81)

In this positive sense, this book is radical, as my basic argument is that US Americans need to change their country *now* to embrace social justice. Law, as experienced in the United States, is, practically speaking, unresponsive to moral urgency. As explained by judge (later Justice) Benjamin N. Cardozo, the law's ameliorative power is gradual, it "goes on inch by inch. Its effects must be measured by decades and even centuries. Thus measured, they are seen to have behind them the power and the pressure of the moving glacier" (1921, 25). Cardozo's glacier metaphor of legal change is worrisome. The people who need food, shelter, health care, and an environment uncontaminated by toxins and social disease cannot wait for an ice age. To insist they wait is to confirm that the law is a tool for social injustice. In sum, the era of change represented by Martin Luther King, Jr. was only the beginning of the work that must be done in this country. Unfortunately, until the United States comes to terms with its past and present, change in the future will be difficult to accomplish. Furthermore, the thought that the future will resemble the present is terrifying, particularly in the post–September 11 political culture.

On September 11, 2001, the United States experienced firsthand the discomfort with which much of the world lives on a regular basis. This was unfortunate, as is any violence of this magnitude. Since the late nineteenth century, however, the United States repeatedly has acted in ways that are equally reprehensible. This position is not anti-American, nor does it excuse the September 11 attacks. Rather, it does make those attacks more understandable, particularly for Americans who do not comprehend what their government represents around the globe. What makes September 11 interesting is less the fact that the United States was attacked and more the potential to think differently that could have followed from this event (ie, the cultivating of a progressive American moral consciousness).

In the most positive sense, the attacks in New York and the Pentagon were an invitation for the United States to change—to recognize that peace in the world depends upon a restrained, less imperialistic nation, sensitive to the human dignity of others. If the United States remains selfishly rich while enacting policies that force much of the rest of the world into extreme poverty, then we should not be surprised to find ourselves the target of the world's collective frustration. If Americans learn to care about the suffering of others (which entails recognizing the pervasive suffering that our government causes in other countries), then something great could come out of America's collective sadness—a reordering of values along socialist-humanist lines. Fundamental to this reordering is a sincere commitment to an equitable world economy in which everyone has access to healthy food, clean water, sanitary and secure living quarters, and basic health care. Instead, the opposite has occurred; since September 11, the United States has grown more militaristic, antagonistic, and more cruelly determined to dominate the world for its own material advantage.

In the months following September 11, the United States threatened preemptive nuclear strikes on seven nations, including Russia and China (Tyson, 2002). Then the United States attacked and occupied the weaker nations of Afghanistan and Iraq, setting up regimes friendly to itself. The fact that Afghanistan and Iraq both had morally despicable governments does little to justify the US invasion, for the United States has overthrown governments that were morally courageous and socially progressive. Consider, for example, the history of military campaigns by the United States to suppress popular movements and governments in Central and South America.

While US intervention in Central and South America dates back to the Monroe Doctrine, the modern era of belligerency began in the 1950s when the United States overthrew the elected Guatemalan government to prevent it from reclaiming lands previously appropriated by the United States. With this land, the Guatemalan government intended to grow crops to feed its starving people. Similarly, in the 1970s, the US government overthrew Chile's social democracy because, as in Guatemala, the government was popular and committed to improving the lives of the Chilean people (which necessarily interfered with US hegemony and economic interests). Military intervention peaked in the 1980s with President Ronald Reagan's war against the peoples of Nicaragua and El Salvador to reverse (in the case of Nicaragua) and to prevent (in the case of El Salvador) progressive political change.

US policy in Central and South America was, to a large extent, shadowy—covered up by the compliant press. For example, most Americans are unaware that Nicaragua took the United States before the International Court of Justice, which ordered the United States to stop its attacks (*I.C.J. Reports,* 1986; see Ward and Green, 2000, 84). The United States, which repeatedly ignores international law when the law conflicts with US interests, simply ignored the World Court (as it ignores the illegality of its embargo against Cuba).

However, as a result of the Iran-Contra scandal, which exposed Reagan's illegal foreign policy (Reagan's policy contravened the Boland Amendment, passed by Congress in 1983 as a result of public pressure against Reagan's foreign policy in the region), public awareness, for a time, increased. Central to this scandal was Marine Lieutenant Colonel Oliver North, who was responsible for coordinating Reagan's war in Central America. North defended himself before Congress and the American people on the grounds that the actions of the United States in the region were justified for the sake of "protecting the Constitution." With this argument, North became a hero for many Americans who accepted the crimes of the US government in the name of patriotism (North's conviction for obstructing justice, destroying documents, and perjury was overturned). North and others involved in the scandal served little or no prison time and received pardons by President George H.W. Bush, who had been vice-president under Reagan. North then became a viable (but unsuccessful) candidate for the US Senate, as well as a wealthy entrepreneur of military supplies and a Washington, DC, radio talk show host.

To take a more recent example of the moral poverty of much US foreign policy, George W. Bush touts his "war on terror" as supporting the common good, but it will be used to suppress many forms of resistance to the United States around the globe. This is particularly clear in South America, where the US military aid to the Columbian government has dramatically increased since September 11. Military aid had been high prior to September 11, but was couched as support for the "war on drugs." This facade has now been dropped, and the money is overtly being used in direct counterinsurgency support against the Columbian leftist rebels in Columbia's four-decade–long civil war.

Bush exploited the rhetorical opportunity presented by the attack on the United States to bifurcate the world into two camps—our allies and our enemies. Either a nation supports the United States or is at war with the United States. Bush then ordered the world to choose: "Every nation and every region now has a decision to make," Bush declared, "either you are with us, or you are with the terrorists" (Fornek, 2001).

Since no military power on the planet exists to resist the United States, the United States has taken for itself the right to attack anybody, anywhere, and for any reason. Indeed, the "disappearance of the Soviet Union . . . means that there is now no effective counterweight to US and Western predominance in international relations" (Miliband, 1996, 15; see Rorty, 2003).

Our leaders' arrogance is palpable. No nation "has the authority or the competence to determine by force the social and political structure [of another], no right to serve as international judge and executioner" (Chomsky, 1971, 86). Yet, our leaders assume this power, and many Americans accept and celebrate this power as they recoil "from the prospect of a world in which America's political and economic frontiers would become coterminous with her territorial frontiers . . . a world in which the American example and American influence would become irrelevant" (Tucker, 1980, 264).

What patriotic supporters of the United States do not realize is that relevancy and influence should be earned, not assumed or taken. The United States, in assuming for itself the "right" to have influence, has not earned this influence through the practice of good deeds.

While political systems worse than that of the United States surely exist, this does not excuse the practices of the US government—a government more powerful than any other in terms of economic and military might. With such power comes responsibility—a moral obligation to use that power for the good of humanity (ie, a *substantive* good measured by increasing poor people's access to life-sustaining resources, as opposed to rhetorical appeals to an undefined and simplistic notion of "freedom"). Sadly, many Americans mistake material power and wealth for spiritual and moral superiority (as in "Manifest Destiny"). Yet, as judged by its foreign policy, the United States is not a moral country and seldom has been, although the United States is an excessively rich country capable of great benevolence. This great, largely concentrated, wealth—proof enough of social injustice—is the result of systematic theft by US elites from both their own people and from much of the rest of the world.

## ✴ NOTE ✴

1. Rorty condemns many intellectuals for not being "patriotic enough to see their country as a symbol of social hope" (1991b, 71). I confess to being this type of intellectual, recognizing, along with Voltaire, that "in order to be a good patriot one often has to be the enemy of the rest of mankind" (1977, 124). Since the early 1990s, Rorty has expressed less enthusiasm for the ability of the US political and economic systems to improve on their own accord.

# CHAPTER 5

## OUTLINING A NEW VISION OF LAW, SOCIAL JUSTICE, AND POWER

The fifth and final framing device situating this book is the conflict (or nexus) between law, social justice, and power. There is often a correlation between the "will-to-law" as practiced in the United States—the rigid law and order ideology—and the pervasiveness of social injustice. The law serves many masters, only one of which is justice; other masters include power, wealth, privilege, and social control. Although the popular discourse of law often speaks in the appealing name of justice, citizens should become more discerning. Justice, after all, is nothing more than an idea, culturally defined; in the United States, at least, the law is limited by the lack of our moral imagination. Justice is, first and foremost, an issue of community and, thus, can be analyzed in critical communication terms (see, Frey, Pearce, Pollock, Artz, and Murphy, 1996, 114).

The proposition that law is often a source of injustice runs contrary to common sentiment in the United States, where law is often elevated to the status of a state religion. Critical law students often find this disturbing. The professors and the majority of students, as well as the judges and Justices in the court cases students read, tend to assume *a priori* that the legal system is facially just and that any perceived flaw in the system is an anomaly to be redressed by further law. This goes unquestioned, although students read many cases codifying social injustice.[1] Although students are encouraged to interrogate the reasoning of any specific holding, they are discouraged from extrapolating to any larger critique of the system. Most students do not resist this quietism and passivity, as resistance could compromise their anticipated $110,000 year (or more) starting salaries, useful for paying off the more than $100,000 average debt that students incur at the best law schools in the United States.

Rather than becoming inspired by their law school experience, some students are horrified by what they study. Even those that come to law school already critical of the United States, but with an open mind about the beneficence of the US legal order, learn to understand more clearly that "the law" is not something to be respected in the abstract. Although some law in the United States strives for social justice, such as when municipalities provide the civil rights that the federal government denies to homosexuals, the legal system, as a whole, is fundamentally skewed against the interest of social democracy. Although classical Marxism has an overly reductionist view of law—dismissing law as merely a tool for ruling class oppression—this view is not entirely inaccurate. Legal norms and institutions do derive, at least in part, from superstructural phenomena such as modes of economy, security, privilege, and social control—the instruments of the elite. Reducing law to economic influences is simplistic; however, acknowledging this does not preclude viewing law as serving the dominant interests of the ruling elite. This was particularly evident to me in law school. With only a few exceptions—most notably Justice Thurgood Marshall (an anomaly resulting from historical factors that are unlikely to be repeated)—judges and Justices in the United States shamelessly serve class and systemic interests, effectively stifling social justice. My law school experiences further reinforced my belief that there is little difference in practice between the two-party system found in the United States and one-party systems of other nations. Lee Artz and Bren A.O. Murphy illustrate a similar point by what they call "two parties, one hegemony":

> The Democrats and Republicans do not really compete but, rather, collude against the public, as institutional representatives of hegemony, they share dominant ideologies, such as patriotism, deregulation, cuts in social services, and support of individualism and consumerism. (2000, 247)

For the above reasons, legal norms should be interrogated constantly so that the most egregious instances of codified legal immorality can be purged from society, along with the privileges of the elite protected by these norms. For this task, we should not rely too heavily on lawyers because they are also the problem; it is difficult for society to use the agents of the law to address the limitations of the law. As noted by Anthony Chase:

> The American legal profession [is] one of the most extraordinary enclaves of essentially private power in the modern world. The influence of law and lawyers in contemporary American social life has done little to alter public perception that there is a disturbing inequity in access to justice, that delay remains an

> inescapable feature of reliance upon law, or that the technicalities of law and the specialization of legal practice make the system virtually impossible for most citizens to even understand, let alone master. (1994, 1970)

The system will not likely be changed unless US society begins to produce a new type of lawyer—the critical lawyer—unwilling to swear an oath of allegiance to the Constitution and the property interests protected by this system. There are more than one million attorneys in the United States, only a handful of whom are similar to Clarence Darrow or William M. Kunstler. Darrow and Kunstler both spent their careers defending high-profile US political dissidents from government repression. Because an oath of allegiance to the Constitution is a necessary condition for receiving a law license (as well as for university employment in many states), there is, at the onset, a significant barrier to the practice (or teaching) of critical law.

## ✶ TOWARD A CRITICAL LEGAL PERSPECTIVE ✶

When people think about the law in a traditional sense, they usually contemplate a system of rights and obligations that they have vis-à-vis others and the State. In Anglo-American legal culture, the law helps to structure how people act in ways that are considered acceptable, informing our expectations as to how other people will treat us. In common parlance, it is the law "which makes regularized political life possible and which provides for the implementation and maintenance of policies" (Palley, 1978, 3). As defined in this way, the law places people in society, securing the relative privileges of citizens from the vicissitudes of wanton government and private interference. But to conceive of law in this way is to deny or to downplay the violence that this social structuring enacts and aggregates. For example, outside of general tax obligations, people in the United States are encouraged by the law to ignore the world around them when there is no duty-bound connection between their prosperity or health and the suffering of others. This is the world that exists under what feminist scholar Carol Gilligan (1982) identified as the "ethics of justice." This is a masculine ethic and can be contrasted with a feminine perspective, known as the "ethics of care."

The ethics of justice involve ethical reasoning focusing on abstractions such as rights, principles, and rules. Under this view, the Rule of Law has its own special status outside the context of human affairs. Women, however, are more likely to address moral issues by focusing on concrete examples—specific relationships, communal needs, and the mutuality of responsibility. Under the masculine view, justice is blind and carries a sword. Under the feminine view, justice is discerning, grounded in humane values, and caring. Justice carries not a sword but a plowshare, which nurtures the growth of community.

Feminists use the famous case of *Yania v. Bigan* (1959) to illustrate the importance of the distinction between the two moral positions. In *Yania*, the court held that the defendant was *not* liable when he stood by and watched a man, with whom he had been having a conversation, drown. In other words, within the Anglo-American legal tradition, a person has no affirmative duty to rescue or to help another (absent a special relationship). Society, according to this view, has no tangible interest in structuring how people react to the misfortunes of others. Although people, as individuals, are free to make moral and ethical choices to help others, these moral and ethical questions or motivations are considered by society to be extralegal. US society refers to this as *individualism*, which is considered a foundational principle in our culture.

There are sufficient policy reasons to ground a society in such an ethic of individualism. Human autonomy and respect for the individual are central to the functioning and success of many societies. However, as feminists and other critical legal scholars point out, there are limits to the amount of individualism a society can tolerate before that society's preference for individual rights leads to widespread suffering. Such suffering exists in US society and has been rendered invisible under a system of social dominance in which law expresses and reifies what is legitimate at the expense of that which is deemed illegitimate.

The marginalization of social suffering can be described as *objectivism*. Roberto Mangabeira Unger describes objectivism as "the belief that the authoritative legal materials—the system of statutes, cases, and accepted legal ideas—embody and sustain a defensible scheme of human association" (1986, 2). Such objectivism, as applied to the *Yania* case, denied the social and economic relationships embedded in the context of the case.

These relationships—such as between the drowned Yania and his wife and children—are arguably far more important than the legal relationship that the court found lacking between Yania and Bigan. Bluntly stated, the interests of Yania's family in Yania's continued health or Yania's interest in living a longer life were not recognized by the court as being important. The court was able to reach this conclusion because these values are not part of the law's normative vision. As described by Mary Midgley:

> The independent self of the social contract lives in a world modeled on that of seventeenth-century cosmology. It is a solitary atom gyrating in a social void, a radically solitary rational entity moving among a crowd of others with whom it has no real connection. This is a world which does not easily find room for non-rational humans such as babies and a world which can scarcely accommodate non-human nature at all. (2001, 147)

More specifically, as argued by Leslie Bender:

> [The law teaches us] to reject [our] emotions, instincts, and ethics, and to view accidents and tragedies abstractly, removed from their social and particularized contexts, and to apply instead rationally-derived universal principles and a vision of human nature as atomistic, self-interested, and as free from constraint as possible. (1988, 33)

As an alternative, the ethic of care focuses attention on the unique context of the dispute and on the parties' ongoing relationships and interdependencies. As Bender explains:

> The care-oriented problem-solver examines the connections between and among people, looking at their interpersonal responsibilities and needs. Preventing hurt, preserving relationships and developing cooperative solutions rooted in the concrete particulars of the conflict are objectives of a care-oriented ethical analysis. (1990, 37)

Traditional law's fixation with extreme individualism overlooks important social and communal values that need to be recognized in our legal system, as well as in our society. As critical lawyers argue, there are moral or ethical issues that the law needs to mediate, particularly the relationship between the affluent and the poor. Therefore, a law of social justice must address questions about the day-to-day influence of law in the life of everyday people, particularly people who are victimized by law. Such people have been rendered invisible. To even contemplate the idea that the law can "victimize" is itself a challenge to many people's conceptualization of law. As a consequence, society tends not to consider the plight of the poor when making many decisions regarding the allocation of resources and the practical legal issues of the day. Simply, providing for a fair distribution of society's wealth is not recognized as a legal question; instead, there exists the widespread recognition of an important truism in our world—that there must be restrictions on theft (Hart, 1997, 91).

For the idea of theft to be meaningful, however, there must first be some common idea of property, and an important function of all legal systems is to provide such a definition. Hence, although the general prohibition against theft is important, this importance is different from what most people assume. From a critical legal perspective, *prohibitions against theft are a violence that the law does to the dispossessed by defining the needs of other people (those who possess property) as more important than the needs of the poor for a life of dignity.* This is simply another way of saying that those "with power in civil society . . . design its norms and institutions, which become the status quo" (MacKinnon, 1989, 238). When the necessity arises to solve problems of economic injustice, the law often turns its shoulder. An alternative exists, as explained by Unger:

> Law practice should be, and to some extent law is, the legal defense of individual or group interests by methods that reveal the specificity of the underlying institutional and imaginative order, that subject it to a series of petty disturbances capable of escalating at any moment, and that suggest alternative ways of defining collective interests, collective identities, and assumptions about the possible. (1986, 111)

Law could be—and is from a critical legal perspective—about creating the possible rather than codifying and perpetuating the extremely intolerant society that we were in the eighteenth and nineteenth centuries. As Henry Giroux explains, "Justice is not merely the application of procedural rules to varying contexts; it is an attempt to understand how moral sensibilities are formed amid human suffering and the struggle for liberation and freedom" (1988, 93). In other words, "Justice is not organized around an appeal to abstract principles but is rooted in a substantive project of transforming those concrete social and political structures that deny dignity, hope, and power to vast numbers of people" (1988, 93).

As opposed to traditional legal theorists, critical legal theorists seek, in jurisprudence, "a theory of the relation between life and law" (MacKinnon,

1989, 237), explicating the law as lived by the people who drink daily from law's bitterness and wince from law's lashes. Legal order always comes at a cost. One reason most US Americans reject totalitarianism is that the cost of a totalitarian legal and political order is simply too high for most of our legal and political sensibilities; US Americans, however, have a greater tolerance for accepting their own legal and political victimization which they do not characterize as injustice. The time has come when they can no longer consistently reject totalitarianism and simultaneously refuse to engage critically with the harmful ramifications of the US system.

## ✶ A THEORY OF POWER: DUALITY AND COMMUNITY ✶

In the West ever since Aristotle, power has been analyzed systematically from multiple perspectives. In the remainder of this chapter, a naturalistic notion of power is contrasted with the imperial use of power as practiced by the United States. As argued here, power is healthy when used to constitute holistic and inclusive communities, when people equally share in the nurturance of power. This notion of power is horizontal, flowing among people; in contrast, imperial power is lateral, selective, and exclusionary. Moreover, such power is hurtful and constitutive of much social and political disease.

### The United States as Empire

As argued by Susan Owen and Peter Ehrenhaus, contemporary US America "is best understood as empire" (1993, 170). This empire can be viewed in two different but interconnected ways. The first is the traditional notion of empire as conquest. In US law, conquest became a constitutionally sanctioned method for bestowing property rights when the US Supreme Court formally extinguished the property rights of Native Americans, who had been dispossessed of their land through white colonization. According to the court, "Conquest gives a title which the courts of the conqueror cannot deny . . . The title by conquest is acquired and maintained by force. The conqueror prescribes its limits" (*Johnson v. M'Intosh*, 1823; reprinted in Dukeminier and Krier, 1998, 9).

The second sense of empire to which Owen and Ehrenhaus refer involves "the intricate orchestration of American cultural, political and economic institutions, and . . . their attendant social practices" (1993, 170). This empire, they argue, is organic; it is a living, growing, self-conscious force concerned with consumption and expansion and "has voracious appetites; it thrives by feeding upon those less well positioned in the world and its perpetuation requires domination over those both within its boundaries and without" (1993, 170).

Until the latter part of the twentieth century, empire was established and maintained through military force and accepted by the colonizer's legal system. The Athenians, Romans, Spanish, Italians, Danish, Portuguese, French, British, and Germans were all at one time expansionist societies, conquering, exploiting, and enslaving much of the world. Currently, the world has evolved such that traditional military conquest is difficult to maintain, and the practice of empire has become largely internal, involving the financial manipulations of economies and the colonization of minds through mass-mediated propaganda and the promotion of consumer escapism, what Michael Carbone calls "our anti-critical mass culture with its managed information" (1988, 8). As Owen and Ehrenhaus explain:

> American empire accomplishes its hegemony largely through the creation of diversions—distractions of desire that integrate the individual into the broader constellation of institutional relations: consumer, voter, spectator, patriot, fan, etc. Empire thrives precisely because of the given consent, complicity, and absorption of those upon whom it feeds. (1993, 171)

A similar position has been articulated recently by Michael Hardt and Antonio Negri (2001). They view the United States as embodying progressive ideals, such as the protection of civil liberties, but they also argue that the United States fails to enact a democratic society. The United States has become a flourishing global empire, as Owen and Ehrenhaus suggest. Fundamental to this empire is communication, which "not only expresses but also organizes the movement of globalization" (2001, 32).

One result of this empire is the fragmentation of identity among citizens, both domestically and internationally. Such fragmentation is often mistakenly characterized as a symptom of a new vision of the world, captured by the term postmodernism. Many critical scholars today are suspicious of this term and argue that the postmodern world is little more than a hypermodern world, a world of "turbo-capitalism" in which the worst aspects of capitalism no longer face the restraints of the socialist challenge. As explained by Ben Agger, "There is absolutely nothing 'post' about the current modernity, which is fundamentally continuous with capitalism from the mid-nineteenth century in the sense that capitalism is characterized by private property, sexism, racism, and the domination of nature" (1990, 6).

The age of empire is not over, for we have not gotten to the "post" beyond that which was ill with the "old" world. What society is increasingly losing, however, is the ability of individuals to identify with others for progressive transformation. Because critical transformation is grounded in a communal identification with others, the loss of this identification makes a critical practice more difficult. The fact that the critical theory of the Frankfurt school was situated in the context of a communication paradigm (loosely speaking) is not surprising, as the critical persona, communication, and community are all interrelated phenomenon (Burke, 1984).

Hardt and Negri are optimistic, however, when they note that "the passage to Empire and its processes of globalization offer new possibilities to the forces of liberation" (2001, xv). In other words, the US empire presents humanity with an opportunity to move beyond the provincialism of nationality and the territoriality such nationality fosters. The political left long has dreamed of a pronounced internationalism in which people transcend religious, ethnic, and national boundaries and unite for the cause of the greater human good. Tragically, the left has failed in this vision, whereas the political right has succeeded in globalizing its hegemony.

Nevertheless, with globalization comes the potential for worldwide solidarity to emerge. Throughout the twentieth century, groups of people developed a progressive consciousness independent of other groups, with little coordination between them; consequently, most efforts to create a socialist society have failed. With the globalization of empire, however, a profound homogenization is emerging among nations and people (which is not the same as a critical or communal identification). If class-consciousness (ie, a critical identification) ever reemerges as an important historical force, as I hope to encourage, the emergence of this consciousness will be perceived much more uniformly around the world; class solidarity will no longer be subsumed by nationalist identification (as was the case with the Second International).

In resisting US values and practices, people globally have an opportunity to rethink culture and the importance of a healthy community.[2] In pursuit of such community, the task of criticism is to respond to empire—to demystify empire—and to denounce the definition of life imposed by empire and to replace that definition with another:

> Power creates both the appearance of controversy, and the contexts within which oppositional voices may be heard, but it does so in ways such that disruptive potential is defused, controlled, domesticated. Thus, critical study must focus on the discursive practices of empire—its discourses of power—that shape social consensus and social integration. Critical study must locate and demystify the social formations which enable various discourses of power to be reproduced and to legitimate empire's "natural" right. (Owen and Ehrenhaus, 1993, 172)

The growth of the US empire began with the transformation of US society following the Civil War, in which the United States began to grow as a world power. In recent years, this power has been increased and extended to dominate almost every nation on Earth. So pervasive is this power that, even before September 11, 2001, staunch supporters of US global influence recognized this influence as "imperial" (Ricks, 2001, A01). Since the September 11 attacks, however, many US leaders and elites have become more comfortable in embracing the imperial identity of the United States (Packer, 2003). Too often, critiques of Western imperialism are improperly dismissed for sounding Marxist. Such dismissal is anti-intellectual: there is nothing inherently wrong with a Marxist critique and there is accurate non-Marxist historical documentation of the existence of Western imperialism (Smith, 1981).

The classic expression of US imperialism was articulated in a famous 1898 speech by Senator Albert J. Beveridge ("The March of the Flag"). Beveridge, an ardent supporter of the annexation of the Philippines by the United States and the pacification of its inhabitants, argued:

> God has not been preparing the English-speaking and Teutonic peoples for a thousand years for nothing but vain and idle self-contemplation and self-admiration. No! He has made us the master organizers of the world to establish

> system where chaos reigns . . . He has made us adept in government that we may administer government among savages and senile peoples. (cited in Sloan, 1973, 131)

To effectuate control, the US military occupied and cruelly administered the Philippines. The Filipinos put up a fierce resistance to the US occupation. In an infamous quotation, the US general in charge of the military campaign to subdue this resistance declared: "It may be necessary to kill half the Filipinos in order that the remaining half may be advanced to a higher place of life than their present semi-barbarous state affords" (cited in Murphy, 1997, 319).

This sentiment is alarming for nations, such as the United States, which claim justice and equality as definitive ideals. All the great empires of history—Greek, Roman, Spanish, British, French, Japanese, German, and the like—were established on the principle that one race, culture, or economic class has the right to conquer and to subjugate as many other nations as possible. This sentiment is typified by Beveridge when he claims that it "is God's great purpose made manifest in the instincts of our race, whose present phase is our personal profit, but whose far-off end is the redemption of the world and the Christianization of mankind" (cited in Sloan, 1973, 130).

Although the United States and other historic empires have (or had) the ability to invade and to occupy other nations, each mistook its power for a mandate that was often couched in religious or eugenic language. The use of power in this way is contemptible, and all US citizens should rue the imperial ambitions of their government, as well the part of themselves that is compliant with such ambitions.[3]

## ✶ POWER AS CONSTITUTIVE OF COMMUNITY ✶

Central to this book's theory of power is that the mere possession of great power is, in itself, not enough to justify the tremendous suffering caused in its acquisition. Power is not inherently virtuous (and power is not inherently corrupt either). What matters most is how power is collected and utilized, and how it becomes expressed in the construction of human life. As Andrew King urges, power must "be exercised humbly and responsibly rather than arrogantly" (1987, 107). To dignify the use of irresponsible, hurtful, and self-serving power with the term "progress" (as expressed in late nineteenth and early twentieth century industrial narratives) is to betray fundamentally both language and morality.

After acquiring great power, people face a choice. First, people can pursue power to the limits of power's *telos*, sweeping aside peace and community to satisfy their own greed. To pursue this goal is to succumb to power as a disease, a corruption of nature. With such power, humans violate the natural world (ie, the world of brute phenomena) as concretely as they violate the conditions of their humanity: Such people fail to recognize that humans are a part of nature. Humans live in the world, as part of the world, and not above the world. To utilize power in the corruption of life is to deem one's self a demigod, to remove one's self from the nurturing fluids of consubstantial human interaction. Demigods have no need for the love and understanding that arises through shared suffering and the moral bonds of community that such suffering creates. Demigods remain above such suffering, often contributing to the perpetuation of suffering. Such people reify Friedrich Nietzsche's claim that no "act of violence, rape, exploitation, destruction, is intrinsically 'unjust,' since life itself is violent, rapacious, exploitative, and destructive and cannot be conceived otherwise" (1956, 208).

Although Nietzsche's statement is ontologically correct, humans can judge power conceived in such a manner as corrupt. In other words, I agree with Nietzsche in his assertion that human beings are nothing more than animals, that we have invented notions of justice, and that the natural world is a difficult place in which to live. Nevertheless, although humans are ontologically deprived of inherent meaning, we are free to construct what I call localized "meaning shelters," contingencies by which moral, spiritual, and social meaning within particular communities are situated. These meaning shelters are similar to spiderwebs. As spiders weave webs, humans weave meaning, and both species attain sustenance through their creations, which, in the case of humans, can be judged by critics. A person need not look further than the visions and values that animated the American Revolution to find grounds to repudiate Nietzsche. The pursuit of justice—a better life for the masses of human beings—and not the pursuit of wealth for its own end, constitutes (in a populist, if not mythical, sense) the original expression of the US ideal.

The above is how many good-willed Americans like to think about the US Revolution. Just communities are not constructed through wealth, but through a power grounded in the will of people to enact a world of genuine equality and fundamental fairness (although wealth and equality are not necessarily exclusive, a community's wealth, if not spread across the community, precludes equality and fairness). If the US Revolution does not stand for this, then the conflict was an ill-fought war between two undeserving forces.

Power, however, can be utilized in a different manner from the one evoked by Nietzsche. As opposed to the brute flexing of power, people can learn to express power in a more nuanced, feminized (ie, natural) fashion as a method for bringing forth and nurturing life, as unconditional love, conciliation, integration of diversity, and rejection of machismo and moral vice. This feminized power is a diffused force, resisting concentration—resisting the urge to consume. Such power is restrained in its punitive capacities and is self-questioning—tempered by its effects and wise to past abuses. The nature of such power is to flow—to never rest long in any individual hand—moving as air between communities and, thereby, expanding human potential. Power conceived in this way is not monolithic: Power ebbs and flows with the conditions of life, lessens as human dignity is smothered, and becomes revived and strengthened with the individual liberation of every person's potential. Use of such power affirms life and is affirmed by life. Such power is, as Andrew King observes, reciprocal and "must be exercised according to the nature and situation of 'the other'" (1987, 22). The wielders of such power meld back into humanity rather than become elevated above their fellow humans. This use of power rejects a fundamental misconception popularized by Nietzsche:

> To expect that strength will not manifest itself as strength, as the desire to overcome, to appreciate, to have enemies, obstacles, and triumphs, is every bit as absurd as to expect that weakness will manifest itself as strength. A quantum of strength is equivalent to a quantum of urge, will, activity, and it is only the snare of language [what Nietzsche calls "ethics"] that blinds us to this fact. For, just as popular superstition divorces the lightning from its brilliance . . . so does popular morality divorce strength from its manifestations, as though there were behind the strong a neutral agent, free to manifest its strength or contain it. (1956, 178)

As much as I respect Nietzsche, I do not consider my expectation that strength temper itself absurd. The history of humanity has not been exclusively that of master and slave; other relationships have been enacted. Power may be seen not as a triumph, but as a transformation. Sunlight does not triumph over the cold and darkness; rather, the cold and darkness become transformed by the sunlight. Furthermore, strength does not need enemies, as Mahatma Gandhi and Martin Luther King, Jr. demonstrated. Strength grows through support, through reaching out, through the unleashing of potential.

By positioning justice as the misguided attempt of the weak to transform intellectually their suffering into virtue (Nietzsche gives an example of lambs who theorize the immorality of large birds of prey), Nietzsche's view belittles and cripples what I call the human *will to justice*. This will to justice is nothing more than a respect for life and for the system of nature containing life. Although this system itself contains violence and struggle, this strife is part of a much larger ecology, the highest expression of which is a profound harmony. The power animating the universe, although destructive at times in the cyclical ebb and flow of time and space, is fundamentally grounded in balance. Justice, therefore, cannot be a regression, as Nietzsche suggests (1956, 155). Justice is that which ensures harmony and balances different forces and is, thus, the parallel of life itself.

In sum, power expressed to the ends of its *telos* is power that is soon expended. Power expends itself when ungrounded from its fundamental source—the conditions of nature and the expression of that nature in human industry. Such power, in expending itself and the life sustained through power, is fundamentally corrupt. The Christian conceptionalization of such corruption is "evil." Transplanted from a Christian vocabulary to my own, evil can be said to exist in the wielding of concentrated power—power that consumes voraciously, rather than creates sustainable, fair, holistic, and interdependent communities.

# ✶ NOTES ✶

1. Paradigmatic cases of injustice include: *Dred Scott v. Sandford* (1857), (declaring slaves are the constitutionally protected property of their masters); *Fong Yue Ting v. United States* (1893), (upholding the Chinese Deportation Act of 1892); *Plessy v. Ferguson* (1896), (constitutionalizing racial apartheid); *Lochner v. New York* (1905), (preventing states from interfering with an employee's right to contract with their employer); *Korematsu v. United States* (1944), (finding constitutional the internment of Americans with Japanese ancestry during the Second World War); *San Antonio Independent School District v. Rodriguez* (1973), (holding that the Constitution does not guarantee a fundamental right to education); *Bowers v. Hardwick* (1986), (upholding the right of states to criminalize homosexuality); and *FDA v. Brown & Williamson Tobacco Corp* (2000), (holding that the US Food and Drug Administration cannot regulate tobacco products).

2. An example of this is the Slow Food Movement, an organization with chapters in 55 nations with more than 65,000 members. The Slow Food Movement emphasizes local and decentralized conservation advocacy grounded with the aim of making food more healthy for people and for the environment. Their Web address is: http:// www. slowfood.com/cgi-bin/SlowFood.dll/slowfood_com/scripts/default.jsp.

3. In the context of French imperialism, Roland Barthes wrote sarcastically, "What does it matter, *after all*, if Order is a little brutal or a little blind, when it allows us to live cheaply?" (1957, 42).

# PART II

## INTELLECTUAL AND CRITICAL ASSUMPTIONS OF THE PARTISAN CRITIC

The four chapters of Part II delineate important assumptions that ground my analysis in this book. Writers and scholars have the power to change the world through their writing, regardless of the outlet (there is no reason disciplinary outlets should preclude social influence). This assumption is a variation of the cliché that "the pen is mightier than the sword." The pen is mightier because the world of human beings is defined by the power of ideas as expressed through language. Organized human strength—such as the military or the police—exists only in relationship to and dependence on human ideas. Although the sword may impede the implementation of ideas contrary to the person who holds the weapon, such obstruction is impermanent: The sword yields when the hand that wields the sword falters. Implicit in this influence is the importance of materiality as a challenge for professional criticism, a critique of power and equity, and a commitment to the underprivileged.

# CHAPTER 6

## ACADEMIC SCHOLARSHIP IS OFTEN A CONSTRAINT TO SOCIAL JUSTICE

Scholars compose merely one type of writer. As scholars write, they express a particular perspective and, thus, are no different from any other writer. According to convention, however, scholars are supposed to produce more definitive texts (ie, normative and authoritative) than other writers whose work is considered inferior, lacking in status and prestige. Such elitism is intolerable for critical scholars, which is why academic professionalism (as well as medical and legal professionalism) must be *deflated* so that academics can learn to see themselves as contributing to society on the same level as do poets, novelists, artists, and, indeed, bookkeepers.

By naming professionalism as a problem to overcome, this book does not mean to undermine the goal of excellence in research or practice. Rather, it seeks to deflate the egos of the intellectual elite so as to reemphasize their role as cultural workers who have a symbiotic relationship with those they serve. In the narrative of this book, professionalism does *not* equal excellence. This is a departure from commonly held expectations. Scholars are expected to be more restrained, detached, careful, methodological, and less judgmental than the much-maligned polemicist. Where the polemicist is considered manipulative and mystifying, the scholar is expected to be honest and clear. As Francis-Noel Thomas and Mark Turner suggest, the scholar is supposed to discern, note, and report. Where the polemicist calls things as he/she wants them to be, the scholar is believed to identify what things are. Scholars, therefore, adopt "the stance that [scholarship's] purpose is presentation; its motive, disinterested truth. Successful presentation consists of aligning language with truth, and the test of this alignment is clarity and simplicity" (1994, 4).

Practical distinctions between the polemicist and the scholar are useful; for scholarship to retain its credibility as *scholarship*, what a scholar produces must adapt to the constraints of the academic genre. These constraints, however, often resemble a ritualistic dance, as well as the dogma of an organized religion. Note the similarities between academia and the priesthood: rites, secret enculturation rituals, arcane language, multiple layers of hierarchical authority, and a claimed access to truth. Furthermore, to acknowledge the practical distinctions of a disciplinary identity in principle is to overlook the fact that, in practice, such distinctions are often oppressive, leading to a breakdown of intellectual cooperation and civility. When this occurs, the *form* of scholarship grows more important than the *substance* of what is written. Intellectual and social progress is thereby hampered.

Disciplinary scholarship does not necessarily have to fit the above model. The more flexible disciplinary scholarship becomes, the more similar such scholarship grows to critical scholarship. Furthermore, the relationship between disciplinary and critical scholarship is not binary. As critical scholarship becomes more disciplinary and disciplinary scholarship more critical, a pragmatic medium will be attained and academic life will grow more culturally significant and pleasurable.

## ✶ THE EXAMPLE OF "SEXTEXT" ✶

A useful example of the politics of the academic genre and its corrosion of disciplinary intellectualism and civility occurred in 1997 when Frederick Corey and Thomas Nakayama published a provocative essay in *Text and Performance Quarterly*. The essay (entitled "Sextext") was controversial because the essay was a first-person fictional narrative describing graphic homosexual pornography, albeit in a way that was theoretically sophisticated and insightful. As Corey and Nakayama (2003) explain:

> The narrative ["Sextext"] conjoined the politics of pornography with the politics of academia. The ideas were derived from French psychoanalytic theory but focused on American sexual identities. The central ideas of the text included eroticism and melancholia, liberation and repression, whiteness and marginality, maleness and subjection. (331)

For some scholars, this was just another article, of no particular concern to their specific research agenda. For many others, however, particularly people associated with ethnography, performance criticism, queer studies, ideology, and thirst for stimulating scholarship that challenged disciplinary limitations, the publication of "Sextext" was a watershed event. For me, the value of "Sextext" was its ability to communicate a homosexual subjectivity to nonhomosexuals. The essay, therefore, had a humanizing influence in promoting a wider understanding of the perspectives of at least one homosexual—the mythical "Mark Stark." Along with many other readers, I was uncomfortable with the sexual explicitness of the narrative, but that says more about my prudence and inexperience than it does about the appropriateness of the language in an academic journal. To paraphrase the motto of Karl Marx, I am both a humanist and a human; therefore, nothing human is precluded from my view of scholarship.

Needless to say, this view is not shared by everyone in the communication discipline. Immediately after "Sextext" appeared, a vigorous online debate erupted on CRTNET, the official email news and dialogue service of the National Communication Association.[1] As characterized by Peter M. Kellett and H.L. Goodall, Jr. (1999), the discussion was uncivil and exclusionary of "discursive plurality." In other words, the exchange was less a dialogic search for mutual understanding and more a series of diatribes defending or condemning a point of view. The intemperate nature of the discussion was due to the stakes involved, for "Sextext" sparked a controversy over what was the "nature" of scholarship in the discipline. Thus, the stakes were perceived as being very high. Kellett and Goodall note:

> At stake are what people consider or do not consider to be "scholarship" in our field, defined operationally as what and who deserves to get published. This discussion is therefore always also about the powered interests of who gets to be productive and how scholarship should be consumed, as much as it is about what counts as appropriate scholarship in the community. (1999, 164)

Soon after the publication of "Sextext," disciplinary authorities gathered to consider abolishing *Text and Performance Quarterly* for publishing "Sextext."[2] Concurrently, a larger discussion was initiated to discuss the ramifications of "Sextext"; these discussions were subsequently published online by the American Communication Association.[3] I turn briefly to these comments to elucidate a fear many feel in allowing nontraditional scholarship to appear in scholarly outlets. Such fears overstate the perceived threat that intellectual diversity offers, and are evidence that the discipline is too concerned about how we are perceived, as opposed to how we influence others.

Two well-known scholars in this exchange presented paradigmatic arguments for why "Sextext" should not be considered scholarship. Ted Wendt, a vocal critic of "Sextext" during the CRTNET discussion, sought to delineate "the nature of scholarship within the field of communication." Wendt considers essays such as "Sextext" as an abandonment of clear criteria "by which we might judge the intellectual utility of our research." This is important because, according to Malcolm Parks, no "question is more central to our identity as scholars than the question of what counts as scholarship." For Parks (as well as for Wendt), the "meaning of scholarship evaporates if we are unwilling to entertain the notion that some things are *not* scholarship." Both desire to demarcate true scholarship from everything else.

Arguably, Wendt and Parks misrepresent the urgency with which the field must respond to Corey and Nakayama's "transgression." "Sextext" does not constitute a threat to the discipline in the way that should be of concern to even the most traditional scholars in our field. For instance, Anthony J. Palmeri argues that "Sextext" "is too solipsistic and limited in focus to be of much help to anyone truly active in a left project to liberate society"; further, the text "might ultimately work against left activists because the existence of the work allows publishers and the academy to advertise themselves as 'tolerant,' 'pluralistic,' and 'open' to new ways of thinking" (1997, 39).

The point of critical scholarship is not to reduce all research to politics, sex, ideology, racism, gender, and the like, but to enrich the field's current methodologies and perspectives by moving beyond our disciplinary boundaries without sacrificing important values. As Robert Hariman provocatively suggests, "Perhaps every tradition has to move through but then beyond disciplinary organization; perhaps disciplinary critique and breakdown are signs of successful disciplinary maturation" (1989, 223).

After many years of reading Richard Rorty, I have learned to adopt some of his vocabulary. Thus, instead of asking whether *X* is scholarship, I argue that we should be asking whether *X* will inform our research and teaching so that our professional identities can advance more strategically the cause of an inclusive human community. Because "Sextext" helped me to become a better scholar and teacher, providing me one additional resource in my struggle to advance an inclusive community life, I accept "Sextext" for what it is, a well-meaning discourse by two scholars who apply theory to culture in an effort to reformulate our experience of both. For that, I am grateful.

## ✦ THE TRADITIONAL DISCIPLINARY PERSONA ✦

A disciplinary resistance to writings such as "Sextext" continues to exist in the form of what can be called the *traditional disciplinary persona*.[4] The constraints of the traditional disciplinary persona involve many expressions, including the theoretical, political, historical, economical, and/or idiosyncratic. Critique of this persona has been offered by many scholars. The following paragraphs engage with many of these critics, both focusing on and amplifying their calls for disciplinary reform and for an increased commitment to socially engaged critical scholarship (ie, scholarship that does no preclude examples such as "Sextext" or a social democratic or socialist/humanist revisioning of US society). Although many of these critics speak from a specific discipline—that of communication studies—the larger arguments made here apply across disciplinary boundaries throughout the humanities and social sciences.

### Systemic and Edifying Criticism: An Engagement with Disciplinary Dissent

An early critique of research in communication studies in the tradition evoked by this book was offered by Lee Thayer. In an influential special issue of the *Journal of Communication* (1983) called "Ferment in the Field," Thayer argued that research is guided by prejudice, both for and against some questions or ideals. Specifically, what "counts" as research must be couched within the schema of vested methodological and conceptual interests; the owners of such interests are the senior members of the rsearch community—those with the most invested in "invisible colleges." Such colleges are "made up of the mentor and former graduate students who continually reinforce the importance of their work to one another" (Nothstine and Copeland, 1989, 24). What these gatekeepers sanction as "knowledge" often reflects their idiosyncratic private egos, as well as field-wide "fashions." Furthermore, the process of recruitment and tenure and the ways in which committees constitute and perceive professional criteria have a chilling effect on scholarship (see Blair, Baxter, and Brown, 1994). To appease these gatekeepers, newer scholars must adapt themselves to the normative discipline they seek to join as a necessary precedent for the privilege of conducting research at the university (Thayer, 1983, 82). Thayer argues that this machinery of academia is itself a form of institutional anti-intellectualism; furthermore, this machinery often is a significant barrier to inspired, creative scholarship. Such critical scholarship is anathema to an academic culture that systematically domesticates deviant intellects and reproduces preestablished research agendas.

Thayer's critique of disciplinary "democracy" is, in many ways, analogous to the larger normative political democracy of the United States. As a result of both—in which many layers of filtering prevent those with unorthodox beliefs from acquiring power and influence—intellectual creativity and dissent are rendered cautious, constrained, and ineffectual. In both politics and research, the citizens with unorthodox views are often unwilling to call attention to themselves; consequently, the breadth of insight and the potential for both disciplinary and societal growth is compromised. In Thayer's terms, such compromise contributes to a culture of mediocrity in scholarship:

> To avoid appearing unseemly in print, one avoids undertaking the study of anything very important and any appearance of having intended to make anything more than an appropriately modest contribution to a research cause that is invariably "larger" than oneself. The results, like the approach, are wishy-washy. (1983, 85)

When understood this way, scholarship comes to resemble a form of party politics in a centralized and authoritarian political system (see Flacks, 1991, 10).

Obviously, such characterization is not categorical because there are examples of disciplinary scholarship that challenge such caricature. Nevertheless, such scholarship, to the extent that it does exist, comes at a price. For every Philip Wander, there are many others who have been effectively purged (ie, denied academic employment). Furthermore, Wander has acknowledged the difficulties he faced in advancing his view of scholarship (1994, 383—388). For instance, in discussing his essay "The Rhetoric of American Foreign Policy," Wander explains that he intended the project to be "an antiwar speech with footnotes" (1994, 385). Not surprisingly, Wander had great difficulty publishing the essay in the early 1970s. As he explains, he "sent an early draft" of his essay to *Philosophy and Rhetoric*. The essay was rejected and an anonymous reviewer for the journal wrote: "What if one shoved Nixon's Vietnam speech of 1969 in Wander's face" (1994, 385). As a result, the manuscript remained in a drawer for more than a decade before Wander reformulated the essay as "historical scholarship," deemphasizing its status as politicized scholarship (1994, 385). The essay was eventually published in the premiere rhetoric journal, the *Quarterly Journal of Speech* (1984a).

The history of Wander's manuscript illustrates the negative aspects of disciplinization. Although Wander's published essay is an example of criticism that makes a disciplinary contribution, the fact that it was published *only* after the public controversy that stimulated it was ten years in the past mocks the values animating the humanities (eg, analysis of the human being within society, including the relationship between citizens and their government). As Michael Carbone states, "If it were truly critical in the tradition of critical theory, liberal education would become a subversive activity (to use an old phrase). It would stand as a challenge to the corporate culture and its nullifying effects" (1988, 8). Instead of contributing to this promise, disciplinary pressures are often an affront to the intellectual freedom that human self-expression and self-governance requires. In the face of such constraints, the promises of a progressive, enlightened, and educated society are severely hampered. In the political realm, Saul Alinsky describes his frustration with his career as a criminologist:

> The experts agreed that the major causes of crime were poor housing, discrimination, economic insecurity, unemployment, and disease. So what did we do? We went in for supervised recreation, camping programs, something mysterious

> called "character building." We tackled everything but the actual issues. (Cited in Sanders, 1970, 25)

Thayer's critique of disciplinization was extended by scholars in a special issue of the *Western Journal of Communication*, edited by Wander, the theme of which was "Ideology and Communication." In his introductory essay, Wander addresses a yearning felt by many critical scholars by offering them "freedom from the field" (1993, 106). When I was a graduate student and reading Wander's introduction for the first time, what he wrote seemed incomprehensible to me; I was working hard to get *into* the field. What I needed was *discipline*, not *freedom*. Yet, after struggling for four years after my doctorate to obtain an academic position, I came to appreciate that there is no "field" to "get into"; there are only conversations to join. Furthermore, the more I struggled against the constraints of other people's conversations, the more I realized that I was losing my voice, my vision, and my sense of what communication scholarship could accomplish. Now that I have an academic position, I seek ways to escape the hegemony of the larger, systemic conversation.

In sum, for over fifteen years, I have longed simultaneously for inclusion and freedom; I wanted my place in the discipline, but I wanted to earn that place on my own terms. Although I am a proud child of the discipline, I insist that I am more than my disciplinary persona. Simply, I do not owe the discipline my intellectual life; students have a duty to transcend their teachers. An important end of education is for students "to surpass their need for the teacher, to render obsolete the teacher's superiority in knowledge, and to escape from the hierarchical setting of the educational system" (Rawlings, 2000, 24). I refuse to be limited to what the discipline considers important. Wander's introduction, along with the essays he commissioned, speaks to my need for both disciplinary service and for moral service to the larger society (see Schiappa, 1995).

Wander introduces his special issue by acknowledging that there is "something fundamentally wrong with the way academic journals are organized," including the way that they are refereed (1993, 105–106). This organizational system leads to many publications that are "trivial and, if not trivial, so abstruse that only four or five people (usually one's friends from graduate school) can understand [them] and want to" (1993, 108). The problem is that most of the articles published in our discipline are unreadable by students and literate citizens (1993, 108). If we are not writing for these people, I wonder for whom are we writing. Our mandate as professors clearly implies that our occupation is to teach students and uplift society, a process Kennedy calls "generational improvement" (1997, 68). Specifically, the university provides an opportunity "to give others the personal and intellectual platform they need to advance the culture, to preserve life, and to guarantee a sustainable human future" (1997, viii). We work, after all, in the *humanities*, the area of intellect most likely to involve the active participation of the wider community. Yet, as Wander notes, this community, and our students, largely could care less about what appears in our journals (1993, 108).[5]

According to Wander, part of the problem derives from the experience of graduate school training, where students are discouraged from engaging in controversial discussions that inform substantive political issues. Once students leave school, they enter the professorate, which often treats controversy and politics as a "professional dead end" (1993, 108). Consequently, the practice of much scholarship in the humanities resembles that found in oppressive totalitarian societies. As Wander notes, an essential part of the "joy and the responsibility of 'scholarship' [is] saying what ought to be and needs to be said, even when no one is ready to hear it. There is no guarantee that such speech will get into print, but if scholarly discourse can sustain the harsher truths, a small, public platform remains" (1994, 387).

For Wander, no necessary gap exists between the professional identity of critics and their moral beliefs. Along with Steven Jenkins, Wander argues that criticism "means coming to terms with an object in light of one's values" (1972, 441). These values are internal to the critic, and the critical act requires the critic to come to terms with who the critic is or would like to be (1972, 441). In other words, Wander argues that criticism is far reaching; criticism "directs our attention to beings beyond the claims of morality and the bonds of compassion. It does so not only in the past, but also in an age of genocidal weapons, in a future of generations yet unborn whose claims on the present grow increasingly faint" (1984b, 216). Under such conditions, critics have "an obligation not only to oppose the state, but also to undermine the existing order" (1984b, 197). Such comments are doubtless extreme, but what other word should be applied to criticism with an attitude, a *telos*, an agenda of influence? Such criticism, notes Wander, "leave the asylum offered by a world of ideas to confront the world of affairs, [involving] the sensual, material is of everyday life" (1984b, 199). This practice of blurring the "purely" academic from the "purely" social is not unique to Wander's approach to criticism; even more mainstream analysis engages in this tactic. As Brenda Dervin notes:

> There is little doubt that even the best of feminist scholarship is tough sledding for some readers. There is also little doubt that a fair quantity of feminist work is, without admitting it, more polemical than scholarly in orientation. Feminist scholarship sometimes chooses the opportunity of scholarship in order to express very angry feelings. These things get confused and muddled whenever oppressed people try to speak. The scholarship and the anger and the wish to talk about your experience all get merged when evaluated by normative standards. (1987, 114)

When I realized that there was no monolithic "field," only many small conversational communities in Stanley Fish's (1989, 93–94) sense, I recognized that we, the conversationalists, define our disciplinary identity through our commitment to intellectual diversity. A plethora of definitions and perspectives on the parameters of our research is fundamental to who we are (Spitzack and Carter, 1989). This search for cohesiveness and respectability, however, is part of the problem. In perhaps the most compelling metacritical essay in recent communication scholarship, John Rodden (1993) explores this problematic of self-conceptualization. According to Rodden, the communication discipline is ill-served by its efforts to remake itself in the image of the more dominant disciplines (eg, psychology and sociology). Specifically, he questions the efforts of the field to struggle for a single identity or to define a single problematic that belongs distinctly to communication.

If we resist this tendency, the communication discipline has the potential to offer systemic change for academic life. However, the discipline, notes Rodden, is facing a "hardening" due to the hostility of the more mainstream disciplines. The communication discipline, according to Rodden, "once had an impassioned mission: to empower students to express themselves as whole persons. We must recover that mission. If we can do so, we shall have taken a long step toward recovering our vocation as seekers and sharers of wisdom, 'generators' of a living knowledge" (1993, 128). Instead, however, we have lost track of this vision:

> Having defined ourselves by our careers, nothing else matters. Having acceded to a system in which we gain respect or professionalism just by writing, we write chiefly for those reasons—which often poisons our relationship to writing, because we're not doing it for the activity itself. Academe conditions us to write for extrinsic reasons—such as hiring, promotions, awards—rather than for the joy of self-expression or communication or creation. The system teaches us to write for success, not for self-fulfillment, and so there is a weariness and frustration. (1993, 132)

There is, in other words, much disingenuousness and a sense of communal impotence that characterizes academic culture. Although many academics claim to respect such great iconoclastic thinkers as Albert Einstein, Jean-Paul Sartre, Simon de Beauvoir, Albert Camus, Linus Pauling, Michael Foucault, Frederick Nietzsche, Kenneth Burke, and many others, few strive to emulate them. No doubt, many of the people who inspire and influence us were geniuses or exceptionally gifted, but that is not enough to explain their greatness. The important fact is that each and every one of the intellectuals just named, and many others that could have been named, cared in ways that few intellectuals care today. They gave all of themselves to the common good, reinventing humanity. None of us has to be a genius to follow in their footsteps. A person's genius is not a prerequisite for greatness; greatness is not an "is," it is a "doing." Nobody, regardless of intelligence, is inherently great; greatness is a matter of will, perseverance, and determination.

Consider a major disciplinary angst; the well-recognized fact in the communication discipline that we have been unable to produce any internationally great thinkers:

> Why have there been no great rhetorical theorists since Kenneth Burke? Why has the field of speech communication *never* produced a widely influential thinker? Burke doesn't have a Communication Ph.D. (or even a B.A.!) and he doubtless wouldn't have been Burke if he had. What is required is the daring to go our own way, as Burke did, along with the capacity to speak to other disciplines in their terms. (Rodden, 1993, 119)

Rodden's general sentiment is collaborated by Peter Goodrich:

> [T]he social space of intellectual success and of international recognition does not stem from institutional academic conformity but rather from marginal disciplines and from the polemical work of the institutional outsider—the researcher or writer who defines her social identity in terms of writing rather than in terms of academic commitment or institutional service. (1993, 394)

In other words, disciplines may conserve, but they do not necessarily contribute—at least in the humanities—unless they offer its members the freedom to think outside of community norms. As Rodden notes, "If you know only one perspective, you think that's all there is. You assume that no alternative exists, that the way you live is the only way to live" (1993, 119).

Rodden suggests solutions to reanimate our discipline; specifically, he challenges us to consider "what might the university be like if more professors *lived* their professed beliefs?" (1993, 112). If we did, we might even decide that we no longer wanted to play what he calls the "University Status Game." As he muses, "Could it be that our mission might be to do *something completely different* ?" (1993, 123). The question is, can we be scholars and intellectuals? Put another way, as Wander asks, can "criticism address public issues and still satisfy a professional audience of editors, referees, academic committees, and colleagues?" (1990, 279). For Rodden, this is an important issue because the academic persona and the persona of the public intellectual are often positioned as being in conflict with one another. At the very least, the two exist in an uneasy and unequal relationship: If scholars are excellent at the first, they may be tolerated when they practice the second. This, however, takes a toll on the critical scholar:

> You can't conform outwardly and live rightly inside. Speak up or get out. You can only please the droning voices—or bow to the "Research 1" institutional orthodoxy—at the price of abandoning your vision. The task of wresting free from fatal hypocrisy and the green worm [envy] demands commitment to a vision, one to be pursued with graciousness, humility, and unceasing determination. (Rodden, 1993, 133)

Rodden dreams of a professional identity that "encourages us to purse insights wherever they lead us, to bring back knowledge from wherever we find it; that urges us to sail beyond all artificial, institutional boundaries, for we know not the riches within us and know only that great-souled work lies always beyond the horizon" (1993, 134). The point, as raised by Rodden, is not merely to generate knowledge but also to have an impact on people's souls (1993, 135).

Rodden presents the field with a choice between being "knowledge generators" or "wisdom seekers" (1993, 126). Obviously, these two categories are not mutually exclusive; practically, however, we often act in the discipline as if they were. Rodden, himself an active researcher, confesses that rather "than pursue specialized research, I would deliberately reduce my intensive cultivation of any one field, in order to expand the context and significance of my life as a whole" (1993, 121). This view is shared by Carole Blair and her colleagues who admit that, although they adhere to disciplinary guidelines, they find them "increasingly difficult to justify them to students" or to themselves and are now "finding *inter*disciplinary attitudes and conversations far more interesting and rewarding" (Bach, Blair, Nothstine, and Pym, 1996, 400). Blair and her coauthors offer an appealing vision of what our academic community could entail:

> Such a view might mean that writing would be a means of offering a different perspective to our disciplinary community or even to other or larger communities, not merely a means for authors to validate their own positions or a certain view of disciplinary history. That is, we might write for and to students, scholars in other disciplines, or non-academic audiences. Under such a model, professional writing—understood in this broader sense—might be more highly valued, possibly even more inviting, than we now take to be narrowly professional writing. Writing might be seen again as a form of communication in which the writer might care about reception (rather than a vita entry). (1996, 414)

An important point made by Blair and her coauthors is that disciplinary constraints do not allow for "the delights, values, or responsibilities of scholarship; the political significance of writing; the self-understanding that scholarship may offer; the social value of an exchange of the products of intellectual labor" (1996, 402). In other words, the disciplinary constraints effectively "de-motivate" scholarship (1996, 402).

In an underappreciated essay published in the *Quarterly Journal of Speech*, Carole Blair, along with Leslie A. Baxter and Julie R. Brown, brought to the forefront of our disciplinary consciousness the "smoking gun" of exclusionary politics. As these authors note, there is often a cynically reductionistic view of scholarship and its purpose: "*That* writing occurs is somehow more significant or influential than *what* is written or *how* that writing is read. This unidimensional portrait of scholarly activity insults both writers and readers by rendering their labors invisible and irrelevant"

(1994, 390). To be successful, professional scholarship should be politically neutral, respectful toward science, mainstream, and politically deferential (1994, 398). Scholarship that diverges from this standard is often "quarantined at the disciplinary border and ultimately deported" (1994, 402).

As I wrote previously in defense of the Blair, Brown, and Baxter essay, there are boundaries to the critical position that scholars may embrace. As long as critical scholarship remains in the realm of theory, the writing is acceptable:

> The problem arises when scholars try to apply their theory to affect the lives and material practices of people in a direct way. Theory by itself is innocuous, even stultifying to the mind that chooses not to apply it. To take theory seriously is to invite praxis, and therein lies the conflict with established authority. One critique that people frequently have of critical theorists is that they are insincere. As long as critical theorists remain "insincere," they are considered safe: they do not "practice what they preach." Blair, Brown, and Baxter ran afoul because they took feminist theory from out of its abstract (safe) conditions and used it for a disciplinary critique that involved specific material practices. (Swartz, 1997, 253)

The importance of such engagement, however, is exactly what WenShu Lee advocates when she argues for a critical approach "grounded in real social problems—contradictions experienced by ordinary people in everyday life" (1993, 223). Fundamental to this approach is "a refusal to accept, on faith, an agenda set by the social science establishment" (1993, 223). Although Lee is specifically addressing only one side of our disciplina community, her critique is relevant for our entire discipline and for academia in general. For Lee, an important imperative is for scholars to begin asking questions that target ideological problems; for instance, scholars must learn to discern who benefits from their research agendas, who is excluded, possible alternative conceptualizations to a research question, and who, ultimately, is responsible for the solution (1993, 221). Questions such as these give scholarship a substance and a potential otherwise denied scholars when they ignore the relationship among power, the authority to define social issues, and the control of the resources to effectuate solutions (1993, 221).

Lee argues that our research agenda are defined by elite interests existing through many levels of the academic-complex and throughout the larger society (1993, 222). Subsequently, the notion of "academic freedom" appears less substantial than academics commonly assume. As noted by Ben Agger:

> Much of the bravado heard about the autonomous academic life is an exaggeration. In the university, specialized writing has largely replaced public discourse. This is not, as some pedants would have it, simply because professors write cumbersome, leaden prose but because literary craft in the university setting has been subordinated to the requirements of disciplinary advancement, scientific replication, and picayune scholarship. (1990, 77)

What Lee calls for is a critical scholarship, one that has a direct and applicable effect on the lives of the majority of people and not just on the elite who have defined the parameters of legitimacy in their own image:

> Without such efforts, given our academic agenda, theories are little more than reified instruments serving to promote academic status (ie, publications, tenure and promotion at the university). The new purpose of research, therefore, is not knowledge for academic success, but knowledge for the improvement of lives (the powerless and the powerful). Ordinary people, learning about scholarly knowledge connected to real life, may learn on their own to challenge existing ways of solving problems and mobilize concerned efforts to pursue alternative solutions. (1993, 223)

In sum, Lee argues that the world of academia is situated within society and, therefore, is not above the needs of society. The generation of theory and the perpetuation of publications only serve to somehow make academics appear deserving of their special status (1993, 223). To this, Lee responds that there is an alternative: "To reach out and put knowledge to social use" (1993, 227).

Central to the foregoing analysis is the notion that the disciplinary apparatus governing communication research is, arguably, too insular (speaking only to itself and to the provincial interests of its most normative scholars). Indicative of this is the fact that there is too much jargon in our field. The effect of such writing "mystifies the scholarly enterprise, obfuscates our message, exaggerates our self-importance, overly qualifies and therefore limits the breadth of our conclusions, and communicates that we are somehow above the fray" (Hollihan, 1994, 233). With such a style, how can communication scholars claim to have a wide influence? An important move for scholars, notes Thomas Hollihan, is to engage in dialogue with communities other than their own to become part of a larger intellectual community with a broader social impact (1994, 233). This is especially important for those in our discipline who identify themselves as critics:

> Critics who ignore the moral implications of rhetoric thus perform support for the mystery that preserves the social order. Those critics, on the other hand, who engage the moral issues in rhetoric act to illuminate the implications of the mystification, peel back the mystery, and thus raise the issues that can lead to social change. The act of criticism involves moral choice, and reveals the moral force of the discourse under study. Critics, merely by doing their work, spark a moral debate, for the very act of rhetorical criticism places the values of the social culture at risk. (1994, 230)

This process of moral engagement is inevitable. The language that critics use is itself moralistic and criticism enacts a morality (Klumpp and Hollihan, 1989). This leads some people to worry about a scholarship that potentially undermines important social values, considering such activity an inappropriate form of scholarship. Celeste Michelle Condit isolates a poignant form of this fear:

> Among humanists, rhetorical critics face an unusually large problem with charges of political bias. Because the texts and contexts we routinely focus upon are self-evidently political, many of our conclusions will instantly and obviously be of greater service to some political constituencies than to others. To protect our jobs as academics, therefore, rhetorical critics have had to respond to intimations that our efforts are generated *merely* by political interests rather than by any unique academic skills. (1993, 182)

Hollihan, however, suggests a solution to the problem identified by Condit. He argues that the "critic's loss of moral detachment emphasizes the importance of the critic's character in the evaluation of his or her arguments" (1994, 231). In advancing the moral engagement of the critic, Hollihan highlights the importance of the critical attitude discussed throughout this book. As Hollihan notes, evidence is audience dependent; the same, however, could be said about truth and what is needed to persuade a given audience of what are a set of "facts." Thus, critics ought to feel free to make whatever claims they can persuade their readers to accept, challenging their audiences to expand their perspectives. These various audiences—internal to academia or external—are all the "reality-check" we need to stipulate:

> Rhetorical critics do not work in the wilderness. They write from the perspective of a particular culture and ideology, and they write with a conception of their

> audience in mind. As members of a discipline, critics also learn the appropriate argument style [or styles] for the conduct of interactions in that field. The evidentiary standards are thus created by the participants in a field as they seek to control discourse practices within their ranks. (1994, 232)

The problem, however, with discipline-specific standards is that what becomes privileged are the conceptual or theoretical contributions at the expense of the social edification or influence derived from the analysis. As noted by James Darsey:

> We celebrate Ernest Bormann for his "fantasy themes," not for what he told us about the Eagleton affair. We celebrate Walter Fisher for his work on narrative rather than for his insights into Gilgamesh, Michael McGee for "ideographs" and his notion of "the people" more than for anything he told us about the fall of Wellington. (1994, 177)

Darsey, who served for one term on the editorial board of the *Quarterly Journal of Speech*, examines two ways that rhetorical studies have been positioned by the disciplinary nomenclature. First, scholars may study rhetoric so as to contribute to its "essence" in the sense proposed by Karlyn Kohrs Campbell (1970; 1974). Scholars who take this route attempt to show how rhetoric works—its form, function, and psychological appeals. Second, scholars may provide new insights into an important text. Within this schema, little disciplinary room exists for other conceptualizations of rhetoric, such as social criticism and popular edification (eg, cultural and societal advancement from a partisan perspective).

To make matters worse, Darsey notes that "the presumption in favor of research in the service of theory is so well established at this time that, in my experience, the failure to conform has been used as the primary reason to recommend against publication" (1994, 173). As evidence for this claim, Darsey cites an associate editor at *QJS* who, in rejecting an essay, cited as his/her reason the author's concern with the text and context at the expense of advancing rhetorical *theory* (1994, 173). Such a standard, notes Darsey, is "narcissistic," preventing critics from applying their talents to real-world engagement. Instead, this standard requires critics "to bring the real world into our circle as illustrative of various theoretical propositions" (1994, 174). This issue is important, focusing on what Darsey calls "a question of motive" (1994, 168), or what I term *attitude*. As Darsey highlights, what is evoked in this discussion implores us "to examine the purposes of our scholarship, and it revives ancient questions about the essential nature of the humanities and the sciences" (1994, 168).

## Conclusion

The foregoing paragraphs reviewed criticism of disciplinary assumptions of scholarship within the communication field. In contrast to the limiting dominant view, I encourage other perspectives for communication scholars. Fundamental to these different perspectives is the notion of what Hariman identifies as the "rhetorical perspective [that] replaces disinterestedness with advocacy, balances specialization with generality, and confronts expertise with an assertion of voice" (1989, 213). This is the position advocated in this book. The point is to transform academic professionalism from a "repressive" to a "productive" power (1989, 212).[6]

Productive power is essential if critical scholars are to reverse the trend noted by Russell Jacoby, in which the disciplinization of intellectuals has privatized them and removed them from public life (1989a, 274). Jacoby suggests that such repositioning has led to an inverse relationship between academic funding by governmental and industrial sources and the freedom of faculty to engage in public critical activity. The more faculty depend on outside grants—as is becoming increasingly the case—the more faculty "cease to function as critics" (1989, 280).[7]

Critical scholars must bind together to resist this trend. Whether we call ourselves *rhetoricians, philosophers, socialists, feminists, postmodernists, critical race theorists, critical legal theorists, queer theorists*, or some other such label, we are all engaged, as critical theorists, in a common anti-disciplinary struggle. This is the same struggle that feminist scholars have engaged successfully with for more than thirty years as they gained an increased acceptability in communication scholarship. As noted by Sonja K. Foss, Cindy L. Griffin, and Karen A. Foss, "To see through a feminist lens, for us, means that we must call into question all aspects of our lives, including our scholarly products and practices" (1997, 133). Criticism, as envisioned in this book, embraces this heuristic and transformative point.

## ✱ NOTES ✱

1. See http:www.natcom.org/Publications/CRTNET%20News/ home.htm.

2. See http:www.natcom.org/Publications/CRTNET%20News/ home.htm.

3. See http://acjournal.org/holdings/ vo l 1/Iss2/curtain.html.

4. This terminology, I recognize, is essentializing. I offer this construction not as a metaphysical truth, but as a rational, historical, and, above all else, *practical* distinction. Along with Kenneth Burke, I face the challenge of using language while, at the same time, trying to minimize the tendency of being *used* by language.

5. Possible alternatives to the peer-review process as currently conceptualized are suggested by Allen, Orbe, and Olivas (1999), who discuss the publication of their essay. As they engaged with their editor, they "recast the review process as a collaboration and an opportunity for mutual engagement, not only with each other's work but, more importantly, with each other. They co-wrote a small part of the essay with the editor, but more importantly, both the authors and editor felt a momentary intimacy and mutual supportiveness against the common deprivations and institutionalized isolations of life in the academy" (426). The marginalization of our journals is a problem that transcends the provinciality of the communication discipline. As noted by Donald Kennedy, across the entire academy, "more than 75% of all papers are never cited at all, and in certain fields that percentage of noncitation is even higher" (193).

6. Murray Edelman uses the term "professional imperialism" to denote the propensity of professionals to use special jargon to define, extend, and maintain their authority (1988, 119). This is part of the repressive power of academia that I reject.

7. For a more extended argument, see Jacoby (1987).

# CHAPTER 7

# Materiality Is an Important Challenge for Professional Criticism

This chapter addresses the issue of the purpose and practice of criticism, locating the partisan style within an established disciplinary tradition and reviewing some prominent critiques of that position. Specifically, Celeste Michelle Condit (1993), Sonja K. Foss and Karen A. Foss (2003), and Sonja K. Foss and Cindy L. Griffin (1995) have articulated a critique of partisan criticism and have urged scholars to enact an "empathic" or "invitational" rhetorical strategy to better effectuate social change.

Ten years ago, Condit cautioned against what she labeled "partisan" criticism.[1] She argued that such partisan criticism propagates a mythical "oppressor-oppressed" narrative that is unreasonably reductionist and simplistic in that "it is no longer so easy to identify single categories of victim and victor" (1993, 187). She asserted that by perpetuating such categories—as partisan critics often do—critics forward overgeneralizations and moralizations unconnected to real-life politics. In contrast to partisan criticism, Condit offered what she called "empathic communication." Such communication "begins in the recognition of the tenet, held by many human groups, that the central value is care for all living things" (1993, 187). According to Condit, this view "does not encourage the critic to adopt a partisan stance that favors some human groups and dismisses others" (1993, 187). A core assumption that Condit makes is that "there are very few happy, empowered oppressors. Even the average American white male of the upper middle class is a tortured unhappy beast" (1993, 187). Social change occurs less from confronting such "beasts" and more from understanding and working with their fears and needs in a language that they understand.

Condit's perspective has been given a renewed emphasis in recent scholarship by Foss, Foss, and Griffin, advancing a theory of "invitational communication." Foss and her cowriters advance the view that certain rhetorical styles (or communicative stances) are more appropriate than others for increasing the quality of community life (see also Gearhart, 1979; Freeman, Littlejohn, and Pearce, 1992). They argue that "invitational rhetoric" (discourse that addresses social problems through the creation of relationships as opposed to positing an antagonistic resistance to already established relationships) is an example of such discourse:

> If you want the world to be an environmentally sound place, for example, you seek out, appreciate, and encourage instances where you see sound environmental practices going on around you. If you want a world where workers are paid equitable wages, you look around and find examples where workers are being paid fairly. You applaud and affirm these cases when you find them. You use these examples to try to recreate these conditions when you have opportunities in other places. (Foss and Foss, 2003, 19)

Implicit in this understanding of invitational communication are a number of assumptions, two of which are relevant to my critique. First, communicators who engage in this form of discourse approach communication as an attempt to achieve a level of *understanding* with another person (Foss and Foss, 2003, 9). The idea is to learn as much as possible about the other to appreciate how that person views the controversy; to do so involves refraining from judgment of the other person's moral choices. Such an assumption is often useful, as when a divorcing couple negotiates child-rearing responsibilities in a situation in which the lifestyle of one parent is considered abhorrent by the other.

Arguably, the most famous example of this situation is *Palmore v. Sidoti* (1984), a child custody case. At issue in *Palmore* was whether the state could divest a fit, Caucasian mother of custody of her young child on the grounds that her marriage to an African American was "harmful" to the psychological development of the child. In *Palmore*, the ex-husband and father of the child was a Caucasian who took offense that his daughter was being raised in the home of an African American. In more recent years, cases such as *Palmore* have been typical in family law when the issue is not race but homosexuality (for example, *Bottoms v. Bottoms*, 1995, in which a lesbian mother was divested of custody on the grounds of her active homosexuality; and *Roe v. Roe*, 1985, in which a father was declared "unfit" because his homosexuality was held to impose a psychological burden on his child). Under such circumstances, a confrontational approach will not easily lead to a productive resolution of the conflict. Although one party may receive custody, the other party is, correspondingly, shamed, denigrated as a human being, and removed from the community of those "equal before the law." The children of these legal battles are also severely injured, often because the ostracized "deviant" parent is, in fact, the better or more committed parent. These cases turn on the fact that *but for* the presumed "deviancy," the defendant parent otherwise would retain custody of the child.

As the above example illustrates, confrontational or partisan rhetorical strategies often result in a polarized community and destroyed families. Families and larger social groups cannot help but experience strain when they suffer a legal inequality based on another's moral condemnation. Unfortunately, the case law in family litigation is filled with such tragic, divisive, and hurtful examples.[2] Thus, an invitational or empathic rhetorical strategy can be useful, as an important goal in these cases should be for all sides to understand the subjectivity and uniqueness of the other. Doing so would help each side of the conflict to perceive how the other side feels and, thereby, focus concern on the most important issues, such as the best interests of the child. For example, one party can ask what he or she can do to help the other feel more comfortable in believing that the child will not be hurt by his or her homosexuality. Invitational or empathic communication suggests that conflict can be avoided when parties learn to speak to the concerns of the other, differentiating between those concerns and the stereotypes in which the concerns are expressed.

A second requirement for an invitational or empathic communication involves equality in that to be successful; both parties must be equal in areas that are deemed important to the parties (Foss and Foss, 2003, 9). In the family context, for instance, expecting this perception of equality is not (or should not be) unreasonable. Beyond this context, however, it is not clear whether invitational or empathic theorists privilege a *formal equality* at the expense of a *substantive equality* in which important differences between people preclude a *genuine equality*. As a result of my reading of the literature on invitational rhetoric, as well as on my many personal conversations with Sonja K. Foss, I am led to believe that invitational communication assumes a liberal formal equality, one in which all individuals are presumed equal by virtue of their inherent agency, and that such agency is perceived to be sufficient to overcome any material limitations of that person's ability to actualize his or her goals. This notion of equality, which is dominant in the United States, is unacceptable from my social justice point of view.

In the feminist legal literature, for instance, the existing legal regime of formal equality has been criticized from the point of view of substantive equality. Central to formal equality is the constitutional mandate that similarly situated individuals or groups be treated similarly (see *Reed v. Reed*, 1971). On its face, this position is reasonable, as formal equality did not exist for women before the historic decision of *Reed* in1971 and is not an achievement at which to be scoffed. However, formal equality is not enough. Many feminists and critical scholars have pointed out that a *de facto* inequality may become masked by an apparently neutral and formally equal relationship. For example, contract law treats all parties alike, glossing over the fact that an immigrant farmworker does not come to the contract with the same degree of power as does a multinational corporation. Although both have the same rights before the law with regard to the contract, few people would argue that the bargaining power of the immigrant worker is equal to that of the corporation. The formal equality guaranteed by the federal constitution is not violated by this arrangement, because the equal protection clause does not guarantee that a law be equitable in its impact.

In *Personnel Administrator of Massachusetts v. Feeney* (1979), for example, the Supreme Court upheld a state law giving hiring preferences to veterans for state jobs, even though the preferences had the effect of permanently denying promotions to the plaintiff, a female state employee with high seniority. The plaintiff made a concerted effort to attain a higher paying position, but in each instance, the position was filled by a newly hired male veteran, each of whom had fewer objective qualifications. The Court reasoned that the purpose of the law was not to discriminate against women; therefore, the disparate impact against women was not a violation of equal protection. The purpose of substantive equality is to avoid this kind of legal conclusion; however, because substantive equality may interfere with principles of formal equality, principles of substantive equality have only a marginal influence in US jurisprudence. This can be contrasted with Canadian jurisprudence, which, in the last two decades, has been much more proactive in establishing a commitment to substantive equality (Bavis, 1999).

The advantage of substantive equality is that the perspective considers the results or effects of a relationship. In other words, I cannot assume that *A* and *B* are equal because the law states they must be treated as if they were equal. More essential to an understanding of the relationship between *A* and *B* are the substantive differences in the relative power of each. The goal is to avoid outcomes that are patently unfair because they involve a gross inequality in bargaining power. For example, African Americans have been granted formal equality, but few would agree that, on a substantive level, African Americans are able to compete equally for social resources:

> Almost one in four black men between the ages of 20 and 29 is either in prison, jail, on probation, or parole on any given day. This means that there are more young black men in the criminal justice system than the total number of black men of all ages enrolled in college. For every one black man who graduates from college, 100 are arrested. (Platt, 2001, 147)

Constitutional law is unconcerned about the condition of young black men, as long as no black plaintiff can point to a specific instance of government sponsored discrimination. Therefore, a commitment to substantive equality would lead a person to support affirmative action and other ameliorative policies intended to create a society in which all people could compete equally for a respectable place in the national community. To take another example, "dominance theory," as articulated by Catharine MacKinnon (1987), explores the imbalances of power between men and women, which become encapsulated in social and legal norms. MacKinnon criticizes the taken-for-granted assumptions in our society that place individuals in hierarchical relationships, usually at the expense of women (for examples, see Bartlett and Harris, 1998).

In sum, understanding, empathy, and dialogical heart-to-heart interaction with people in power do not necessarily lead to the type of social transformation that theorists such as Condit or Foss, Foss, and Griffin would like to see enacted. Thus, it is surprising that these theorists contrast transformational rhetoric with these more malignant coercive or confrontational rhetorics (Foss and Foss, 2003, 7—9). Certainly, theoretical distinctions in this area exist, and naming them is useful. Less useful, however, is to assume, even implicitly, that there is something wrong with coercive, confrontational, conversionist, or, in other words, partisan persuasion. These scholars, however, disparage such a rhetorical stance on the grounds that such an approach may exacerbate conflict. They also suggest that the motives of a partisan critic may be compromised. As Foss and Griffin claim, "Embedded in efforts to change others is a desire for control and domination" (1995, 3). Although this critique has, in the abstract, some validity (Boyd, 1999, 398), the condition is unavoidable when much of American society suffers from alienation.

Foss and Griffin conclude that a confrontational or conversionist rhetorical stance may not only be counterproductive, but, according to the invitational rhetoric paradigm, might itself be positively harmful, helping to perpetuate the various ills against which partisan critics struggle:

> A number of scholars and activists from different fields suggest that creating what you want is much more effective than resisting what you do not want. They explain that resistance and opposition are ineffective options for creating change because what we resist persists. To resist something grants it life and establishes it more firmly in place. Whatever you give your attention and energy to in the form of communication thrives and grows. Communication is creative—it generates or produces the nature of the reality in which we live. When you talk about what you do not want, you create more of it in your reality. By communicating about it and bestowing your belief on it, you reinforce it as reality, you strengthen it, you become its accomplice, and it remains a part of your life experience. (Foss and Foss, 2003, 19)

In sum, transformational rhetoric, unlike confrontational or partisan rhetoric, seeks to generate what Foss and Foss suggest can be a "genuine understanding" among people who hold potentially incommensurable positions. As noted by Foss and Griffin, "Change may be the result of invitational rhetoric, but change is not its purpose" (1995, 6).

Although this position clearly has merit, there are times when social change is not about understanding people who think differently. Conflict is often necessary for significant moral growth and change (Stewart, Smith, and Denton, 1989). Materiality is often separate and distinct from rhetorical action. In the material world, communities often pursue narrow self-interest and take advantage of others to effectuate that goal (through rhetoric and/or otherwise). Weak parties often seek to persuade stronger parties to treat them better but find their efforts wasted when the hearts of their oppressors are closed to them. As a result, persuasion must be supplemented by strategic coercion to create the impression that, until the weaker party is treated fairly, that party will agitate, sabotage, bomb, or otherwise disrupt the peace enjoyed by the stronger, oppressing group. For instance, what the State of Israel and George W. Bush disingenuously label "terrorism" is often the dramatization of Arab oppressed groups' frustration and their attempt to destroy the complacence (what the dominant group calls *peace*) by which the world ignores their displacement (Kennedy, 1999; Madriz, 2001, 46). So-called terrorists may be no more guilty for their actions than the larger society that calls forth the cultural conditions that make terrorism a sensible option for a significant subgroup. To demonize such subgroups, to blame them for their noninvitational communication patterns, is simply to condemn them to their oppression.

The materialist critique is, of course, not unknown to advocates of invitational communication. As Foss and Foss clearly acknowledge, we live in a noninvitational world, in which equality is seldom achieved and justice is determined by the amount of money a person possesses. In this world, hierarchy and oppressive social relationships are the norm. Yet, although Foss and Foss acknowledge these norms, they tend to portray them as *rhetorical themes* that dominate our communication habits and suggest that the communication habits are, in fact, the *cause* of the oppressive realities (2003, 7–9). Although Foss and Foss write that confrontational and aggressive rhetorical strategies are "legitimate and valuable options that help achieve particular communication goals in many situations" (2003, 16), this is only because material success in this world entails their use. It is better, they argue, to change this material condition by first changing our communicative patterns:

> Because we most often choose conquest and conversion rhetoric as default modes of communication, we create and experience a particular kind of world. Communication isn't just words and sounds and gestures that reflect our world. It is the means through which we create that world. By the choices we make in our use of communication, we create our reality. (2003, 7)

In terms of the philosophy of communication, Foss and Foss are correct: Rhetoric is epistemic and communication does contribute to the creation of social reality. Nevertheless, the reality created by communication is often material, deadly, and is not reducible to the communicative practices of any particular human being. Although individuals such as Martin Luther King, Jr. or Mahatma Gandhi were able to have an influence on human culture by advancing an invitational communication paradigm, both faced insurmountable obstacles as they tried to reinvent community life. Although what both King and Gandhi accomplished was invaluable, both largely failed as invitational speakers because material conditions allowed for only a certain type of moral and spiritual evolution to emerge in society during their lifetimes. Both men were inspiring and had an effect in certain areas, yet neither achieved the type of world that their teachings advocated. To acknowledge this is not a sign of disrespect for either man; rather, it is to note that invitational rhetoric, although important for many tasks, is not the answer for every political task. Furthermore, I do not assert that the symbolic has no effect on the material or that the symbolic mechanistically follows from the material but that politically progressive human evolution involves a combination of both. Although this point is certainly not novel, the materiality underpinning discourse is underrecognized in empathic and invitational criticism. Simply, Foss and Foss's framework "for cultivating, responding to, contributing to, and enjoying the diverse perspective [people] encounter" (2003, 2) does not capture all the worthy potentials for rhetoric and social movement persuasion.

Foss and Foss give an example of how their position can work in a delicate social and political context. This example is both compatible with, as well as problematic to, partisan or confrontational criticism:

> If you can come to an understanding of why a neo-Nazi perspective might make sense to someone, you are more likely to understand the conditions that are likely to produce such a perspective. You then can help to create different kinds of environments in which that viewpoint has less opportunity to flourish. By understanding how perspectives that are abhorrent to you make sense and are attractive to someone else, you can set about creating an environment in which individuals are likely to make other choices. (2003, 18)

Clearly, we need to understand the people that our culture teaches us to demonize; in this way, invitational criticism supports my larger argument that condemning the Nazis as "evil" or demonizing "terrorists" as evil is unproductive. A more productive task is to understand that these personas were created, often by the same forces condemned in this book, eg, the selfish policies of the industrialized world and, in particular, the United States (McCaughan, 2001).

Rather than blaming others for the problems that plague the contemporary world, a more useful tactic is to see the origin of this trouble within our own ideology and practices as a nation. I suspect that invitational theorists would not disagree with my rhetorical strategy if they understood that I have a productive goal that I am advancing with my criticism—social justice as embodied in democratic socialism (see Nielsen, 1989). However, for my constructive goals to become clear, I have to argue against the prevailing attitude that condemns socialism, as well as uncritically accepts normative US culture. In short, I have to argue against the prevalent belief that no viable alternative exists to the political status quo.

A further way to respond to empathic and invitational criticism is with Dana L. Cloud's (1994) notion of a "materialist ideology of criticism." As Cloud argues, the point of criticism is its material effect—that is, criticism's ability to help people in the material world. In such a world, most human groups do not—contrary to Condit—"care for all living things." Furthermore, in *this* world, the conditions of material oppression render prudent our favoring of some human groups and our dismissal of others (eg, siding with the Jews against the Nazis and siding with the Chinese against the Japanese during World War II). If the upper-middle-class, white males of this world feel tortured, unhappy, and beastly, as Condit suggests, that is unfortunate; however, it is unlikely that the two- thirds of the human beings on Earth that live in a structured, lethal poverty shed tears for these people. Famine, which is often grounded in a politics benefiting upper-class, white males and their privileged colleagues in the developing world, is "the most common form of violence in today's world" (McCaughan, 2001, 40).

Many US Americans also feel no pity for the "suffering" of the elite. If this sounds harsh, it is unavoidable. Moreover, this claim is far less harsh than the material conditions that the wealthy and privileged have created for the bulk of humanity (Anderson, 1992, 352–353). If the wealthy were to extend solidarity to the poor, then I would reconsider this position: the poor and dispossessed do not hate the wealthy because the wealthy have money; rather, they hate the wealthy because the wealthy are responsible for creating and sustaining poverty. The onus, therefore, is on the rich to do something to abolish poverty.

Moreover, the critical attitude of partisan scholarship is, in practice, *human*. As Wander and Steven Jenkins note, "If the critic is willing to speak of things outside the language of his essay and beyond the academic boundaries of criticism, he becomes less a role player and more of a human being" (1972, 446). Although empathy is an important part of being human, moral indignation, rage, vengeance, and a sense of a consuming struggle, are, at times, equally important. As Brenda J. Allen, Mark P. Orbe, and Margarita Refugia Olivas observe, it is often necessary to "embrace our emotionality as a central component of scholarship" (1999, 406). To be empathic is to understand a situation fully, and such understanding is often not possible in the messy struggles of everyday politics. Of prime importance is to act against injustice and not waste time in coming to terms with why the oppressor feels justified in perpetuating his/her oppression.

As scholars, what we have to work with are texts. Texts are useful because they provide the raw material for analysis. However, textual fetishism, what Thomas Farrell identifies as the "textualization of politics" (1993, 148), obscures the fact that the point of criticism is to have a material influence—that is, to help people (particularly *poor* people). Although discourse practices, indeed, constitute many of our problems, we should not forget that *people* do the suffering. As Cloud insists:

> It is not only discourses and codes from which many people need liberation. A politics of discourse, even where the project is grounded in the critic's commitment, assumes that those who are oppressed or exploited need discursive redefinition of their identities, rather than a transformation of their material conditions as a primary task. The project of ideology critique, modernist as it may be, is the only critical stance that suggests discourse may justify oppression and exploitation, but texts do not themselves constitute the oppression. (1994, 157)

Engagement with social texts, however, can be *part* of the liberation, a point that is fundamental to the task of criticism. Although criticism is political, the critic is not necessarily an urban guerrilla. As discussed by David Fraser:

> A law review article is hardly a car bomb, leaving violence and destruction in its wake, but it is one of the few forms of "armed propaganda" open to those of us

> who believe in a fundamentally different world and who live and work in the heart of the legal academy. In a very real sense, legal scholarship, as an act of "interpretation," is an act of calculated and relentless violence. It is an imposition of meaning, a will to power in a world of the word. (1990, 778)

In other words, legal interpretations, as well as other textual interpretations, do matter:

> A judge articulates her understanding of a text, and as a result, somebody loses his freedom, his property, his children, even his life. Interpretations in law also constitute justifications for violence which has already occurred or which is about to occur. When interpreters have finished their work, they frequently leave behind victims whose lives have been torn apart by these organized, social practices of violence. Neither legal interpretation nor the violence it occasions may be properly understood apart from one another. (1990, 779)

Likewise, the partisan critic realizes that language does matter—that language supports material conditions in which people are not treated equally and are indeed seriously mistreated—and takes a side. After all, "Moral violation [may] take on the guise of literary form" (Lang, 1988, 350). To condemn injustice is to condemn the agents of injustice, as well as the instruments of injustice and the mute or compliant witnesses. When injustice is tangible, when the materiality of suffering cannot be denied, then criticism is just when criticism acts as moral critique.

## ✶ RORTY ON CRUELTY AND STRUGGLE ✶

The partisan response to invitational rhetoric can be made clearer by engaging with Richard Rorty on the issues of cruelty and struggle. Coactive persuasion is not always enough to create a better world and confrontational rhetorical strategies, in which there are winners and losers, are often a necessary part of political progress. Along with Rorty, I seek to construct a world in which humans cease being cruel to one another. To accomplish this, people have to experience a widening of their moral imaginations and learn to extend to everyone the benefits of civilization. Thus, everyone, *without exception*, is entitled to food, shelter, education, health care, and a chance to explore and actualize his or her self-potential, among other things. Denigrating any human being for any reason or elevating one group of people over another group is a crime against humanity, although localized restraints are often necessary to prevent individuals from harming others; for example, society rightly imprisons pedophiles and the poor rightly have a claim against the rich for a fair share of the world's wealth. Distinctions between individuals are primarily symbolic and do not justify elite privilege or the dismissal of large segments of humanity as "surplus." Simply, the injunction against cruelty requires a vision of community that values what I have described. This is not to say, however, that there is no room for violence and force in effectuating change. Obviously, the more we rely on violent methods, the more we achieve violent ends, but to censor emphatically violent or coercive persuasion is to allow ourselves to be subjected by other communities that choose to adopt these tactics. By acknowledging that we had to use force to stop the Nazis, we admit that we have failed in an important task, as we must confront our own responsibilities for their creation, having lost the people who became Nazis from our moral universe. Nazis are made, not born, as are all cultural identifications. Only because *other* moral identifications lost their credibility was it possible for the German people to be persuaded to model themselves into the image that Hitler offered them.

For instance, one of the stronger scenes in Leni Riefenstahl's famous *Triumph of the Will* involves the segment, early in the film, in which morning breaks on the tent city that houses the million people who gathered from throughout Germany to attend the Nuremberg party rally. The tents are well ordered and the camera focuses on pots of milk that are overflowing, large cauldrons of porridge, and endless strings of sausages. Viewers are overwhelmed by images of happy people eating and laughing, and strong, virile, even sexy bodies. In subsequent scenes, that virility is emphasized, signifying that people are able to attend to "higher" social needs now that their basic needs have been met. Such scenes were extremely poignant at the time to a people who had recently experienced an enforced starvation by the punitive victors of World War I and they remind us that it is useful to study the Nazi social movement with the perspective given by Leland Griffin, who argues that "to study a movement is to study a striving for salvation, a struggle for perfection, a progress toward the 'good'" (1969, 460). In this case, the Nazis associated themselves with feeding a starving nation and by bringing about the leisure and security by which the finer things in life could be contemplated. As exemplified in *Mein Kampf*, literally "My Struggle," the Nazi party presented itself as a moral movement, a battle for the purification of Germany. By positioning the Jews as the enemy of order, the Nazis were able to convince people that by attacking the Jews, they were defending something precious about themselves, that they were protecting the homeland of the (authentic) German people. Because such appeals are difficult to resist, the ultimate ends of Nazi agitation assumed an aura of legitimacy in the minds of the German people. Closer to home, the US ideology of anticommunism was based on this same appeal (Parenti, 1969).

When faced with a Nazi (or a "terrorist"), Rorty would attempt to persuade that person that he or she is wrong, that a better persona to adopt is to be nice and creative rather than cruel and destructive, and he would point to the death camps and to the destruction of Europe as evidence of his point. In so doing, Rorty would not be appealing to their "true" inner moral worth, upon which their capacity for invitational rhetoric is grounded. What he would be practicing is old-fashioned conversion or confrontational persuasion, the type of intellectual activity that the classical Greeks popularized. The Nazis had, after all, an inner moral worth, one that was not "false" but productive and creative in Foucault's sense of power. The Nazis' "inner moral worth" was a great strength to them, particularly when the trials of world conquest and the pressures of the Holocaust grew heavy for the Germans. The Nazis' war of conquest and extermination demanded a clear sense of moral priorities and an inner stamina to be able to withstand the recriminations of their victims and the stench of burning flesh.

The inner moral stamina of the Nazis was indispensable to them, particularly in the onerous work that many otherwise decent Germans had to perform to make sure that the mass killings proceeded smoothly and efficiently. Transits of prisoners and supplies had to be organized, ovens had to be cleaned, gas chambers repaired, prisoners processed, corpses stripped of hair and teeth, and hundreds of other little things had to be taken care of daily for the Nazi machinery to process corpses at a factory pace. In fact, the Nazis were processing death, and the actions of this dirty business had to be done in spite of whatever non-Nazi moral reservations that the morally "weaker" Nazis may have felt. This is similar to the "moral stamina" that led scientists and technocrats in the United States to design atom bombs and napalm and to order them dropped on civilian targets during World War II and in Vietnam. As Kenneth Burke noted, "An overwhelming amount of the damage done by our ingenious, spendthrift, modern weaponry in Vietnam was made possible by humble, orderly, obedient, peacefully behaving job-holders, who raise their families in quiet suburbs, and perhaps do not even spank their children" (1982, 42). This is not to say that "moral stamina" does not exist. On the contrary, moral stamina is very real, evident in periods of war as much as it is evident in times of peace; the problem is that such stamina is not always grounded in values that privilege a social justice perspective.

Failing to persuade the Nazis to give up their violent ways, Rorty would run (in light of a probable deportation to a concentration camp), but he would not allow himself to hope for the Nazis to find within their hearts the slumbering truth that would allow them to engage in invitational discourse. He would not hope for the Nazis to reawaken morally and to call off their horror. Rather, Rorty would place his hope, especially if he was caught and interned in Dachau or in Auschwitz, in an impending Soviet liberation. The interest that Rorty would have in a Nazi heart would be to have that heart stop beating; there is nothing to which Rorty could hope to appeal to in order to save himself besides luck and whatever individual survival skills he happened to possess. Inside Nazi hearts is Nazi ideology, and this provides norms for action and for definitions of goodness. The "good" Nazi may act piously, as do, presumably, Islamic suicide bombers.[3]

When Rorty ponders the potential of a renewed Nazi or neofascist consciousness, he turns first to the discourse that Foss and Foss champion. In turning to our citizens as they contemplate fascism and genocide, he would appeal to everything that is good in a nonfascist world (liberal beliefs, human dignity, state accountability, etc.). I would do the same thing when discussing politics with a would-be terrorist. I would say, along with Foss and Foss, that by perpetuating the cycle of violence, the potential terrorist is only contributing to the larger hate and negativity in the world, perpetuating unhappiness, and moving the world that much closer to destruction. I would insist that there was another way, and I would urge the potential terrorist to work with me as his or her brother to change the world nonviolently. However, I realize that potential terrorists would stare at me incredulously and tell me that the only thing the Western world seems to respect is violence, that the darkness engulfing the developing world was a planned effort to bleed those nations, and that the industrialized world has no plans to alter its behavior. Although I prefer my narrative and desperately want to believe in the inevitability of moral social progress, I know that the potential terrorist is correct, that in the absence of goodwill toward the developing world, the West cannot expect anything but hatred in return (see McCaughan, 2001, 40).

Failing to convince my disadvantaged brother to reject terrorism ends my attempt at communication, just as this failure ends Rorty's attempt to persuade the Nazis that the world would be a nicer place if they adopted Western liberalism. I agree that the world *would* be nicer if everyone converted to Western liberalism *and* if Western liberalism embodied all of the features Western liberalism claims to endorse; however, Western liberalism does not, and we do not fool the developing world.[4] Thus, the "terrorists" pick up guns, and the rest of us are left with two options—fleeing or fighting.[5] In the face of horror, we are left with difficult choices for which there are no "right" answers. What we are left with is a relative spectrum of "better" or "worse" options for response, with the criterion for evaluating them being "what works" in *this* context for alleviating suffering.

The term "struggle" is a key component of analysis in this book. Struggle is celebrated as a necessary response of repressed people to situations of suffering created by others. As noted by Jason Ingram, "Communication and community formation are works in progress, as are attempts to articulate particular struggles to dominant symbols and persuasive discourses" (2002, 12). Although struggle has the potential for creating more of what people resist (Gearhart, 1979), that is not the fault of those who struggle. For example, the fact that the Palestinian struggle to resist thirty-two years of military occupation increases the violence brought against them by the Israelis should not be taken to mean that the Palestinians are creating the conflict; the conflict will end when the Israelis (shamed and exhausted) withdraw to their original borders, compensate Palestinians for the land stolen in creating the Jewish state, and outgrow the racism associated with Zionism. Although communication strategies are essential to mediating and resolving conflict, the fact remains that, at some point, the oppressing power must refrain from oppressing. In short:

> What is required is a complete reassessment of the current global economic system, with the goal of promoting genuine human security and development. Global financial institutions, such as the World Trade Organization, that do not promote these goals must be revised or scrapped completely and replaced with a system based upon principles of equity, peace, and democracy. (Staples, 2000, 22)

In every historical struggle, people have acted inhumanly: In battle, few humans are ever blameless—the saints and martyrs of the world all have warts. Yet, just causes (*bellum justum*) have and do exist—when becoming a soldier is morally necessary. For example, China's fight to expel the invading Japanese army represents a profoundly just cause. During Japan's military occupation of China in the 1930s and 1940s, the Japanese murdered over 25,000,000 Chinese (Murphy, 1997). Given the gravity of the Japanese threat, any atrocity committed by an individual Chinese against any Japanese solder is, although regrettable, morally inconsequential in terms of the larger struggle, for the Japanese were the unqualified aggressors and retained the power to withdraw their forces and end the human suffering that they caused. They, not the Chinese, were responsible for the death and carnage that took place in China.

I am not a soldier and I do not advocate violence. However, if I were living in Nazi-overrun Europe during the Second World War, in China in the late 1930s, or in Central America during the 1980s, I would do what was necessary to protect my community from the atrocities of the marauding invaders, as the Nazis, Japanese, and United States plainly were in those circumstances, respectively (Gibney, 1997; Herman, 1991). Caring people should find untenable the claim that the misbehavior of people fighting for a just cause belittles the moral significance of their struggle. Although such misbehavior is to be avoided, only with extraordinary naiveté can a person maintain that, in the pursuit of justice, no vile deeds are ever committed. In the words of Victor Hugo, "If the soul is left in darkness, sins will be committed. The guilty one is not he who commits the sin, but he who causes the darkness" (quoted in King, 1987, 7).

No individual is perfect; within the best people lie corrupt motivations. Rather than condemning people for their imperfections, a more useful task involves recognizing that the drive for perfection is responsible for many human travesties. With this perspective, critics can avoid judging the human ambitions of organized labor or socialists by their human failures. As

Rorty notes, "If we look for people who made no mistakes, who were always on the right side, who never apologized for tyrants or unjust wars, we shall have few heroes and heroines" (1998a, 45). Although it is impossible to collectively agree on who is or is not a hero or heroine (one person's hero is another's villain), it is essential to recognize that without inspiration the human spirit withers. Thus, we should embrace the history of struggle and the attainment of past victories as a constitutive source of contemporary hope.

In the future, there may exist a culture in which moral persuasion will keep greedy and selfish people from starving or torturing children. With many others, I long for such a world and am prepared to do something to achieve it, even if this means maintaining the language of struggle and conflict, because struggle and conflict are what constitute the world today. I also recognize that, within this struggle, organized labor and its political parties (the heroes of this book) have been guilty of unfortunate compromises and misdeeds, even cruelties, that must be acknowledged and condemned to avoid a reoccurrence of what Albert Camus once called "the socialism of the gallows" (1960, 171).

Specifically, the international repudiation of political Marxism and of the larger socialist tradition should not blind scholars to the heuristic utility of Marx's critical insights or the insights of other critical scholarship. The work of writers such as Marx, members of the Frankfurt School, Rorty, Foucault, Nietzsche, or any other philosopher are only tools. The utility of these tools is their ability to document poetically the inconsistencies of a culture, name essential tensions creating suffering within that culture, and guide humans toward reinvention. The writings of these people and of many others help to rejuvenate human culture by reanimating the notion of community and, thereby, reminding us of our humanity.

## ✷ NOTES ✷

1. The modern origins of the debate between partisan and objective criticism in the communication literature can be traced to a disciplinary discussion that arose out of a speech given by Richard Nixon on November 3, 1969, as well as by the later publication of Wander's (1983) landmark essay, "The Ideological Turn in Modern Criticism." A chapter-long synthesis and reengagement with this discussion appears in Swartz (1997a, 91-134). At a deeper level, the issue involves the scientizing of criticism. See Black (1978) Nothstine, Blair, and Copeland (1994).

2. Perhaps the most egregious example of hostile custody battles over the lifestyle choices of a fit biological parent is *Painter v. Bannister* (1966). In Painter, a loving and highly capable father lost custody of his son to his son's maternal grandparents. The mother and sister had been killed in a tragic car accident, and the maternal grandparents successfully took custody of the surviving son, in spite of the fact that the son wished to remain with his father, on the grounds that the father was a "hippie" and that the child's grandparents could provide a more stable and religious environment for the child.

3. Although the self-immolation of suicide bombers may appall us, it would be disingenuous to condemn them for their single-minded commitment. In the United States, we employ a highly professional army that utilizes high-tech weapons to do our killing for us. I see no meaningful distinction between the carpet bombing of Vietnam by the United States and the crashing of two airlines into the World Trade Center by terrorists. Both are equally wrong, and until we learn to condemn the one, we are disingenuous when we attempt to condemn the other. Other scholars are more discerning; see Simon and Benjamin (2001).

4. I grew up believing that I was a liberal, and would still like to think of myself as a liberal (in the New Deal sense), but liberalism today has moved so far to the right that for me to discuss the issues that I care about, I have to use the language of social democracy.

5. In a story told to me in 1991 by Professor Don Abbott, he and the noted theorist of rhetoric Chaim Perelman once drove in a car together. In light of Perelman's experience in the Belgium underground during the Second World War, Abbott asked Perelman if he would have shot a German soldier. Perelman responded, "Of course. There are some things for which rhetoric does not work."

# CHAPTER 8

# PARTISAN CRITICISM HAS A COMMITMENT TO LABOR AND THE POOR

Labor, what this book calls the "working class," has been and continues to be systematically excluded from normative political representation in the United States and is allowed little opportunity to contribute to the terms and conditions of its social existence (Henwood, 1987; Moberg, 1992). Although few workers today resist such marginalization, this has not always been the case. During the formative period of US labor consciousness (from the end of the Civil War until the First World War), the political alienation of labor was routinely challenged by workers who relied extensively (and illegally) on collective self-help in their pursuit of economic justice. With this method, labor achieved many gains—including the eight-hour workday and a federally guaranteed minimal wage. These welcomed developments attest to the power of worker militancy and collective action (Zinn, 1990b, 181).

In our current neoliberal political environment, however, these gains continue to be eroded as working class power wanes (Chomsky, 1998). Such erosion exacerbates economic inequality, which stands at the highest level in US history (Phillips, 2002). Crucial future gains are dependent on a political cohesion that derives from a renewed working class self-identification grounded in a collective sense of mutual aid and community (see Kropotkin, 1989, 300). Therefore, in order for "average" citizens (defined as individuals who lack normative political or economic power, labor under unsatisfactory conditions established by others, and/or possess little or no bargaining strength) to have a collective say in the utilization and distribution of public resources, an essential goal of the working class and partisan criticism must be to reanimate the labor movement. Such a movement seeks the creation of a strong progressive government and the establishment of an economic democracy in the United States.

## ✷ DEFINITION OF THE "WORKING CLASS" ✷

Owing to its long history and its imprecise usages, a specific definition of the "working class" is difficult to articulate. The concept has become "deterritorialized" (Guattari & Negri, 1990, 22). The classic experience of the working class during industrialization in the nineteenth and early twentieth centuries has given way to more complex and less theoretically discrete relationships between labor and capital. As Felix Guattari and Antonio Negri explain, "Deterritorialized production signifies that work and life are no longer separate; society is collapsed into the logic and processes of capitalist development" (1990, 22). As capitalism becomes the defining force in society, the identities of the workers it creates become less connected to the traditional binary between the "creative" and the "appropriating" classes. The symbols and culture of the middle class have proliferated to the point that many individuals are both the exploited and the exploiters. In other words, exploitation and social insecurity have become a more accepted part of our political and moral communities (ie, internalized by more people as natural or inevitable). We are, as Edward Said (1994) once suggested, all complicit to a degree with the crass inequities that define our contemporary world.

In less postmodernist terms, Carolyn Leste Law highlights the conceptual problems involved in delineating the boundaries of the working class. She asks, "Is income a viable marker of class? Should we define 'working class' by level of parents' education . . . or by how dirty or dangerous one's job is? Can a small business owner . . . be considered working class?" (1995, 8). Along with Law, this book recognizes that attempting to answer these questions is divisive and unproductive to the struggle for social justice. Rejecting terminological inclusivity as unnecessary frees us to accept a pragmatic understanding of working class suffering. The goal, after all, is not to capture the "essence" of the label, but to provide a critical construct by which to engage in cultural criticism and political action. Rather than imposing any definition, a way out of this quandary is to stress the importance that individuals themselves attach to this identity. For example, Law concludes that people are "working class if they say they are" (1995, 8).

Similarly, what this and subsequent chapters identify as the "working class" is intended to be inclusive of a wide community of workers in the

United States. The community envisioned by the use of this term is comprised of everyone whose health, happiness, and security are dependent on working conditions established by a hierarchy insensitive (or antagonistic) to individual and humanistic needs (see Meehan, 1997, 165). Although not every working class person is degraded by or unhappy with his/her working conditions, most clearly are. In the United States, people largely work to survive and seek personal fulfillment in their off-hours. More specifically, the *working class* is comprised of those communities of people who must labor under the authority of another and who are dependent on market conditions to define the terms of their employment. Fundamental to an individual's working class identification is the desire to "reclaim mastery over work time, the essential component of life time" (Guattari & Negri, 1990, 16).

For the purposes of this book, if individuals resonate with certain cultural cues, or are negatively impacted by classism, such people will understand "the sense of displacement" and the "complex ambivalent feelings it represents" (Law, 1995, 8). The key to making such a conceptual move is, as Duncan Kennedy notes, to transcend simplistic distinctions between "productive workers" and "idle capitalists." Instead, the "main problem is not how to expropriate the capitalist class, but how to overcome the unjust and unnecessary inequity of power and reward among those who work or want to work, and the patterns of behavior that reinforce and legitimate that inequality generation after generation" (1983, 86). By defining the working class in as broad a set of terms as possible, this chapter encourages readers to recognize their own interests in the issues discussed below and to imagine ways by which gross structural inequality can be abolished. All workers, regardless of their political and cultural identifications, benefit from understanding the history of labor and the current struggles to create a political environment where the human dignity of all workers is respected.

## ✶ THE IMPORTANCE OF EQUITY IN LABOR RELATIONS ✶

In principle, democratic culture demands equity among citizens and does not privilege private property above all other values. Equity does not mean a forced equality that ignores individual strengths and weaknesses, as all citizens are not similarly situated in terms of motivation, intelligence, moral character, or physical stamina. Equity must not be equated with a crude social leveling. The goal of a progressive society is not to make everyone poor; rather, the goal of a progressive society is to provide for the basic material and cultural needs of all citizens and allow them the intellectual freedom to explore, reorganize, critique, and debate (Dorfman, 1989, 146).

At the most fundamental level, equity involves a profound social commitment to the human community. A person's lack of wealth is as irrelevant to that person's status as a human being as is that person's sexuality or ethnic identifications. The individual human should be respected, and that respect should be unconditional. The hostility toward the wealthy expressed in partisan criticism should not be taken as a sign of disrespect for individuals who happen to be rich. The term "the wealthy" is an abstraction, as is the term "the poor." But beneath the abstraction is a reality situated (although imperfectly) along structural class lines. Partisan hostility is directed toward the existence of these lines and not to individuals who occupy a particular status within an unjust system.

Class distinctions should be viewed—along with racial, religious, cultural, and gender distinctions—as regrettable symbolic provincialities that interfere with the creation of a just society for all humans (hence, my reluctance above to reify a definition of the working class). All people are fundamentally the same, as all other species of animals are fundamentally the same among members of their classification. Thus, we should reject all metaphysical assumptions of the inherent importance of any exclusive community and work toward creating a society grounded in pragmatic assumptions of solidarity, cooperation, kindness, and reciprocity. In other words, for sustained progressive change to occur in the United States, a practical sense of hope must be forged. Social and economic justice are not inevitable. Moral evolution is seldom driven by top-down initiative. When such evolution occurs, the driving force of change is usually the result of community vision and mass struggle. By definition, such vision is grounded in hope. With hope, vision achieves its strength in the ability of individuals to imagine a better life; this imagination, subsequently, becomes the blueprint for progressive change.

Social hope can assume many forms. In the past, organized labor attempted to create and to communicate the possibility for hope. In so doing, labor founded an inspiring tradition grounded in the solidarity of the working classes. An important lesson from this tradition is that popular resistance to inequality is necessary. This resistance can take many forms, including that of communication; "the most critical function of communication is transformation, or the capacity to suggest new possibilities for individuals to be together" (Eisenberg, 1998, 100). Such resistance, however, should not be reduced to communication because it often assumes other forms. As Peter Kropotkin once noted, "Without the menace contained in. . . revolts, no serious concession has ever been wrung by the people from the governing classes. Without such risings, the social mind was never able to get rid of its deep-rooted prejudices, to embolden itself sufficiently to conceive *hope*" (1995, 103).

My unqualified commitment to—and respect for—the individual human acknowledges that among all classes of people there is a fundamental interdependence (which, admittedly, becomes obscured when struggle and resistance are exemplified militarily). This interdependence is an essential nutrient for the health of collective life and represents an important normative value in progressive politics. Out of respect for the fundamental codependence of all humans, the different social classes strive to provide each other the necessities for a life of dignity. No single class of people can survive independent of all other classes. Human potential is dependent upon cultural diversity for its realization; human beings blossom only in the context of other humans. Thus framed, class cooperation is the *topos* of the economic vision advocated by a partisan criticism. This vision is offered to replace the antagonistic "class warfare" model of economic relations now practiced on a global level. Thus, as Amardo Rodriguez argues, the new goal is "to foster human relations that engender empathy, cooperation, diversity, and equality" (2001, 108).

Under this new model of political economy, industry can continue to organize for the production of social goods, and important incentives remain for motivated people to amass a comfortable level of *useful* wealth (as opposed to *superfluous* wealth). This distinction is pragmatic, not metaphysical. Wealth should be used to reduce human suffering in the world.

When squandered on decadence, wealth doubly harms the under-resourced. Usable wealth is wealth that people utilize to secure necessary items such as food, shelter, health care, clothing, as well as some modest material comforts. Superfluous wealth, on the other hand, is wealth wasted on "conspicuous consumption" (Veblen, 1998) such as multimillion dollar celebrity weddings, multimillion dollar bonuses for corporate officers, or houses valued at tens of millions of dollars, all of which insult the dignity of the working class and highlight the moral poverty of the non-working class elite.

Part of the current malaise in US society is that Americans are more offended by restricting the opportunities of the affluent in how they spend their money than they are offended by the condition and suffering of the poor (for example, the repeal of the Estate Tax and tax breaks for the superwealthy). In contrast, the economic model that partisan criticism supports provides for an equitable distribution of society's wealth and opportunities (c.f. Feldstein, 1999, who argues that the increase of wealth for the wealthy is not at the expense of the poor, and is therefore justified). When this economic change occurs, the class tensions that plague the current economic arena will be recast into *relationships of mutuality*. Relationships of mutuality recognize the fundamental consubstantiality of all human beings (Burke, 1969a, 1969b). Such relationships can help mediate the effects of the arbitrary—yet inevitable—symbolism that divides human communities. In mediating such effects, relationships of mutuality deny US elites a rationalization for structural inequality.

Within relationships of mutuality, the working class will continue to produce goods and services, as this is their important contribution to society. However, rather than hoarding that wealth for themselves, management and owners will invest that wealth back into the well-being of the workers, their families, and their communities. This act constitutes industries' essential contribution to society:

> [T]oday a business can no longer be seen as a creator of wealth solely for its owners. The role of business as a creator of wealth is broader than that. Business is the principal engine for generating wealth for society as a whole—for the entrepreneur and the owners, but also for the employees who must receive fair salaries, for the community which receives tax revenues to fund schools and other public institutions, and for suppliers and sales organizations and their employees up and down the business stream. (Maresca, 2000, 161)

Under the working class industrial model proposed here, the concerns of labor are essential for management, as the health of the industrial enterprise would be correlated to worker satisfaction. If the producers themselves are not satisfied, the production process becomes a sham and the objects produced cease to be a societal benefit. No product, no matter how necessary, can be considered a benefit if the methods of production offer no quality of life to the producer—the historical nexus of sugar and slavery is a paradigmatic example (see Dunn and Nash, 2000). Labor that does not affirm humans and, instead, reduces them to objects for manipulation is a form of oppression. Humans labor to live and to construct community; they do not live to labor for the sole gain of another.

Under a system of equity in which mutuality of relationships is established, industry would still be encouraged to generate "profit," but the profit generated would be socially focused. Because society supports the conditions for industrial wealth, the profit from such enterprise properly belongs to society. Managers and owners are merely stewards of this wealth. Although such classes are entitled to compensation for this responsibility, their fundamental duty is to channel their power toward ends supportive of society that make their enterprise possible.[1] The end result of this system is a more just society, marked by increased citizen satisfaction and overall productivity. Historically, labor unions have worked (however imperfectly) toward such a vision. As Richard Rorty notes, at "their best, labour unions are America at its best. Like the civil rights movement, the union movement is a model of Americans getting together on their own and changing society from the bottom up—forcing society to become more decent, more democratic and more humane" (1999, 256).

Under the equity model of labor relations, the greatest countries would not be those that create concentrated wealth, but the societies in which the most low-level workers are guaranteed that their economic and social needs are firmly met. This move is not intended to turn paupers into princes, but to construct a world in which neither extreme is acceptable. Without such guarantees of economic equality, without economic justice, the protections of political equality that US citizens respect are not secure; in fact, much of this political equality has been steadily eroding as the public realm becomes increasingly subjected to unrestrained market forces and the concurrent growth of economic disparity (Bruner, 2002).[2]

Critics of the equity model might argue that being rich is inherently virtuous, and that free markets can help the entrepreneur become wealthy; the entrepreneur, in turn, spreads the wealth (hence the idiom, "The rising tide raises all boats"). Yet, although tremendous wealth has been generated by free markets, this wealth—with few exceptions—creates social problems like immorality, gluttony, depletion of vital resources, social isolation, and cultural callousness. Moreover, the wealth generated by world markets has not been rationally or fairly distributed. Simply, markets make few rich and most poor. As of 2002, for example, the developing nations had a total debt of approximately $2.5 trillion (Sharma and Kumar, 2002, 45). A few people in the developing world have become billionaires, but their wealth does little to uplift the conditions of their impoverished compatriots. Thus, the market's focus on the material wealth of a select group misses a fundamental point about humans and their needs. Meaningful wealth comes not from BMWs, diamond rings, or nuclear arsenals but from healthy bodies and healthy spirits and from communities that are uplifting and dignifying—meeting human needs for love, inclusion, self-fulfillment, and joy (Goldman, 1969, 55). Karl Marx may have been wrong about many things, but he was correct in warning that people should not mistake money for life.

In sum, the US system of property works best when everyone has some property, and the system works least effectively when a handful of people control most of the property. The underlying assumption behind private property is that people will do their best work with pride and feel integrated into the community when they have the right of sole possession over some resource that cannot be taken from them (See William Blackstone, *Commentaries on the Laws of England*, excerpted in Ellickson, Rose, and Ackerman, 1995, 37-44). The flip side of this assumption is that when people have no property, they have no investment in their community or in their occupation and thus have no reason to do their best work or to invest emotional capital into their surroundings. Under the current system, people without property are alienated, and when millions of such people exist, societies become destabilized, the rich fearful, and governments more punitive in an effort to further entrench the privileges of the aristocracy against the claim of the poor for an equitable share of society's wealth.

When property is highly centralized, a monopoly condition exists, stifling competition, dampening initiative, and destroying the purifying elements of a more inclusive market economy. Simply, so-called "free market" economies are not free (Bruner, 2002, 27). In the face of accumulated economic power and the private rules established by the strongest players, free markets exclude more than they include. Free markets are only free in the sense that rational humanistic control over them has been extinguished. An equity model of economics is intended to introduce rational and humanistic control over the economy. Achieving this equity has been a dominant thrust behind much labor organization in this country and animates the desire of the working class to speak with an impassioned voice. Working toward this equity is as important today as this work has been for the past one hundred fifty years; the barriers to achieving such equity are as significant today as they have ever been.

## * LABOR'S ROLE IN COMMUNICATING HOPE *

For sustained progressive change to occur in the United States, a sense of hope, as discussed above, must be forged. Social and economic justice are not inevitable. Moral evolution is seldom driven by top-down initiative. When such evolution occurs, the driving force of change is usually the result of community vision and mass struggle. By definition, such vision is grounded in hope. With hope, vision achieves its strength in the ability of individuals to imagine a better life; this imagination, subsequently, becomes the blueprint for progressive change.

In the early 1950s, Eric Hoffer observed (almost incomprehensibly today in light of the excessive demonization of communism and the denial of its causes) that if "the Communists win Europe and a large part of the world, it will not be because they know how to stir up discontent or how to infect people with hatred, but because they know how to preach hope" (1989, 9). More recently, Ronald Aronson noted that socialism was "the greatest of human secular hopes" (1999, 471) and that the "worldwide socialist and Communist movements were *hope mobilized, hope in action*" (1999, 473).

People who bring hope to the hopeless are not inconsequential, no matter how marginalized they are by the powers with a vested interest in a widespread hopelessness. Such people—as in Hoffer's communists or Aronson's socialists—are the best prophets in the Western tradition, more so than the theistic prophets celebrated in Western faiths. Unlike the theistic prophets, the secular prophets do not require people to surrender their minds. To the contrary, the goal of a secular hope is to reinvigorate the human intellect to focus on earthly problems: to humanize and energize the moral force of the human will, and to focus the energy of this will on the critical talents of people to create the world that they envision. Secular prophets preach hope for a secular world of justice. The illusion of heavenly justice is rejected as a pretext for the injustice of the existing world:

> God being everything, the real world and man are nothing. God being truth, justice, goodness, beauty, power, and life, man is falsehood, iniquity, evil, ugliness, impotence, and death. God being master, man is the slave. Incapable of finding justice, truth, and eternal life by his own effort, he can attain them only through a divine revelation. But whoever says revelation says revealers, messiahs, prophets, priests, and legislators inspired by God himself; and these, once recognized as the representatives of divinity on earth as the holy instructors of humanity, chosen by God himself to direct it in the path of salvation, necessarily exercise absolute power. All men owe them passive and unlimited obedience; for against the divine reason there is no human reason, and against the justice of God no terrestrial justice holds. (Bakunin, 1970, 24)

Hope, in my sense, is pragmatic, involving strategy, perseverance, and fortitude. Such hope promises not heaven, but a life on earth animated by a widespread dignity and self-worth for all people. Vision and hope, therefore, involve the richness of the human imagination. In the pursuit of community, the human species constructs itself; such construction is the quintessential human act—grounded in both bodily desire and symbolization (Burke, 1970, 305).

Labor's tradition in creating hope must be revitalized and its vocabulary and strategies adapted to meet the needs of a twenty-first century reactionary (ie, right wing) climate. Driving this reanimation is what Chapter 1 called the communicative or communication imagination. This imagination involves the ability to perceive how individuals are placed in history by texts and decisions authored by other people and, thereby, helps individuals to realize that their place in history has not been accidental. Furthermore, the social placement of many people is not what most would choose to accept for themselves. Lacking a communication imagination, most people resign themselves to the condition of their lives and never learn to question the conditions that created their subjectivity. In other words, people adapt to alienation—what Martin Luther King, Jr. defines as "a form of living death" and as "the acid of despair that dissolves society" (1987, 44). Exercising a communication imagination, however, enables workers—creators of wealth, knowledge, and service—to imagine a more egalitarian society designed to enrich human life through inclusive and expansive notions of care, community, and identification. Such imagination is creative, helping individuals to respond more intelligently to their communication environment, as well as to equip them with the conceptual models to construct their vision of the future (as in Brummett, 1984).

By helping people to appreciate the subjectivity of their social placement, the communication imagination makes obvious the relationship between the structure of society and human social consciousness.[3] As Karl Marx noted, "It is not the consciousness of men that determines their being, but, on the contrary, their social being determines their consciousness" (1956, 51). In other words, human beings experience their subjectivities through "the totality of social relations" (1956, 68). Individuals are positioned into often limited and limiting economic and social roles; such positioning affects all aspects of an individual's sense of self and often determines his/her life potential. A great deal of this positioning occurs at birth, as a child's life chances are largely determined (although not exclusively) by the socioeconomic (and racial) status of his or her parents (Kornblum, 2000, 373).

Due to such positioning, social mobility in the United States is largely a myth, although this myth exerts a tremendous influence over society.[4] Social mobility is impaired because every occupation is a status, and that status creates a discipline and culture of being:

> The culture of work is not simply the physical actions of production but a total experience objectively located in social relations, practices, and institutions. The workplace culture provides a distinctive way of life organized with meanings, values, practices, languages, and social relations . . . . For most Americans, work is the principal site of daily activity and the substance of personal identity. (Artz and Murphy, 2000, 256)

Children born to an impoverished working class home usually grow into the limitations of that identity (Willis, 1981). These limitations are reinforced throughout the social network; indeed, many are embedded in the fabric of society. We are, in the words of Ben Agger, "trained to be smart or stupid depending on our proximity and utility to power" (1990, 33). In this way, the clerk at Wal-Mart is as limited in his or her social potential as he or she is limited by the marginalized working conditions of the service sector (see Ehrenreich, 2001). Such workers and their families are conditioned to an experience of life that is fundamentally dehumanizing and hopeless.

To recognize and to name the collective sufferings of people are not insulting or demeaning to them[5]; this naming is a strategy for empowering dehumanized people to change their conditions:

> In naming our reality we comprehend it; we liberate our experience from a world and language community that denies or distorts it. Until it is named and expressed, the experience remains a mute suffering, an inarticulate experience, a vague discomfort, a feeling of confusion. A sense of not belonging, not being affirmed, a sense of being an outsider comes with not having a shared language for this seemingly subjective, personal experience. Naming this experience removes it from the personal, subjective, private realm of the individual while transforming it into a social and public reality. (Bologh, 1991, 38)

Social molding occurs among the professional classes as well, with detrimental effects on the national community. For example, a professor is as much a professor outside as inside the classroom. The enactment of a professor's life reflects the tempering of his or her character. This is as true for a physician or an attorney. A life committed to inquiry and edification requires the critical practice of a staunchly disciplined life. This discipline is so comprehensive that a vast cultural gulf has emerged between the professional classes and the traditional laboring classes, making identification between the two societies increasingly difficult. Unfortunately, the freedom required for professionals to perfect their occupations (as well as the inequitable compensation between the two communities) often results in a segregated social existence. Such distance and privilege encourage an elite ethos and a dispassion toward those who suffer. Social elitism—when divorced from community bonds—can turn elites into "a gathering of birds of prey" (Andrew King, 1987, 45—46), as doctors and lawyers are often portrayed. In this way, the collective intelligentsia of society serves its own interest and not the larger interest of society.

Against these conditions, labor and partisan scholarship struggle for recognition of the essential needs of the larger community, which are great. Many US communities have become materially, spiritually, and culturally dysfunctional. Evidence of such dysfunction surrounds most US citizens: The US has the highest violent crime rates of any industrial society (Kornblum, 2000, 210); drug and alcohol abuse are endemic, decimating entire communities and promoting moral and spiritual squalor; and apathy toward homelessness, joblessness, and institutionalized poverty betray the humanity of all US citizens. As Christian Parenti notes, "When community spaces are dominated by signs of neglect and anonymity, or have become dangerous, social relations soon decline as well. Common spaces are, in a very literal sense, the platform upon which communities and their movements are built" (2000, 46). On a fundamental level, these and other problems serve the political order. As Parenti argues, "crime justifies state violence and even creates popular demand for state repression. Thus, it helps to liquidate or at least neutralize a whole class of potential rebels. Crime also short-circuits the social cohesion necessary for radical mobilization" (2000, 43).

With the exception of people who suffer from neurological brain deformities that render them narcissistic, psychopathic, or schizophrenic, or else suffer from other biological infirmities caused by human-created pollution, malnutrition, and other maladies, what society commonly understands as being "bad" is often socially conditioned. Even the most grotesque human behavior needs to be understood for its systemic causes and not dismissed as an act of "evil." For example, what commonly is described today as "terrorism" is a form of political struggle and must be understood in that context. Although we may reject the justice of a particular struggle, we would be shortsighted to deny that the actors were struggling for a political cause and were, thus, reacting to conditions created, in part, by ourselves. To reduce terrorism to acts of evil is to ignore the causes of the struggle, as well as the effect of the social pressures that create social approval for violence to occur.[6]

In short, socially deformed human beings are made; they are the result of social pollution in the environment, just as birth defects are often the result of toxins in the air, food, and water. The classic expression of this sentiment was articulated by Marx, who noted:

> Labour certainly produces marvels for the rich but it produces privation for the worker. It produces palaces, but hovels for the worker. It produces beauty, but deformity for the worker. It replaces labour by machinery, but it casts some of the workers back intoa barbarous kind of work and turns the others into machines. It produces intelligence, but also stupidity and cretinism for the workers. (1964, 124)

Against this "stupidity" and "cretinism" is the power of labor to create hope—a hope for a better life and healthier communities. This power is grounded in a mature political vision of an equitable society, one free of hierarchy and organized around the common good. As reiterated throughout this book, the *common good* is comprised of a world in which stable societies exist that provide to every human being—regardless of birth, race, sex, nationality, sexual choice, and so forth—the fundamental resources to live life to the best of his or her potential, providing for those with low potential a well-defined and comprehensive safety net that belongs to them as a matter of their status as human beings (see Robley E. George, 2002, arguing for a democracy grounded in a Universal Guaranteed Personal Income as well as a Maximum Allowable Personal Wealth). If not enough resources exist to provide everyone with this security, then society must reduce the birthrate so that no human is born into a world of preventable suffering.

The partisan vision of shared economic resources is a strong bulwark against social and political alienation. With such vision, people learn to question the reification of the status quo and become empowered to act as agents of social change, which is essential for the moral development of society (Cushman, 1996; Lentricchia, 1985). However, in the current political environment (a plutocracy with global influence), cultural elitism and institutional norms within the academy have made it difficult for scholars to champion workers' rights and economic justice (Katz, 2002). Although the normative rule in a democratic society is that citizens have authority to frame the issues and contours of community life, this is not the practice of politics in the United States. In the United States, important decisions with regard to the structure of society are made by corporate and industrial elites that often act in their short-term self-interest and engage in actions and policies antithetical to the health and welfare of most working individuals.

The empowerment of labor and a national commitment to a more just social and economic world does not necessarily threaten to eviscerate elite privilege, nor do these changes necessarily lead to the weakening of US institutions. Issues of social justice do not have to be addressed in binary terms: Enacting social justice does not simply invert the hierarchy. As discussed above, social justice seeks harmony through mutuality and respect for the needs of others. A strong and prosperous United States is not incompatible with a just United States. Even the current US government—as selfishly, cruelly, and corruptly as it often behaves—is not beyond redemption. Although systemic change must occur to the US constitutional structure (as discussed throughout this book), the US political system has potential. Specifically, nothing prevents the government from changing itself if enough political pressure could be brought to bear and if the ferocity of our moral anguish can be wielded into a poignant ideological tool. Given that there is no reason why the US government cannot—on its own accord—alter its course and enact a national and international climate of social justice, moral persuasion could be transformative and the possibility remains that a US President or important members of Congress could become socially conscious, and every effort should be made to help them do so. Selfishness and greed are acquired traits and, therefore, can be consciously rejected or unlearned. The profound hostility to social justice—as historically and currently expressed by the US government—is the source of much social tragedy. By affirming a commitment to social justice, the US government could, instead, enable individual communities to enact their visions of social equality, as many unsuccessfully tried throughout Europe in the years since the Second World War (Kolko, 1990).

In the future, people in power might have no choice. If the US government will not reinvent itself on its own initiative in the name of humanity, other action *must* be taken if we are to have a world in which we would want our children to live. Since no international force currently exists to temper US ambitions, US citizens themselves must hold their government accountable for its breach of the public and human trust. This accountability is the essence of democracy and is grounded in engaged political activity and, if need be, in civil disobedience (Zinn, 1968; Thoreau, 1960). Sadly, many US citizens have historically been derelict with this awesome responsibility and have chosen conformity over confrontation.

This sentiment is reflected in a speech delivered in 1950 by W.E.B. Du Bois:

> The reason why we have not got a democratic government in this land capable of successfully dealing with health, education, transportation, communication, mining, manufacturing and heavy industry . . . is because we do not want it; we have for three generations taught ourselves and our children that politics are nasty; that politicians are thieves; that democracy without corruption and manipulation is impossible and that our government, bad as it is, is the best on earth. (1985, 273)

Many US citizens are themselves responsible for US injustice by not demanding progressive change (as defined in a vision of the common good). This problem, however, has systemic roots. Specifically, the US mass media and educational system often make it difficult for US citizens to view themselves as agents for historical change (Chomsky, 1989; Lewis, 1999). If citizens cannot view themselves as agents for change, then the terms of the future will be written by those superelites that control the present.

The first demand by people should be for the US government to allow democratic communities to form—domestically and abroad. This demand is essential because, in spite of what the anarchists claim, government is necessary for social progress. Although bad government can be murderous, no government is a defense of the status quo in which the strong consume the weak. Therefore, we must construct a *good* government, one that, regardless of form, serves the cause of humanity. To achieve this goal is quite possibly the spiritual apex of humanity as we currently understand ourselves. Although democratic communities offer the promise of this commitment, they have failed largely to live up to this ideal. Although people do not normally consider other types of communities as being able to provide this type of leadership, there is nothing to preclude nondemocratic societies from embracing this commitment. Progressive societies do not necessarily have to be democratic, at least in the sense that people typically think of democracy. Localized communities must be allowed to debate and define the conditions of their social life. If such debates lead to the questioning or the reorganization of localized economic, social, or political life, then the government must yield. A plethora of different economic systems must be allowed to emerge, and everyday people themselves (as opposed to a min-iscule social elite) must control and benefit from these systems. These premises are basic to a healthy community life, and owe their moral imperative to values and virtues that predate the US Constitution. To the extent that the United States fails to live up to these ideals, the expression of democracy purported to emanate from this society is but a pale reflection of a higher form of community cooperation.

## Conclusion

Fundamental to the agency of labor in creating hope is the assumption that, currently, all people do not share equally in the power to coconstruct the world because the elite monopolize this power. By accepting the responsibility for social transformation, labor must strip the elites of this power. Such antagonism is necessary; indeed, antagonism between the classes already exists. The difference in my model is that I recognize, ultimately, that a mutuality between all classes is a necessary prerequisite for an environment where cocreation between free and equal people can occur in a meaningful sense. I welcome such a community should it emerge, which, ideally, would be through invitation from the elites for the rest of us to join into their conversation. However, as the wealthy have systematically ignored and abused the working classes, no one should be surprised when the working classes enact change on their own.

Leadership worthy of respect must articulate the aspirations of labor for an equitable society and create policies to enact them; although imperfect, Roosevelt's New Deal agenda constitutes a paradigmatic example of this leadership. Such leadership can only be effective if it animates the moral consciousness of all US citizens. Although citizens themselves need to develop the moral imagination to demand change, that imagination cannot develop in a culture committed to its negation. Most people in the United States are unaware of the past, miscomprehend the present, and are unconcerned for the future. This is the result of the collective moral imagination being bent inwards and twisted to accentuate base self-interest as the national interest (as in Bush's $1.3 trillion tax cut and rebate). Through persuasion and compassionate policy, the federal government must undo what it has wrought, and that means new partisan, working class political leadership is crucial. When this occurs, the connections between labor, community, and social justice will become obvious. In creating a world in which labor is respected, people simultaneously create a world in which diversity is embraced and communities are affirmed. Because humans constitute their lives through work, respect for labor is nothing less than respect for ourselves and respect for the work of all people.

## ✷ NOTES ✷

1. The officials responsible for the economic rape of Enron employees and other pensioners graphically represent the corporatism and greed that a mutuality of relationship perspective is intended to combat.

2. Few Americans are aware of the fact that large amounts of US political autonomy were turned over to the agents of globalization (Brunner, 2002, 30). The loss of such autonomy threatens the rights and privileges that the US government is supposed to secure for its citizens.

3. In light of our current society, one in which inequality is systemic and profoundly detrimental to people's health and well-being, I cannot help but describe "social placement" as a violence done to people by the elite who benefit materially and in other ways from the status quo.

4. For a critique of the Horatio Alger myth, see Dalton (1996, 127–135).

5. The "system," not my description of the system, causes the dehumanization. My intervention, motivated by my profound empathy, is symptomatic of my identification with the poor and socially maligned and is not intended to express arrogance. As Richard Boyd explains, fundamental criticism of this ethos "is that it assumes the right and responsibility . . . to define and represent critical consciousness for others . . . . [and] assumes the mantle of the expert, presuming to give voice to those whom society has rendered voiceless" (1999, 396).

6. In her response to September 11, for instance, Esther Madriz writes, "It is clear to me that this violence is rooted in institutional and structural violence–specifically, in human rights abuses–that exist in the various countries of the Arab world" (2001, 45). More specifically, the "conditions in the Arab world today constitute a flagrant violation of human rights, especially against women, but also against the majority of its citizens in general . . . . many of the cruel and inhumane policies administered in the Arab world today with US support constitute violations of human rights" (2001, 46).

# PART III

## LAW, LABOR, DEMOCRACY, RACISM, AND COMMUNITY: CASE STUDIES IN PARTISAN CRITICISM

As suggested earlier, the United States often exemplifies the type of power antithetical to humane, inclusive, and equitable community. An important reason why the United States has attained this type of deleterious power stems from the failure of organized labor in humanizing and tempering US power.

The chapters in Part Three apply the model of partisan criticism outlined previously. By studying three working-class movements (trade unionism, anarchism, and reformist-socialism), the next three chapters illustrate how the government responded with excessive military and legal violence to the efforts of labor to better the lives for tens of millions of individuals. Specifically, Chapter 9 confronts the legacy of *Commonwealth v. Pullis*, the 1806 case constituting the first US prosecution suppressing a trade union under the law of criminal conspiracy. Important to an analysis of the case is the discourse of the prosecuting attorney, which successfully criminalized the coordination of labor for collective goals, conceptualizing the worker's needs as antithetical to the "social interest." *Pullis*, therefore, is valuable for its insight into the legal rhetoric of marginalization.

Chapter 10 explores the historical expression of anarchism and the 1886 trial of prominent US anarchists charged with murder in the Chicago Haymarket Riots. Although largely forgotten today, classical anarchism was an authentic and influential expression of popular discontent in the late nineteenth and early twentieth centuries, and was particularly important for the reconceptualization of community it offered. For the anarchists, community was more than a place for the poor to huddle in ragged conditions; it was the source of all prosperity and constituted the social, political, economic, and moral foundations of human society.

Chapter 11 engages the experience of Eugene Debs, the Pullman Strike of 1893, and the reformist-socialist tradition in the United States. Deeply animated by the spirit of social justice, this tradition sparked a nationwide rebirth of a popular commitment to peaceful political and economic change; much of the ethos animating the New Deal era was forged by the dreams and aspirations of individuals working in this tradition. Yet, Debs and reformist-socialism were bitterly resisted by the economic and political authorities. In addition to the state violence and intimidation directed against them, Debs and his reformers discovered that the mere discussion of socialist political theory or social change was criminalized and severely punished.

After the discussion of labor, Part Three explores issues of law and racism, examining the legal marginalization of African Americans from the human community through judicial discourse. Specifically, Chapter 12 explores the nexus between community, race, and the law, highlighting an important process by which social division and hierarchy are codified within legal norms. It also engages with a lingering trait of US society, often mistakenly referred to as "racial tension." Chapter 13 explores specific elements in the historical contextualization of slavery, studying the North Carolina Supreme Court's rhetoric of definition and constitutive discourse by providing an analysis of six legal decisions (1801-1849). Through these decisions, the court struggled to reify slavery as the total subjection of the slave while, at the same time, protecting slaves against specific forms of egregious mistreatment.

# CHAPTER 9

# DEFENDING LABOR IN *COMMONWEALTH V. PULLIS*: CONTEMPORARY IMPLICATIONS FOR RETHINKING COMMUNITY

This chapter reviews the reaction of the government and the judiciary to labor's attempt to organize in the preindustrialized United States. The government argued, and the judiciary accepted, the necessity for alienating organized labor on the grounds that such organization was inherently coercive, undemocratic, without legitimacy, and a threat to the economy. Under this rationale, subsequent courts and legislative policy continued to marginalize organized labor until the time of the New Deal. From the mid-1930s until the mid-1980s, organized labor was allowed into nórmative politics, but within a constrained framework of legal control (Voos, 2000, 244). Since the 1980s, however, the actions of organized labor have been increasingly restricted by conservative administrations and the courts.

## ✶ THE ECONOMIC AND SOCIAL CONTEXT BEHIND LABOR UNREST IN THE UNITED STATES ✶

Opponents of organized labor tend to conflate all labor unrest with the most extreme form of revolutionary activity, but this is historically inaccurate. Most movement for social change in the United States begins as popular expression for mild social reform. Such agitation often seeks political inclusion for a large section of society excluded from the larger community (eg, African Americans). Group agitation is almost always directed against the social and political conditions that reify the status quo, hampering social tolerance, progress, justice, equality, and community pride. Although resistance to the status quo often leads to strife, such strife can be properly viewed as society's growing pains, as progressive social movements seek to expand the moral imagination of a community so as to have themselves included as full-fledged members. This is as true for the labor movement as it is true for the civil rights movement.

With industrialization came uneven economic development—periods of prosperity were followed by cycles of ten-year depressions, lasting until the Second World War (Beaud, 1983, 117–122). As the United States shifted its economic base from agriculture to manufacturing, these depressions became particularly disastrous for millions of farmers and recent immigrants. Shut out of self-sustaining agrarian communities, these people had no source of income and no way to survive except by subjecting themselves to the horrible conditions of factory work. By 1870, 67% of all working US Americans were dependent on such factories for their livelihoods; in the more industrialized states, that number was as high as 85% (Forbath, 1985, 817).

Factory work is not bad in and of itself. The institutionalized production of social goods benefits society; for without such production; human civilization could not have advanced to its contemporary state. Many of the comforts of modern life depend on such work. The problem, however, was that industry treated these workers as superfluous and expendable. Literally, the health and safety of tens of millions of workers were sacrificed. Few contemporary US Americans can contemplate the horrors of working class life during this time and remain unmoved; the benefits of modern US life arose from out of the privation and suffering of these workers.

Cities rapidly expanded as workers migrated from across the nation and world in search of work. Much of this immigration was encouraged by industry, as leaders strategically created widespread unemployment to suppress wages, as well as to provide scabs to replace striking workers (Zinn, 1980, reports that company agents would also travel to Europe and spread rumors and falsehoods about the "opportunities" available in the United States, 261). Those who had work found themselves engulfed in huge industrial enterprises that isolated and alienated the individual (David, 1963, 24–25).

Moral character (eg, respect for individuals as human beings), so important in autonomous, agrarian society, counted for little in the new industrial climate. Labor responded to these conditions by illegally forming the first modern unions. This trend started with the Knights of Labor, founded in 1869 under the slogan "An Injury to One is the Concern of All" (Voss, 1994). The principal idea animating these new expressions of labor solidarity was that labor should unite for cooperation, self-protection, and the remaking of society. This vision was precisely what the prosecution in *Commonwealth v. Pullis* (1806) feared—labor was finding its legs and was beginning to stand. In so doing, labor threatened to shake the foundations of this country.

As labor grew more sure of itself, industrial strife increased dramatically, leading to a series of railroad strikes in 1877 (Stowell, 1999; Bruce, 1989; Foner, 1977). In 1877, the United States experienced the worst year of a major depression. The railroads responded to the weak economy by cutting wages 10% (prior to the cuts, brakemen earned $1.75 for a twelve-hour day; Zinn, 1980, 241). Angered railroad workers around the United States refused to move trains. Transportation was paralyzed as the strike—involving more than 100,000 workers—spread across the country (Zinn, 1980, 246). One hundred people were killed in the government suppression of the strike and 1,000 were incarcerated (Zinn, 1980, 246).

The strike followed a typical pattern: In periods of recession, industry enacted wage cuts. Workers responded by staging walkouts. Management then hired scabs (usually members of a different ethnicity) to break the strike. Fights broke out between strikers and scabs, and authorities intervened and attacked the strikers, ostensibly to protect the right of scabs to "accept work on any mutually acceptable terms, free of third-party coercion" (Avery, 1988, 29). The strikers typically resisted such authority, which escalated the violence, leading to the death of many workers.

In sum, the nineteenth century produced an increasingly profound uneasiness around the country as social elites and the small middle class began to fear that collective action by workers would lead to violence and civil war. This uneasiness is even apparent in the 1806 case discussed in this chapter. In response, broad political coalitions between government, industry, and the clergy formed to meet the challenges of suppressing the labor movement. The clash between such authorities and workers are the subjects of this and the following two chapters, starting with the first judicial suppression of trade unions.

## ✷ THE FIRST LABOR CASE ✷

The context of *Commonwealth v. Pullis* (1806) was that of a new nation on the cusp of a profound industrialization. Society was still primarily dominated by the traditional agrarian and artesian values that animated the original colonies. Thus, the legal troubles of the workers in *Pullis* (known as journeymen cordwainers) were surprising to them, as their actions were consistent with prior labor practice, as well as the ideology animating the American Revolution. In retrospect, the case was a harbinger of the breakdown of traditional community life and the loss of individual autonomy in which such community was grounded. By the second half of the nineteenth century, those norms would change and future generations of workers would grow increasingly conscious and questioning of the law's profound hostility toward them. As industrialization took hold in the United States, peaceful political association for the improvement of the working classes became increasingly untenable. Many workers responded by growing militant. This militancy manifested itself in different forms, ranging from slowdowns to strikes to Luddism (eg, the sabotaging of industrial equipment) to paramilitary activity to revolutionary struggle.

The first example in the history of the judicial suppression of trade unions in the United States was *Commonwealth v. Pullis* (1806). *Pullis* is useful to study because the rationale (or narrative) articulated by the prosecution and the court for the legal marginalization of organized labor continues to have cultural influence, even as the specific holding of the case is no longer valid law.[1] As noted by Dianne Avery (1988), *Pullis* and its progeny had great influence on subsequent jurisprudence concerning combinations of workers (in the form of strikes, pickets, and boycotts) that restrained capitalist production. The discourse in *Pullis* promoted the narrative "that workers were transitory, irresponsible, and dangerous," and were, thus, properly the subject of judicial control (1988, 5). This view remains salient. *Pullis*, therefore, is paradigmatic as it encapsulates recurring themes animating the larger labor movement and its relationship to government and industry.

The goal of this chapter is to revisit *Pullis* and to defend the interests of the defeated workers. By defending the workers' movements of the past, we learn better what it means to defend our current common interests as working people in the age of globalization. The pages that follow provide an overview of the context for the conspiracy charge in the *Pullis* case. The chapter then explores the government's repression of nonviolent labor tactics and engages claims made by the government that nonviolent union action should be repressed as coercion. Fundamental to the issues raised by *Pullis* is the problem of legitimacy and its relationship to "working class republicanism" evoked by the labor movement.

## ✶ CONTEXT FOR THE CONSPIRACY CHARGE ✶

The first expression of the Industrial Revolution in the United States occurred in the shoe industry (Nelles, 1931, 166). In 1794, Philadelphia shoemakers (journeymen cordwainers) responded to the labor hardships of industrialization by forming an organization, the Federal Society of Journeymen cordwainers (FSJC). Through direct action (as described below), the FSJC successfully redefined the Philadelphia shoe industry as a closed union shop, in which only members of their organization could be employed.

Through 1804, the Journeymen cordwainers received moderate wage increases (the workday for the cordwainers was sunrise to sunset for less then $10 a week; Nelles, 1931, 167). These increases were not detrimental to the shoe industry, as the FSJC was sensitive to the larger economics of the business. As one example of this, the FSJC voluntarily accepted a reduction in wages to help the master cordwainers cultivate an export market for shoes to the US American South (Nelles, 1931, 167). Yet, as this very export trade matured, pressure mounted for the masters to reduce the piece-rate wages of their workers. To be successful in this task, the masters had to destroy the power of the FSJC. The masters, thus, founded their own management organization and filed a criminal complaint with the State of Pennsylvania to have the tactics of the FSJC declared unlawful. In a particularly egregious example of justice for sale, the employers, not the government, paid the prosecution's expense (Holt, 1984, 593). The criminal complaint against the leaders of the FSJC was grounded in the English Common Law of Conspiracy, which precluded workers from organizing for the goal of increasing wages or reducing working hours (see *Rex v. Journeymen Tailors of Cambridge*, 1721; Wright, 1887). Eight leaders of the FSJC (including George *Pullis*) were indicted and found guilty at trial "of a combination to raise their wages" (*Pullis*, 236).

The prosecution in *Pullis* was part of a larger political battle being waged in the United States between the forces of *aristocracy* (federalism) and those of *republicanism* (Jeffersonian democracy) (Nelles, 1931, 168, 170–173). Within this ideological battle, which continued with different labels through the early-twentieth century, the working classes argued that Jeffersonian democracy envisioned a society in which the pursuit of happiness and dignity was the right of each citizen. Under this view, equality was grounded in the opportunity for individuals to participate in public and economic life. With the growth of industry, organized labor was necessary to mobilize citizens to retain their presence in the public sphere. Nothing less than the freedom of the individual was at stake (Nelles, 1931, 169). In short, Jeffersonian democracy placed great value on individuals and defined freedom as autonomy and self-reliance:

> The hallmarks of labor and Populist rhetoric were demands for equal rights, anti-monopoly, land reform, and an end to the exploitation of producers by non-producers. These movements inherited an older republican tradition hostile to large accumulations of property, but viewing small property as the foundation of economic and civic autonomy. (Foner, 1984)

This republican view was a radical break from English society and necessitated a rejection of the English legal system.

The Federalists, to the contrary, maintained that the national interest could best be advanced through an aristocracy, such as that found in England. According to the Federalists, men of wealth and accomplishment were the best stewards of the common good. Threatening this common good were the base passions and unrealistic whims of the common person. Because the English Common Law reflected this aristocratic interest, the Federalists were interested in importing much of that tradition into the emerging legal systems of the United States. The debate in *Pullis* concerns the wisdom of applying the English Common Law of Criminal Conspiracy to domestic labor cases.

## ✶ ANALYSIS OF *PULLIS* AND THE CONSTRUCTION OF COMMUNITY ✶

The government opened the case against the journeymen cordwainers by arguing that citizens do not have the liberty to judge their own economic value or to interfere with the valuation placed on them by society. Claims to the contrary violate "just government, equal laws, and that due subordination to which every member of the community is bound to submit" (*Pullis*, 132). The government's argument reflects the change caused by industrialization which was then transforming the United States and under which the autonomy and dignity of small-town agrarian individualism gave way to a more regulated existence necessitating heightened means of social control and new forms of authority. Such regulation was regarded by the Federalists to be the responsibility of the elite. Therefore, the defendants acted unlawfully by combining to "regulate the price of the labour of others as well as their own" (*Pullis*, 132). In combining for the common good of the working classes, the FSJC hampered the stewardship of the elite. In contemporary language, the defendants could be considered partisan actors who argued that challenging elite privilege is fundamental to the development of democratic society and a necessary part of social progress.

The government's argument suffered from one major issue; namely, the actions of the journeymen cordwainers were completely legal if done outside the legal fiction of a conspiracy context. As noted by the defense attorney, "A purpose innocent or lawful in one man, cannot be otherwise in a society or body of men. Supposing, therefore, that the facts charged . . . are true; that the men refused to work but at a certain price, it is no crime, and they cannot be punished for it" (*Pullis*, 145). In other words, the journeymen cordwainers were acting within the liberty generally afforded to people living in the society of the period. Therefore, if the government were to succeed in punishing the journeymen cordwainers, a new principle had to be established, a new discipline had to be constructed.

The vehicle for establishing this principle would be the law of criminal conspiracy. Conspiracy laws are broadly written to punish agreements between two or more people to complete some act that the legislature seeks to discourage—completed acts that are themselves illegal (Bonnie, Coughlin, Jeffries, and Low, 1997, 595–632). For example, robbing a bank is a criminal act. The act, however, does not have to be completed for the action to become a crime, as illustrated by the crime of "attempt." With the crime of conspiracy, however, a crime is committed when a person works in tandem with others to *intend* to rob a bank, even if no attempt is actually made. All that is required for the crime of conspiracy is an agreement to commit an illegal act and for one party in that agreement to engage in an action furthering the agreement. This action can be innocuous, such as renting a car, purchasing rope, or checking into a motel. Note also that conspiracy is different from the law of attempt. The law cannot punish someone both for attempting to rob a bank and for actually robbing a bank, as the completed act subsumes the intent. However, the law *can* punish someone for robbing a bank and for the conspiracy (ie, the agreement) to rob the bank.

Arguably, society has an interest in preventing bank robberies and may legally intervene to break up a gang of robbers who, although preparing for their act, have not in any other way acted illegally. The subject of the conspiracy in *Pullis*, however, was not analogous to a bank robbery, as working-class unity cannot easily be considered illegal or immoral. Such immorality must first be *assigned* to working-class unity, which is the function of the law in this case. As an individual, each journeymen cordwainer was free to reject the conditions of his work and to withhold his labor. Collectively, the journeymen cordwainers sought to exercise the same rights they had as individuals; as a society, they refused to associate with people who did not respect the efforts of the FSJC. In a Jeffersonian world, such action would be appropriate, as democracy is grounded in the belief in the strength of individual citizens who come together as a community and work for the common good. Community life is strong only when individuals of that community are strong. From individual freedom and autonomy does the larger culture assume an ethos of freedom and autonomy. The American Revolution was fought, at least in theory, to actualize this vision of community, and much of the labor movement has been a struggle to remind the nation of this vision.

In securing a conviction under the English Common Law of Conspiracy, the prosecution faced three related hurdles. First, the Common Law crime was clearly perceived by many in society at the time to be a "discriminatory dragnet designed to catch only certain sorts of economic actors at the insistence of others who were being economically hurt" (Holt, 1984, 601). As later labor history would illustrate, the conspiracy law would seldom, if ever, be applied to management organizations that "conspired" to depress wages, nor was it applied that way previously in Britain. Thus, the indictment "seemed arbitrary, unfair and class-oriented when all [the journeymen cordwainers] had done was to attempt to exert the same kind of collective pressure against employers that employers' organization, with their massive control of capital . . . exerted against workers" (Holt, 1984, 594).

Second, the English Common Law rule had not been endorsed by the Pennsylvania legislature in positive law. In other words, the state legislature—aware of the English Common Law rule—did not codify the rule with a state penal statute. In the absence of a penal statute, the application of the English rule to Pennsylvania was considered controversial (Holt, 1984, 602–605).

Third, and perhaps most salient at the time, Pennsylvania had only recently gained its independence from what the former colonies considered British tyranny. Thus, the government faced the political awkwardness of introducing English precedent (overtly biased on behalf of the aristocracy) to the new US working classes of Pennsylvania who had recently fought a war against aristocracy. This weakness is clearly illustrated by the defense attorney who addressed the jury as follows: "If you are desirous of introducing a similar spirit of inequality into our government and laws . . . if you think that the labourer and the journeyman enjoy too great a portion of liberty, and ought to be restricted in their rights . . . such disposition and opinions will lead you to convict the defendants" (*Pullis*, 162).

*Pullis*, as we will see, turns on the manner in which society defines the concept of violence or coercion and acceptable social action. If the union of workers is defined as violent, coercive, and/or unfair, then policy makers are privileging the values of the economic elite over a more socially inclusive set of values that understands that much union mobilization (particularly in the classical period) is the result of social and economic factors that are themselves violent against labor. As argued below, the tactics of the journeymen cordwainers, although coercive in a rudimentary sense, were not violent and were far less coercive and more justifiable than the larger economic and political violence directed against them and subsequent labor organizations.

## Nonviolent Labor Tactics

Central to the history of conflict between labor and government is the issue of violence. As discussed in this context, violence can be understood in two paradigmatic forms: the violence of worker militancy and the violence of the government and industry in suppressing workers (as well as the violence of the system more generally in degrading and harming workers). Although workers have acted violently at times, the overwhelming responsibility for the loss of life in labor disputes lies with government and industry. Throughout much of this country's history, the government used the excuse of worker militancy to justify the violent suppression of organized labor. The government has been so zealous in suppressing organized labor that even when organized labor acts nonviolently (as is often the case), violence is often attributed to it, as well as blame for any violence that may result from governmental provocations.

In this early labor dispute between the journeymen cordwainers and the masters, little violence was experienced, although the prosecution vigorously claimed that the FSJC was a *de facto* coercive organization. Although an objective reading of the trial record does suggest that some limited scuffling may have taken place between the striking journeymen cordwainers and scab employees (and that a shop window may have been broken by a thrown potato), such violence was atypical of the strike. The lack of violence was also *atypical* of future labor disputes, which, in some cases, bordered on open warfare, with tragic fatalities for workers and their families (for example, the Ludlow Massacre of 1914).[2]

What makes the *Pullis* case so paradigmatic is the way that the government and the court defined the strategies of the journeymen cordwainers as violent, when all they did was withdraw their labor and shun both employers and employees who violated the labor standards they articulated. These methods—generically known as "scab law"—were described by a witness for the Commonwealth: "When a Journeyman came from New York or Baltimore, a notice was sent to him, at the house he lived at, that he must come forward and join the society; if he did not his employer was called upon to turn him off; and none of the members would board at the same house with him" (*Pullis*, 95). Then, if a FSJC member failed to follow the rules of the society, or if that member worked for less than the wages established by the FSJC, the FSJC would tell that person's employer to discharge him. If the employer refused, the other FSJC members would leave that employer. As noted by the witness, "Suppose you was scabb'd, and working in Mr. Ryan's shop, all the members would leave him, if they were fifteen or twenty, unless he turned off the scab" (*Pullis*, 90). One master testified that, due to this tactic, he lost more than half of his employees for more than two years (100). As a result, no employer would dare to hire the scab, and he would be "driven out of all manner of work, that is of any profit" (92). With such tactics, the journeymen cordwainers successfully closed the shoemaking industry to FSJC members only.

## The Question of Coercion

As discussed above, the activities of the journeymen cordwainers were based on tactics that cannot be considered violent—people were not attacked, property was not destroyed, and there were no battles with the police or military. The journeymen cordwainers simply cooperated with each other to coordinate a favorable change in their working environment. These tactics were certainly uncivil, but civility is not necessarily a virtue when the continuation of social inequality is at stake. An absence of civility and an element of coercion, although discernable in the actions of the journeymen cordwainers, does not equate with immorality.

In other words, because conditions of individual freedom depend on others working collectively to maximize social conditions conducive to economic democracy, union tactics such as the closed shop are often necessary, even though some workers may feel that the closed shop is an affront to their autonomy. Simply, the closed shop is a useful method for attaining and preserving union strength. In the US economic system, workers are often pitted against other workers so that some individuals can gain personally at the expense of their colleagues. Consequently, workers are not always conscious of their interests and often align themselves with anti-labor politics. Given this situation, the closed shop may be a politically necessary (although regrettable) tool so that the collective power of labor can be used to advance its interests. All employees of an enterprise share in the benefits achieved through collective bargaining; therefore, all employees should contribute toward common strategies and goals.[3]

For the prosecution, however, the fact that coercion was not overtly violent was irrelevant because, in fact, when a new journeyman cordwainer worker arrived in town, he was "required" to join the FSJC. Although the new worker was free to refuse, to do so would preclude him from working or having a place to live. Once in the FSJC, the new member would be obliged to follow the rules established by the society, or else be expelled. Not only would such a member be required to pay dues, but he would have to strike when ordered by the FSJC, even if he preferred to work. Thus, the prosecution defined coercion in language that anticipates later so-called "right to work" legislation:

> If I go into a country I am bound to submit to its laws, but surely I may judge, whether or not I will go there. The society has no right to force you into its body, and then say you shall obey its rules under severe penalties. [Yet the] man who seeks an asylum in this country, from the arbitrary laws of other nations, is coerced into this society [the FSJC] . . . he must leave his seat and join the turnout. (*Pullis*, 139)

As noted by the government, this was the case of a man named Harrison, a state witness at trial:

> [Harrison] was a stranger, he was a married man, with a large family; he represented his distressed condition; they [the FSCJ] entangle him, but shew no mercy. The dogs of vigilance find, by their scent, the emigrant in his cellar or garret: they drag him forth, they tell him he must join them; he replies, I am well satisfied as I am . . . No . . . they chase him from shop to shop; they allow him no resting place, till he consents to be one of their body; he is expelled [from] society, driven from his lodging, proscribed from working; he is left no alternative, but to perish in the streets, or seek some other asylum on a more hospitable shore. (*Pullis*, 139)

A second worker testified that the "name of a scab is very dangerous; men of this description have been hurt when out at nights. I myself have been threatened for working at wages with which I was satisfied. I was afraid of going near any of the body: I have seen them twisting and making wry faces at me, and heard two men call out scab, as I passed by" (*Pullis*, 93).

In responding to the claims of the prosecution, the defense attorney noted that no disturbance was created in violation of any applicable criminal law and that the only offensive behavior of the defendants was "their refusing to work for any master who employed such journeymen as infringing the rules of the society to which they belonged" (*Pullis*, 150). Such refusal may have been "unreasonable," "ridiculous," "capricious," "whimsical," or "illiberal," but that was not enough to support a criminal prosecution (*Pullis*, 151). As argued by the defense attorney, individuals in the United States have both moral and political authority to work with others to achieve common lawful goals. Thus, every "man may chuse his company, or refuse to associate with any one whose company may be disagreeable to him, without being obliged to give a reason for it: and without violating the laws of the land" (*Pullis*, 151).

Outside of slavery (still legal in Southern jurisdictions at the time), forms of indentured servitude, court-ordered child support payments, and vagrancy laws, refusing to work was not a criminal act and should not be so considered. Although contemporary society tends to reject scab politics as unfair to individual workers who do not agree with union goals, it would do well to consider how the existence of a permanent pool of unemployed labor, created by industrial and governmental policy, makes scab labor attractive to many workers who would otherwise support collective action. The unfairness is the systemic cultivation of unemployment by industry to suppress labor costs and not the tactics of labor in responding to the exploitation of the unemployed and the use of their human needs as a weapon against the efforts of the collective to better the condition of all workers. Scab politics is often a necessary response to a larger economic system that embraces coercion (eg, crude physical necessity) as its fundamental economic engine.

In sum, the coercion issue was, for the most part, a red herring. On the face of the trial record, it is not possible to conclude that the actions of the journeymen cordwainers were truly abusive in a way that would be repugnant to a dynamic democratic society. On the contrary, the journeymen cordwainers went out of their way for five years to coordinate their need for labor with the needs of industry (strengthening industry to the point of undermining their own interests). What changed was not the tactics of the workers, but their power. As the Philadelphia shoe industry broadened into an export industry, the Philadelphia workers were hindered by their competition with other producers, such as workers in England. This competition forced down the selling price of shoes. In this new market, the master cordwainers could no longer afford to pay the same wages as when the market was local and the journeymen cordwainers had less competition. The FSJC, therefore, had to be eliminated, which was why this case was brought. If any compulsion can be said to exist in this case, it was the compulsion of industry to lower wages.

## The Problem of Legitimacy

When the charge of compulsion is rejected, another salient issue in the case becomes heightened. This issue, fundamental to the larger conflict between the Federalists and the Jeffersonian Republicans, centers on the issue of legitimacy. Specifically, who are "the people"? Who has the right to speak for the people and to enact laws to govern their development? When do citizens have the right to reject one notion of community and to offer another? These questions are central to *Pullis*, as well as to most subsequent labor solidarity cases.

*Pullis* provided society with an opportunity to develop in terms of democratic inclusion, what William E. Forbath identifies as "working class republicanism" (1985, 816). As discussed earlier, working class republicanism, an expression of Jeffersonian democracy, involved labor's "conviction that the integrity of the Constitution depended on the 'ability of the people to rule'" (816). Such belief "was rooted in a republican tradition that dated back to the Revolution" (816). Working class republicanism emphasized equality and dignity for all citizens.[4] Specifically, this view maintained that "being forced to sell his labor contradicted the worker's status as a citizen" (Forbath, 1985, 768).

Such working class republicanism—as well as future expressions of anarchism, communism, socialism, progressivism, or unionism—are frequently labeled threats to liberty by the defenders of the status quo. With this definitional tactic, the status quo reifies itself as the standard of social truth. The government in *Pullis* exemplifies this phenomenon:

> Shall these, or any other body of men, associate for the purpose of making new laws, laws not made under the constitutional authority, and compel their fellow citizens to obey them, under the penalty of their existence? The prosecution contravenes no man's right, it is to prevent an infringement of right; it is in favor of the equal liberty of all men, this is the policy of our laws; but if private associations and clubs can make

> constitutions and laws for us . . . if they can associate and make bye-laws paramount, or inconsistent with state laws; What, I ask, becomes of the liberty of the people? [These men] ought to submit to the laws of the country, and not attempt to alter them according to their own whim or caprice. (135)

The concerns of the government were not entirely foundationless given that three major rebellions occurred in the United States during the period 1776–1800, challenging the conception of "the people" offered by the new federal government.[5] Furthermore, established states such as Massachusetts were splitting apart, creating new political entities, such as Maine. Other states, such as the State of Franklin, failed to stabilize.[6] In light of these events and others, such as the French Revolution, which frightened US elites (the passage of the Alien and Sedition Acts were the result of this fear), there was much concern during these early years of the republic over what the political boundaries of "the people" meant. As argued by the government:

> We charge a combination, by means of rewards and punishments, threats, insults, starvings and beatings, to compel the employers to accede to terms, they the journeymen present and dictate. If the journeymen cordwainers may do this, so may the employers; the journeymen carpenters, the brick-layers, butchers, farmers, and the whole community will be formed into hostile confederacies, the prelude and certain forerunner of bloodshed and civil war. (*Pullis*, 221)

To talk about civil war, as the prosecutor did, is to forefront the issue of legitimacy. As with legal norms, civil war is neither good nor bad *per se*, and should not be feared simply because it involves conflict. Although such war is a radical expression of a failed community, there are many reasons why a community may fail and significant reasons why conflict is necessary to heal the community. Most of these reasons center on the fact that, for a significant portion of a population, normative state legitimacy has been rendered obsolete. Communities have no *a priori* presence—they exist only through communication and to the extent that common, moral bonds and identifications between members remain strong; community "possesses no fixed, stable referent but is instead an 'essentially contested concept' whose meaning is continuously negotiated in and by cultural performances, as well as other symbolic forms" (Fuoss, 1995, 93).

The health of any community can be compromised by social injustice; social instability arises when a community treats a segment of its population unfairly. Such communities can be transformed so that social morality can be reestablished and no one is allowed to slip through the social cracks. As Sonja K. Foss, Cindy L. Griffin, and Karen A. Foss argue, "The talents of everyone, whatever they are, deserve to be acknowledged and affirmed, even when they do not stand out in dramatic ways" (1997, 124). This belief is grounded in the notion of "immanent value" (Foss, Foss, and Griffin, 1999, 168–169). Because people are inherently valuable, individuals should not be "measured up against an established hierarchy" (Foss, Griffin, and Foss, 1997, 124). Furthermore, the established hierarchy can be engaged so that the immanent value of everyone has a chance to flourish. Social entities (including individuals) that stifle human potential must be engaged so as to negate their deleterious influences. In other words, if, by combining to reduce their suffering, the working classes cause widespread social unrest and dramatic transformation in public life, that most likely means that the current status quo is itself untenable and in need of adjustment to better serve human needs.

Specifically, in a society such as the United States where people's subjectivities are often determined by the amount of money they possess, the concept of immanent value implies that social change may, under some circumstances, be necessary. Politically, however, this argument raises difficult issues. For instance, what status do "the people" have as historical agents for political change? What are the limits of the people's right to gather to better perfect their communities and under what conditions is it permissible to constrain others in the process? More practically, where is the line between civic activism and sedition? For the prosecution in *Pullis*, these questions were easy to answer: If "the people" can create their own regulations and constitution in the context of a republic, then such people create, in effect, a sovereignty within a sovereign (an "*imperium in imperio*"), and the national fabric is correspondingly eroded (*Pullis*, 235). In this way, the government attorney crystallized what would become a major justification for the suppression of organized labor:

> It now rests with the jury, under the direction of the court to say, whether we shall in future be governed by secret clubs, instead of the constitution and laws of the state; a verdict of not guilty, will sanction combinations of the most dangerous kind; a contrary verdict will give the victory to the known and established laws of the commonwealth. (*Pullis*, 235)

Such reasoning raises a further issue that will become much more evident in future labor conflicts: To what extent does an effective political government exist when confronted by a massive capital monopoly? For instance, many government agencies at both the state and federal levels collapsed with corruption under the influence of powerful railroads in the nineteenth century.[7] In the post-Enron world, this is not an inconsequential question. Given pervasive government corruption due to industry influence, neutral observers cannot deny what labor has long claimed: The counterbalance of organized labor is a necessary corrective to the corrupting influences of amassed capital. While a judge on the Massachusetts Supreme Court, Oliver Wendell Holmes eloquently addressed this issue in a noted dissent:

> One of the eternal conflicts out of which life is made up is that between the effort of every man to get the most he can for his services, and that of society, disguised under the name of capital, to get his services for the least possible return. Combination on the one side is patent and powerful. Combination on the other is the necessary and desirable counterpart, if the battle is to be carried on in a fair and equal way. (*Vegelahn v. Guntner*,1886; reprinted in Cox, Box, Gorman, and Finkin, 1991, 23)

Unfortunately, more than four decades would pass before the sentiment in Holmes's dissent would become public policy, as found in Roosevelt's New Deal policies for the reconfiguration of US society. As New Deal—era influence on the US economy has been rendered nearly obsolete in current times, Holmes's dissent takes on a renewed cultural significance.

## Conclusion

Contemporary courts face many obstacles when importing foreign legal precedent willy-nilly, as did the *Pullis* court. Furthermore, prosecutors who assume that a crime has been committed on the grounds that the state's ideological conventions have been violated are now often constrained by public sentiment. For example, through the 1960s, many white prosecutors enforced segregation on the grounds that the white community had the power to protect itself from the "threats" that African Americans allegedly posed. A majority of the contemporary public would no longer recognize the validity of such arguments. However, when a community's identity is in flux, as it was during the first several decades of the United States, convictions such as those found in *Pullis* occur. As the United States and the world enter another such period, *Pullis* remains illustrative. When such convictions serve the interests of a powerful elite, the "bad" law enacted often begets more bad laws, as legal precedent builds on itself. Furthermore, bad laws tend to multiply because a bad law, by implication, often denies normative community to a significant population, and such people often resist their social marginalization. A community's power to reinforce the alienation of a marginalized group often requires a comprehensive jurisprudence.

Obedience to a law, no matter how bad the law, is commanded by the government in *Pullis*. The recurring trope justifying this position is that the United States is a nation ruled by law, not by individuals. Decontextualized, however, obedience to the rule of law becomes a shibboleth that the forces of the status quo often evoke for repressing progressive social change. In Western culture, this argument was eloquently first advanced in Plato's *Apology*, in which Socrates staked his life on his fidelity to the Athenian law that condemned him to death.

However, although the community welfare should be guarded, law *per se* is not necessarily the community's best guardian. At its best, the law can serve this function; however, the law often allows individuals to combine to pursue legal goals that are quite injurious to the general welfare of the community. Thus, such arguments based on fidelity to the rule of law should be approached with a suspicious eye. Law and order often incubate a violence committed against the interest of some people in the name of others. In other words, order, by itself, is not a bad thing, as all societies need a degree of structure to be able to function effectively. But in times of crisis, "order" often becomes operationalized as a substitute for a wider, more socially inclusive political view (ie, "order" for the Nazis meant the exclusion of the Jews). Order is also established according to somebody. Society itself has no "order." Order is the structure that a political vision imposes on a community.

Viewing law and order in this way does not make law and order "bad"; rather, it recognizes that the appeal to law and order is always suspect, which is why legal norms must be constantly questioned. As Michel

Foucault notes, it "would be hypocritical or naïve to believe that the law was made for all in the name of all . . . it would be more prudent to recognize that it was made for the few and that it was brought to bear upon others. . . Law and justice do not hesitate to proclaim their necessary class dissymmetry" (1979, 276). Historical, rhetorical, and legal criticism is particularly necessary when law and order is used as a weapon to prevent progressive social change done for the betterment of society. When law and order discourse is used in a self-serving fashion, society opens itself to the charge that "law is congealed injustice, that the existing order hides an everyday violence against body and spirit, that our political structure is fossilized, and that the noise of change—however scary—may be necessary" (Zinn, 1968, 4). At such times, however, "a cry rises for 'law and order.' Such a moment becomes a crucial test of whether the society will sink back to a spurious safety or leap forward to its own freshening" (Zinn, 1968, 4). The *Pullis* case was one such moment.

## ✷ NOTES ✷

1. Pullis was rejected in *Commonwealth v. Hunt* (1842). See Nelles (1932) and Levy (1957, 183–206). Hunt, however, was soon distinguished by other courts; thus prosecutions for conspiracy continued for many decades. When combined with later labor injunctions (ie, *In re Debs*, 1895), these two legal doctrines were effective in suppressing labor organizations.

2. Particular examples of violence from among ranks of labor cannot be used to discredit the just struggle of a class of people who regard violence as the *result* of struggle and not as the *reason* for struggle. This is particularly important when, in contrast, the government typically views violence as a means to an end.

3. Note that the Supreme Court, in a string of "right not to associate" cases, has repeatedly rejected this argument. See *Abood v. Detroit Board of Education* (1977). "Right to work" laws exist in many states where legislatures–by fiat and with court approval–have outlawed union shops on the grounds that workers have a "right" to not associate with a union.

4. As with the democracy of Ancient Greece, citizenship in the early United States was rigidly constrained. See Hansen (1991).

5. These were Shay's Rebellion (1786), The Whisky Rebellion (1794), and Fries Rebellion (1788). See *United States v. Mitchell* (1795); Taylor (1990, 89–121); Slaughter (1988, 11–27); and http://www. jamesmannartfarm.com/friesreb1.html for a history of Fries Rebellion.

6. In the early 1780s, the short-lived State of Franklin was created in the area of what is now Tennessee. Leaders of the former colonies in that region, alienated by federal economic policy and by the ineffectiveness of the new national leadership in controlling the Native American population, petitioned to join the Spanish empire. By 1789, however, the territory came under US control (*A Dictionary of American History*, 1995).

7. One notable case, the Crédit Mobilier of America scandal of 1872–1873, involved the Union Pacific Railroad, Congress, and the administration of President Ulysses S. Grant See Bain (1999, 675–710). By 1900, the accumulated assets of the various railroads constituted 10% of all US wealth (Hovenkamp, 1988, 1018).

# CHAPTER 10

# The Challenge of Anarchism and Its Lessons for Partisan Criticism

The anarchist movement has been greatly misunderstood. Anarchism was demonized by the press of its day and that demonization has largely remained until the present.[1] The government, courts, and mass media unfairly reduced the anarchist political vision to that of ruthless violence and social degradation (ie, the "cult of dynamite") contributing to a perception of anarchism that justified the government's suppression of the anarchist movement. As Paul Avrich explains, "For a large segment of the population the anarchists had ceased to be human beings. They had become the incarnation of evil, monsters endowed with infernal powers" (1984, 177). Similar to the label of "terrorist" today, or "communist" during the Cold War, the word "anarchist" was used to position a political opponent as evil, a primordial state enemy (Andrew King, 1987, 58).

Although the anarchists were the most radical of the labor activists, their theoretical works and historical practices suggest that they were far less demonic than they have been portrayed (see Goldman, 1970). According to anarchist theory, the state (and its apparatuses such as the schools, the military, and the police) is responsible for the immiseration of the working classes. The anarchists, thus, advocated a more comprehensive degree of political change than other groups that sought the appropriation of industry by the laboring classes. Class oppression, in their view, was systemic to the state itself:

> Anarchists believe that society can function more smoothly and more equitably with everyone owning the land, factories, businesses, and banks in common. Unlike state socialists, anarchists insist that the administration of the economy and of social affairs be done directly by workers and residents themselves, rather than being nationalized into the state apparatus. Under anarchism, economic and social functions would be controlled at the point of production or geographic locality and coordinated on a larger scale through the federation of groups by industry and common interest. (Hong, 1992, 115)

The anarchists, therefore, were not uncivilized barbarians bent on senseless destruction; rather, they represented a new vision for the moral and spiritual evolution of humanity. This vision, although perhaps unrealistic and untenable, is nevertheless noble and grand, deserving of admiration and respect. Such visions—no matter how utopian—are to be celebrated, for they suggest alternative ways of conceptualizing human relations and, at the same time, urge humans to live up to their potential (Johnson, 1991).

Anarchism, also known as "libertarian socialism," is communism without the Communist Party, or at least without Lenin's notion of the political "vanguard." The historical practice of communism, as expressed in places such as the Soviet Union, China, and North Korea, has been hierarchical and authoritarian. According to the anarchists, any utility derived from authoritarian rule is offset by the coercion involved in upholding authority. Therefore, anarchists reject this governance style and maintain that politics is primarily the politics of everyday people struggling together to create just and equitable work and living relationships. As described by Peter Kropotkin: "There must be no disagreeable labour. All labour must be so organized, so distributed, and so diversified as always to be attractive. And no sort of coercion must be exercised. In a society organized on the principle of free association, no sort of coercion could be tolerated, and none would be needed" (1995, 72).

For anarchists, politics is generated at the level of the community, and is expressed through the needs of its individual members. No party or state apparatus is permitted to interpret the needs of the people; rather, political decisions are based on the active involvement of the people affected by the decision. This principle should sound familiar to US readers, for, in theory, this anarchist view is fundamental to the ideology of US democracy.[2] Perhaps the most well-known anarchist leader in the United States was Emma Goldman; other important anarchists include Michael Bakunin, Alexander Berkman, Noam Chomsky, Daniel Guerin, Peter Kropotkin, Errico Malatesta, Pierre-Joseph Proudhon, Herbert Read, Rudoph Rocker, and George Woodcock. Goldman may be the most well known because she was an influential speaker, organizer, publisher, dissident, feminist, and theorist (Drinnon, 1982). Although much celebrated today, Goldman was vilified by the public and the press during her lifetime; many people considered her to be the most hated person in the United States. In 1919,

Goldman was deported from the United States to Lenin's new Soviet Union, where she witnessed the Soviet repression of what had been a significant anarchist presence during the Russian Revolution (Goldman, 1991). As Goldman eloquently expressed in her writings:

> Anarchism . . . stands for the liberation of the human mind from the dominion of religion; the liberation of the human body from the dominion of property; liberation from the shackles and restraint of government. Anarchism stands for a social order based on a free grouping of individuals for producing real social wealth; an order that will guarantee to every human being free access to the Earth and full enjoyment of the necessities of life, according to individual desires, tasks, and inclinations. (1969, 62)

In writings such as this, many anarchists enacted a passionate commitment to a new human renaissance grounded in compassion, cooperation, and solidarity. The anarchists, however, did not believe that they could create such a world through words and declarations alone. Such a world could only be attained through armed struggle. This involved primarily self-protection for the laboring classes. This notion was not based on ideology; but, instead, on empirical observation. As Dianne Avery observes:

> Much of so-called labor violence throughout the early history of the American labor movement was a response to direct acts of violence against workers by employers and their agents, detectives, police, militia, and federal troops; as well as to the more diffuse structural violence of the workplace. (1988, 8; see Cooper, 1980)

When workers—anarchist or not—gathered to express their common concerns, they were often harassed by the police and the military (Schultz and Schultz, 1990). Peaceful meetings were broken up and many thousands were jailed. When strikes were particularly bitter, workers and their families were often murdered by their employers and government agents. The anarchists, therefore, reasonably argued that arming the workers was necessary to protect them from state and private acts of terrorism. The anarchists, thus, disseminated weapons to the workers and formed paramilitary groups to train workers in the use of those weapons. However, although the larger rhetoric of the anarchists anticipated an inevitable war with the capitalist classes, the anarchists did not proclaim a desire to initiate such a war; they simply reasoned that such a war would follow from the effort of the capitalists and the state to resist the social evolution of society into anarchy.

Kenneth Burke cautioned that people should use language carefully, so as not to allow language to use them. This warning is particularly relevant in the context of the phrase "the social evolution into anarchy." As the result of the demonization of anarchism by the government and the media, the word "anarchy" has a strong negative connotation. Because of the successful efforts of the media to vilify anarchy, society is seen as not *evolving* into anarchy; rather, society *decays* into anarchy. For example, the nation of Somalia is frequently described as being reduced to "anarchy," as there is no effective government or system of law and order. In actuality, rival factions and warlords compete for influence. The citizens are impoverished, mortality rates are high, and social stability is absent.

Although I regret the way the term "anarchy" has come to be understood, I recognize that most readers view the term in its current pejorative sense. Historically, however, anarchy meant the exact opposite of what the term now means. As originally envisioned, anarchy was a condition in which there *would be* social structure and a heightened sense of community and responsibility. Although the anarchists rejected "law and order" and the "state" as such, they were prepared to replace such institutions with new ones grounded in human integrity and social inclusion. The societies in which the anarchists of the nineteenth and early twentieth centuries lived were not, under their view, civilized. Other, more mainstream observers have reached similar conclusions; for example, Mahatma Gandhi acknowledged that what passed for "Western civilization" was what he called "diluted Nazism" (1965, 45). Further, he once quipped to a reporter that, in his view, "Western civilization would be a good idea."

War between anarchists and the capitalist class did occur, but not in the United States. In Spain, during the 1930s, a high-profile civil war was waged between the anarchist-controlled republic and the rebel fascist forces of Generalissimo Francisco Franco. As anticipated by anarchist theory, the war was started by the conservative elements of Spanish society—the wealthy classes and the church. This elite faction lost political power when a democratic coalition of progressive working-class parties established an anarchist republic. Murray Bookchin notes that in 1936, before the war, the National Confederation of Labor, Spain's largest and most important anarchist labor collective, registered a million members out of a population of

24 million (1977, 1). In response, the conservative elements attacked the republic in an attempt to expel the progressive coalition. Initially, the anarchists were successful in repelling the fascists and were able to govern Spain for two years before they were defeated. Social development during this period—limited by the severity, brutality, and necessity of the civil war—provides the only historical glimpse of an actual anarchist society (Orwell, 1952). This world, however briefly it existed, was noteworthy for the remarkable cooperation among the Spanish workers and peasants, as well as for a pervasive egalitarianism. Although anarchists never achieved the level of power in the United States as did anarchists in Spain, they managed to garner a great deal of domestic attention and influence, perhaps out of proportion to their actual numbers, which were relatively small (Foner, 1986, 21).

The Spanish Civil War is historically significant. From the beginning, the war had important international implications. Many workers in Western nations correctly understood the conflict in Spain to be a precursor of an even more fundamental worldwide class struggle. With this foreboding, volunteers from all over the world traveled to Spain to join the anarchist cause; the US contingent was particularly famous (Lawson, 1989). In this manner, the working classes expressed their most sustained experience of international solidarity. Although labor has historically expressed itself with idealistic international terms, the practice of labor politics worldwide has been almost exclusively nationalistic. When revolutionary governments emerged, they, too, assumed nationalistic agendas. Thus, the dream of an "international brother and sisterhood" among the working classes has seldom been achieved.

The powerful nations of the time also understood the historical significance of the Spanish Civil War. For example, the United States, Britain, and France diplomatically isolated the anarchist republic and prevented war materials from reaching the anarchist forces. The Soviet Union, although ostensibly helping the republic, imposed Stalinism on the Spanish anarchists, annihilated anarchist leaders, and subverted anarchist military forces. Germany and Italy, which saw in Franco's Spain a fascist ally and junior partner, actively bombed anarchist positions from airplanes in the first air assault on an undefended urban population in history. In addition to the bombing raids, Germany and Italy provided Franco with generous military support, including Italian ground forces (Beevor, 2001); similarly, Portugal and Morocco provided Franco with weapons and funds (Wilkinson, 1988, 5).

When the anarchists were defeated in Spain, Franco established a fascist government that lasted until 1977 (Payne, 1999). Fascist Spain, along with fascist Italy, Germany, and Japan, were all viciously antilabor. For this commitment, each of these nations received, at different times, positive affirmations and degrees of support from the United States and from other Western nations. For example, at the inception of Mussolini and Hitler's regimes, an enthusiastic US government provided both Italy and Germany with military and financial support (Schmitz, 1988). Although this support ended when these countries became enemies of the United States, such hostilities were grounded in other political issues, which came to supplant the shared commitment by all to crush the international effort of labor to organize. Furthermore, in addition to allowing Spanish fascism to survive the "war to defeat fascism," the US government gave extensive protection and support to many German and Japanese war criminals. Two high-ranking US government officials—former Congresswoman Elizabeth Holtzman and former Associate Supreme Court Justice Arthur Goldberg—have protested the unconscionable alliance that arose between agencies of the US government and thousands of Nazi war criminals. According to Holtzman, "as many as ten thousand Nazi war criminals [were permitted entrance] to this country" (1990, 338). Provided with secret identities and financially supported, many of these were actively protected by the United States. The motivation of the United States to protect Nazis—who, in many instances, committed horrendous atrocities—was their utility in intelligence gathering against the Soviet Union (Goldberg, 1984). A similar model was applied to Japanese war criminals—who were equally as monstrous as the Nazis in their abuse of human rights—for their strategic knowledge in fighting the Communist Chinese and the Communist North Koreans.

Many, but not all, US anarchists practiced a philosophy called "propaganda by deed," which involved highly publicized acts of public violence. Anarchists who followed this principle were aligned with Johann Most and his paper *Die Freiheit* (Papke, 1987, 170–173). Similar to the Diggers and Levelers of seventeenth-century England, Most promoted the idea of social leveling, in which the use of dynamite was considered a democratic instrument of force and terror to equalize the balance of power between the state and the individual. Such violence helped workers to gain political control from the institutions that displaced and repressed them. Most wrote a widely circulated book, *Revolutionary War Science*, in which he detailed his methods for urban guerrilla warfare. A well-known example of propaganda by deed was enacted by Leon Czolgosz, an anarchist who was enraged by President William McKinley's formation of US imperialism and by his military conquest of the Philippines. Czolgosz assassinated McKinley in Buffalo, New York, in 1901. In Europe, anarchists were often responsible for the assassination of royalty.[3]

Violence, unfortunately, is an inescapable part of human interaction. Often, without the power to engage in violence (in terms of retribution), groups of people are taken advantage of by stronger groups, as was the case with the US working classes in the late nineteenth and early twentieth centuries and with slaves in the antebellum South. To the extent that a group such as the anarchists has the ability to engage the world through resistance and violence, violence becomes a method for the reconstruction of social life. Although violence is an ugly word, we must remember that when we like the effects of violence, we call it something else (eg, victory, justice, law, discipline, authority, punishment, nature, free markets, or order). Rather than condemning violence outright, we should recognize that violence "is a delicate instrument. It may act as a catalyst, but it can also act as a deterrent; it can even be totally counter-effective" (Chaliand, 1985, 55). Consequently, the question of violence involves tactical considerations for a community's goals.

Communication is always about community, and that involves human social relationships. Violence is one way of establishing or reestablishing these relationships. Consider, for example, the US South prior to the early 1970s. Violence created and sustained most Southern communities within the context of slavery and segregation. In addition, the violence of the Civil Rights era was largely, if not exclusively, the violence of the white community in its effort to maintain inequitable social and economic relationships with US Americans of African descent. Consequently, those descendents of Africans lived in a violent world. By the start of the Second World War, for example, approximately 7,000 individuals, mostly Southern blacks, had been lynched since the end of the Civil War (Graham and Gurr, 1979). African Americans, however, were not merely the victims of violence; rather, the violence of the white community often situated their social existence. Few aspects of African American life were not in some way tainted by the fear or experience of white violence directed against them.

Similarly, society, throughout much of this period, was also segregated along class lines, with violence and fear used to subjugate the poor and laboring classes. To the extent that the normative white and wealthy community fears the violence of the working classes and/or ethnic communities, the elite must realize that the violence they project on the oppressed is the violence that originates in themselves. I do not imply, however, that racial or economic categories are monolithic. My point is simply that the extent to which *anyone* is compliant with the elite white power that creates the context for domestic or international unrest (and many nonelites identify with the elite class), the more they are part of the problem.

In particular, I find it difficult to label as "violence" the actions of African Americans who struggled for their basic human rights and their rights of citizenship, such as when the Black Panthers picked up guns and when others in the ghettos of the United States rioted. In neither case were these citizens trying to limit the parameters of community; rather, in the instance of both, the violence was instructional (ie, rhetorical) and largely symbolic, directed against the constraints that shackled them and against the people who were subjugating them. In this sense, their actions are understandable and can be connected to progressive politics. To recognize this point is to acknowledge that there is a significant difference between the violence of the slave revolt and the violence of the masters in suppressing the revolt, as John Brown and his supporters exemplified (Thoreau, 1969). The violence of resistance, and of resistance persuasion, is an attempt to rethink the way people live under an oppressive situation. This is what makes popular peasant or worker revolutions fundamentally just, even if violence is used to advance the interests of these people against the landed, business oligarchies. When violence is used to expand human inclusivity and to create the conditions for a community's moral growth, that violence takes on a significance that is altogether different from the violence intended to exclude people from a community. Thus, even pacifists, such as myself, can agree with C. Wright Mills when he argues that although wars are tragic, that tragedy takes on a heightened significance when people fight for a just ideal (1963, 295).

For most anarchists, however, the violent rhetoric of class struggle was little more than an inclusive vocabulary to serve as a strategy for group identification and organization. All communities need to communicate so as to create the perception of inclusion. Anarchists were workers excluded from the mainstream political and economic structures, who used a fiery rhetoric to define themselves as different and in opposition to the larger culture (Roderick P. Hart, 1984, 774). The advantage of this strategy was to sharpen issues and to establish clear moral lines. Moral clarity and focused issues are highly persuasive tactics for encouraging others to join in a common goal (1984, 774). The anarchists were, thus, effective in organizing workers who were not themselves anarchists and were central leaders in the larger labor movement during this period.

On the other hand, the aggressive rhetoric of the anarchists made it easier for the establishment to associate labor organization with violence and the overthrow of the government. The events discussed in this chapter occurred years before "communism" was a term that people regularly used, as the Russian Revolution did not occur until 1917. During the late nineteenth and early twentieth centuries, the anarchists (who came from many different European backgrounds) and not the Russian communists were considered the primary threat to US capitalism and elite privilege. These sentiments grew after the Haymarket bombing and trial of prominent anarchists in Chicago in 1886.

## HAYMARKET BOMBING AND TRIAL OF PROMINENT ANARCHISTS

The events described in this section stem from the struggle for the eight-hour workday, involving hundreds of thousands of workers, only a small number of whom were active anarchists. However, the anarchists were often leaders of this movement and played important roles in the organizing of thousands of local strikes. The eight-hour workday was eventually achieved, and the labors of the anarchists were instrumental in achieving this fundamental victory.

Through the mid-1880s, a ten-hour, six-day workweek was the norm in industrial employment, but in many cases, workers were required to work 12–15 hour days (Foner, 1986, 14). Pressure on state and federal legislatures to reduce the workday was ineffective. Political gains, if achieved, were often struck down by the courts. In this context, labor leaders—anarchist and others—agreed that direct action by the workers was necessary. On May 1, 1886, a massive collective strike paralyzed the nation. On the first day of the strike, 400,000–500,000 workers walked off their jobs, 90,000 of whom were in Chicago, where the events of the Haymarket drama unfolded (1986, 27). Many thousands more joined the strike over the following two days (1986, 27).

On May 3, the conflict intensified at the McCormick Harvester plant in Chicago. Relations between labor and management at the plant had been poor for some time. Two years earlier—in the economic downturn of 1885—the industrialist Cryus McCormick cut wages; the workers responded by forming a union, which led a successful strike. In February, 1886, however, McCormick reneged on the terms of his agreement that settled the strike and expelled and blacklisted active union members from his plant. When the remaining workers protested, McCormick initiated a lockout and brought in scab replacements (Foner, 1986, 29). The displaced workers agitated on the factory grounds and McCormick responded, as management often does, by bringing in armed guards, city police, and government soldiers (1986, 30).[4]

After McCormick called in a military force to disperse the protesting workers outside the plant, the crowd grew increasingly agitated and violence soon broke out. Replacement workers were attacked, company buildings were stoned, and the police opened fire, killing four workers (Foner, 1986, 29). The strikers responded with fiery anarchist rhetoric, calling for the arming of the workers. A mass rally was scheduled for the following day and important anarchists were invited to address the crowd. Due to poor weather and a plethora of other scheduled protests, the rally was attended by only approximately 3,000 people (1986, 30).

Toward the end of the rally, around 10 p.m., one of the defendants was drawing the event to a close. The audience at this time numbered around 200 workers (Foner, 1986, 30). With vivid language, the speaker denounced the law for its subservience to the owners. As described by a trial witness, the defendant "spoke of the law and of the oppressive acts of capital which injured the working men, as being the result of the law, and urged his hearers to overthrow the law, to kill it, stab it, to throttle it" (Lum, 1969, 90).[5] A moment later, 180 police appeared and ordered the crowd to disperse (Foner, 1986, 30). Although the speaker protested that the meeting was lawful, the police converged on the audience, scuffling broke out, and then an unknown person threw a bomb into the crowd of police. The exploding bomb killed one policeman and wounded 70 others (1986, 30). The police panicked and began firing their weapons into the crowd of workers. Witnesses testified that the police fired at least 250 bullets (Lum, 1969, 33). When the violence ended, over 70 police had been injured and eight killed (Foner, 1986, 30). The police deaths, excluding the single fatality due to the bomb, were determined to have been caused by their own gunfire (Avrich, 1984, 88–90). Tellingly, there is no record of how many civilians were wounded or killed.

In reaction to the bombing, there was an outpouring of newspaper editorials and criticism by public officials, all of which vividly denounced the anarchists (David, 1963, 178–189). This editorialism fed a frenzy of fear that engulfed the country, leading to the first great Red Scare, in which thousands of suspected anarchists were rounded up and deported or imprisoned. Many of these people were beaten and tortured by the police (Foner, 1986, 31). The rhetoric of the establishment emphasized the extreme threat the anarchists were to the country. As one newspaper exclaimed:

> No disturbance of the peace that has occurred in the United States since the war of the rebellion has excited public sentiment through the Union as it is excited by the Anarchist's murder of policemen in Chicago on Tuesday night. We say murder with the fullest consciousness of what that word means. . . [such] cowardly savages who plotted and carried out this murder shall suffer the death they deserve. (Cited in David, 1963, 183)

Other newspapers called for the "most complete and summary methods of repression" (1963, 183).

The general tone of the press was that the time had passed for tolerance or half measures: The only good anarchist was a dead anarchist (1963, 187). Eight prominent anarchists—Albert Parsons, August Spies, Samuel J. Fielden, Michael Schwab, Adolph Fisher, George Engel, Louis Lingg, and

Oscar W. Neebe—were hunted down and charged with the bombing, despite the fact that only two of these defendants were present at the rally (Foner, 1986, 25). The resulting trial—which was extraordinarily corrupt—was perhaps the most infamous political trial in US history.[6] The defendants were all found guilty and four were hung, one committed suicide, and the others imprisoned.

A brief note on William Perkins Black, the main attorney defending the anarchists at their trial, helps to exemplify the extreme hostility directed toward the accused. Black was a Civil War hero and a founder of the Chicago Bar. For years, Black worked as a successful and respected corporate attorney; by all accounts, Black was a significant legal figure in Chicago. When word spread that Black was defending the accused anarchists, his clients left him and his partnership dissolved. Black was relegated to the margins of the legal community for the remainder of his career. He remained undaunted by his treatment, and, in the eulogy he delivered for the executed men, he defiantly declared: "We do not stand here by the bodies of felons. There is nothing disgraceful about their death. They died for liberty, for the sacred right of untrammeled speech and for humanity. We are proud to have been their friends" (quoted in Foner, 1986, 38).

## Justice Corrupted Is Community Denied

The criminal justice system is a definitive force in the creation and maintenance of society. The system's basic purpose is to assure the security of all citizens, for without a well-functioning system of criminal justice, no society can remain stable. If the government does not provide for the collective security, citizens will likely engage in self-help, forming paramilitary militias or engaging in vigilantism (see Bonaparte, 1899). As lynching and vigilantism contribute to increased lawlessness, cruelty, and the proliferation of violence, they should be strictly avoided through a system of just and equitable laws. Such laws, and an effective system for policing them, are, therefore, necessary. However, if the criminal justice system is not itself just, the moral grounding of the social order is compromised and the law becomes a haven for the corrupt. When this occurs, society also suffers from a proliferation of violence. Unlike vigilantism, however, such violence is systemic and inseparable from larger social institutions—the police, the military, the schools, the press, and the economy become violators of human dignity. Under this condition, "it is not the lawbreaker we must fear . . . as much as he who obeys the law" (Dwight Macdonald, quoted in Jacoby, 1989b, 189). In such a world, the fundamental order of community justice is inverted—the poor become more impoverished, corruption flourishes, the police become criminals, and those whom society labels as criminals are often prophets (eg, Martin Luther King, Jr., Mahatma Gandhi, and Nelson Mandela). Community life ceases to become a basic good and is transformed into a struggle between the strong and the weak. Social stability is attained through incarceration and state violence against dissent, as when, for example, nearly 2,000,000 people are incarcerated in the United States, 90% of whom earned less than $25,000 the year before they were sent to prison (Easterbrook, 1999) and two thirds of those incarcerated are people of color (*Racial Equality*, 2001). This world of legalized gangsterism was particularly acute in the late nineteenth and early twentieth centuries. For example, at the trial of the eight anarchists—who stood accused of murdering the police officers—no evidence was introduced to connect any of the accused to a single act of violence. Rather, the defendants—who were all found guilty—were convicted solely on their ideology, as bluntly stated by the State's Attorney at the close of the jury trial:

> Law is on trial. Anarchy is on trial. These men have been selected, picked out by the grand jury and indicted because they are the leaders. They are no more guilty than those thousands who follow them. Gentlemen of the jury; convict these men, make examples of them, hang them and you save our institutions, our society. (Cited in Foner, 1986, 34).

Throughout the trial, the spoken and written words of the defendants were presented in detail to the jury. This material consisted of extensive newspaper literature—written or edited by the defendants—concerning anarchist theory and contemporary political criticism (Lum, 1969, 171–173). Anarchist material written by others, such as Most's *Revolutionary War Science*, was also presented to the jury as evidence against the defendants (Lum, 1969, 79). Moreover, the speeches and private utterances of the defendants, none of which were incriminating, were routinely offered as evidence of their guilt (1969, 79).

The jury was also inundated with evidence that all the defendants were known to have attended socialist and anarchist meetings (Lum, 1969, 79). This fact was deemed conclusive of their guilt for the bomb attack on the police. No proof of any conspiracy among the defendants to cause the death of the policemen was established. Instead, the trial court determined that the Haymarket meeting was intended to be peaceful and that the meeting was, in fact, peaceful until the police initiated the violence (Lum, 1969, 133). Nevertheless, the theory of the prosecution, which the jury accepted, was that since anarchists in general advocated armed resistance to the state, the eight anarchist leaders on trial were responsible for any anarchist-related violence that occurred anywhere. The State asserted that "the defendants for two or three years had been engaged, as the leaders, in a gigantic conspiracy against law and order, of which the meeting on Monday night was but one step" (1969, 73).

Finally, sensationalist objects were entered into evidence by the prosecution to arouse the fear and indignation of the jury. These objects included dozens of bombs not alleged to have been in possession of the defendants, bloody police uniforms and emotive descriptions of police injuries, and red flags and banners that the defendants used at their meetings and rallies (Lum, 1969, 172).

Other trial defects were salient in this case. First, none of the evidence collected from the defendants conformed to constitutional or statutory criminal procedure; searches and seizures routinely occurred without warrants or probable cause (Lum, 1969, 163). Second, testimony from police investigators was profoundly contradictory; the police could not agree as to the quantity, nature, or location of the evidence seized (1969, 99, 126). Third, eyewitness testimony from the crime scene was resolutely discredited by the defense—most notably, the report of the prosecution's star witness was contradicted by forty-six different witnesses and impeached by nine others (1969, 158). Fourth, witnesses who did not understand German testified to conversations by the defendants most likely to have been uttered in German (1969, 158). Fifth, when testimony by a witness for the prosecution undermined the prosecution's case, the witness "mysteriously disappeared from the city" (1969, 153). Sixth, evidence of the intent of the police to initiate violence at the Haymarket meeting was suppressed by the judge (1969, 150). Seventh, the judge, over the objection of the defense, routinely forced the defendants to testify extensively to their political beliefs and thus serve as witnesses against themselves (1969, 132). Eighth, the prosecution, in full hearing of the jury, frequently addressed the defendants as "loathsome murderers," "wretches," and "assassins" (1969, 173). Ninth, the police paid state witnesses undisclosed amounts of money during the course of the trial (1969, 165). Tenth, the trial judge, Joseph E. Garry, was publicly known for vehemently opposing the labor movement. Eleventh, and most importantly, the jurors were profoundly biased against the defendants.

Of the thousand people brought in as potential jurors, most had preformed opinions that the defendants were guilty of murder as charged and they freely expressed their disdain for anarchists, socialists, and communists (34). During *voir dire*, for example, one potential juror stated, "The police should have shot them [the defendants] all down," that the defendants were entitled to no rights, and that "if I was on the jury I would hang all the damned buggars" (63). Another, when asked if he harbored any prejudice against the defendants, replied, "I think I would be prejudiced because my feeling [toward them] is very bitter" (57). A third, acknowledging that he had discussed the Haymarket bombing many times, said, "I believe what I have read in the papers—believe that the parties are guilty" (54). A fourth potential jury member testified that he would "find the defendants guilty upon less evidence than if they were law-abiding citizens" (50). Comments such as these were typical of the trial record. In each case, potential jurors were challenged by the defense *for cause*, and each challenge was overruled by the court. The defense, therefore, was forced to use up its limited peremptory challenges in removing the most hostile jurors.[7]

The final jury array was not representative of the defendants. Most of the defendants were German-born and all were industrial workers, but none of the jury appeared to be foreign-born, and none were industrial workers (Lum, 1969, 60-66).[8] Moreover, most of the jury strongly identified as being Christian. In the context of the era, it was widely known that anarchism was profoundly hostile to Christianity (Bakunin, 1970). In addition, the jury was composed of managers, salesmen, contractors, and businessmen (Lum, 1969, 66). At the end of the trial, before the jury was dismissed, the judge told the jury that they "deserve some recognition of the service you have performed besides the meager compensation you are to receive"

(1969, 188). Shortly thereafter, public calls appeared in the Chicago press for the creation of such a fund to increase jury financial compensation (1969, 188).

## Conclusion

The farce of the trial did not go unnoticed. For instance, John Peter Altgeld, the Governor of Illinois, received petitions signed by 60,000 people requesting an executive investigation (Zinn, 1980, 266). As a result of this investigation, Altgeld declared the trial a miscarriage of justice and pardoned the three surviving anarchists (four of the defendants had already been hung and one had committed suicide the night before his execution; Foner, 1986, 38). The working people in Chicago were incensed by the trial and executions. Nearly half a million people appeared to witness the funeral procession of thousands of marching workers carrying the caskets of the executed men to their gravesites (1986, 38). Later, in 1893, workers erected a large monument to the martyred anarchists, which still stands today. At the base of the monument is an inscription of the last words of August Spies, one of the executed men, "There will come a time when our silence will be more powerful than the voices you strangle today" (Foner, 1986, 38).

The events of May 4 and the public condemnation of the violence that occurred helped to crystallize the belief that anarchism was an illegitimate expression of labor dissatisfaction (Dubofsky and Dulles, 1999, 112). The violence and the subsequent trial caused many to question the association of unions with militant activity. In this way, the experience of anarchism in the United States highlights an important reason why US labor lacks a developed and vital workers' party. This absence exists, in part, because the paradigmatic labor movement in the United States in the late nineteenth century was anarchist, not socialist, as in most of Europe. The extreme rhetoric and ideology of the anarchists made them a relatively easy target for establishment derision and suppression. Furthermore, their vision of community alienated many, particularly compared to the more reform oriented and accommodating community offered by the socialists.

## ✷ NOTES ✷

1. A modern expression of anarchism has emerged from the global resistance to the World Trade Organization (WTO). As perceived by these anarchists and others, the WTO is a powerful global agency that functions as a "supreme court" of international commerce, overruling laws or procedures that restrict international trade. Although extra-governmental, the WTO undermines national sovereignty due to its power to force countries to change laws enacted to protect the environment, public health, and domestic production (Staples, 2000, 19). In other words, the WTO is not democratically accountable (proceedings of the WTO are held in secret); instead, the WTO serves the interests of multinational corporations while, at the same time, its policies impact all aspects of life on this planet (Bruner, 2002, 29–30). The WTO tramples labor and human rights and is destroying the environment. One result of the WTO is the worldwide increase of extreme poverty and deprivation.

2. For an overview of the connections between anarchist thought and the articulation of US democracy found in the philosophy of John Dewey, see Manicas (1982).

3. After participating in an earlier failed assassination attempt of a notorious industrialist, Goldman repudiated such assassinations while, simultaneously, recognizing what she identified as the "psychology of political violence." See Goldman (1969, 79–108).

4. Throughout the history of labor struggle in the United States, there has been, as Howard Zinn (1990a, 80) observes, a "firm connection between entrenched wealth and political power, manifested in the decisions of government, and the machinery of law and justice." A deadly example of this occurred in the Colorado coal mine strikes of 1914. In the Ludlow Massacre, "sixty-six men, women, and children–mostly workers or families of the workers–[were] killed by federal troops and private police" (99). The most gruesome aspect of this massacre involved federal troops, who intentionally burned to death eleven children and two women in the Ludlow tent colony where the striking workers, evicted from the company town, had gathered for shelter (79).

5. All quotations from the trial record were taken from Lum (1969).

6. The full court proceedings and related documents can be found in the Haymarket Affair Digital Collection, Chicago Historical Society Website at http://www.chicagohistory.-org/hadc/index.html.

7. Generally, in all jury trials, both sides are allowed a limited number of peremptory challenges by which they can dismiss a potential jury member for any reason. This number fluctuates based on jurisdiction and on whether the trial is criminal or civil, with a greater number of peremptory challenges being granted to parties in criminal trials. In addition, both sides to a legal action have an unlimited number of challenges for cause, in which they must persuade the court that the potential juror is unfit to serve at trial, although the court has the discretion on whether to dismiss the potential juror. In the Haymarket trial, the court systematically denied defense claims that potential jurors were unfit (Lum, 1986, 48-66).

8. Ten of the twelve jurors have their place of birth listed in the court proceedings.

# CHAPTER 11

# EUGENE DEBS, REFORMIST-SOCIALISM, AND THE PULLMAN STRIKE OF 1894

With the waning of anarchism as a political force, cultural space appeared for the development of alternative labor movements. Over time, these movements would splinter, further weakening the chances for a progressive working-class labor party to emerge. Throughout the twentieth century, for example, dozens of worker political parties sprang up in the United States, including the Communist party, Socialist party, Socialist Workers party, Maoist International Movement, Democratic Socialist of America, Social Democrats, Socialist Labor party of America, Revolutionary Communist party, New party, Workers World party, Freedom Socialist party, New Liberty party, World Socialist party of the United States, and the Progressive Labor party. Aside from the Communist party and the Socialist party, both of which had significant influence in this country, the other groups remained marginal, fighting each other as they became increasingly irrelevant.

The most influential of these movements, the Socialist party,[1] was led by Eugene Debs. Debs had grown up as a working class youth in Terre Haute, Indiana. While employed in the railroad industry, Debs became appalled by the working conditions. In 1893, along with others, Debs created the American Railroad Union (ARU). Within a few years, the ARU was crushed by the US government and Debs was imprisoned. In prison, Debs began reading socialist literature and concluded that more fundamental social change was needed in the United States, so Debs created the Socialist party of America in 1901 (Papke, 1994) and became "the most popular and effective socialist figure ever to appear in America" (Cochran, 1969, 63). Debs typifies the desire of labor to gain a systemic national identity in an era that "departed from the traditional republican definition of the workingman's liberty in favor of a narrower, more strictly liberal definition [where] the workers' freedom rested simply in his ownership of his capacity to labor" (Forbath, 1985, 769).

As discussed below, even the mainstreaming of dissent, as found in Debs, was bitterly crushed by the US government. As Dianne Avery explains, "Economic harm became blurred with physical harm; peaceful economic coercion became synonymous with coercion through violence. The talk of violence both masked and revealed the judges' real fears: fears of great union strength and autonomy, of class warfare, of anarchy, of loss of control, of change" (1988, 12). Because the US government historically has been quick to equate the economic harm of industry with working class sedition, and because the government has been (and continues to be) slow to recognize the economic marginalization of the working classes as an affront to their human dignity, any government assertion of neutrality in future labor disputes should be immediately challenged.

## ✶ COMPARING REFORMIST-SOCIALISM AND ANARCHISM ✶

Debs and his movement differed from the anarchists in several important ways. First, and most importantly, unlike the anarchists, who viewed the state apparatus as inherently tyrannical, the reformist-socialist tradition was fundamentally committed to achieving political and economic reform through democratic politics and electoral victory (Eric Foner, 1984, 71). Through such elections, more than a thousand socialists served in local, state, and even federal office (Klehr and Haynes, 1992, 8). The strategy of these reformist-socialists was to create social justice through progressive and well-intentioned legislation. As Debs argued, "The ballot means that labor is no longer dumb, that at last it has a voice, that it may be heard and if united shall be heeded" (cited in Stewart, 1973, 162).

The anarchists, on the other hand, flatly rejected electoral politics as a solution for working class oppression. Such tactics were considered foolhardy and ineffective for the more complete social liberation they imagined. The anarchists "feared that when workers were elected to parliament and translated to bourgeois living conditions, they would cease to be workers and turn into Statesmen, becoming bourgeois, perhaps even more bourgeoisie than the bourgeoisie itself" (Guerin, 1970, 19). Thus, few if any anarchists sought or attained systemic political power in the United States. From the beginning, the anarchists used confrontational tactics to undermine state legitimacy and to shatter the myth of state invincibility. In contrast, the reformist-socialists, who often found themselves in confrontational situations, regretted such confrontation and viewed it as evidence of their profound political marginalization. The activism of the reformist-socialists was not aimed at sedition; it was intended to dramatize their political marginalization and to elevate the moral consciousness of the nation. Such tactics predate a major strategy of the civil rights movement; in the words of Martin Luther King, Jr., "The oppressed must never allow the conscience of the oppressor to slumber" (1986, 212).

Second, by positioning themselves as enemies of the state, anarchists were committed, at least in theory, to the violent overthrow of all existing state apparatuses. Fundamental to anarchist strategy was the recognition that political violence directed toward the industrial classes (as well as sabotage of state property and industrial organization) was necessary. This belief, coupled with bitter rhetorical attacks on the state through anarchist publications and discourse, heightened the fear of eminent class warfare, and thereby threatened state security. The target of anarchist rhetoric was a trinity of evil: capital, the law, and the state. For the anarchist, true freedom could only be achieved with the abolishment of all three (Kropotkin, 1995, 19).

The reformist-socialists held an entirely opposite view. According to this tradition, the state was not inherently bad; rather, it was a tool for the management of class relations, which could be utilized for the common good. Their fundamental question was not by what authority state power could exist but in *whose* interest that power would serve. The reformist-socialists concluded that the various jurisdictions in the United States had been captured by wealthy private interests. The wrong was not the state *per se* but the state's subservience to a minority elite. Thus, with popular support, the various laws that repressed and impoverished the working classes could be revised to allow for a widespread industrial democracy. Shoji Ishitsuka calls this political movement for social change the "socialist enlightenment," which helped to realize the "idea of equality" in this country and throughout the world (1994, 25).

The reformist-socialists did not reject private interests so much as they rebelled against the profound injustice and misery that flowed from the callousness of such interests. They imagined a world in which economic development could be directed toward the well-being of an ever-increasing majority of citizens. The creation of such a world would not extinguish the privilege of the wealthy, but it would make the affluent more accountable to the rest of society. To achieve such a society, the reformist-socialists needed the support of a widely inclusive community; since subversive violence against the state would position the reformist-socialists antithetically to those goals, they were rejected. What these socialists attempted to capture was the moral soul of the nation—the conscience and heart of the US people, which could not be achieved through widespread violence and class warfare.

The third important difference between the movement inspired by Debs and the movement inspired by the anarchists was demographics. The anarchists were primarily foreign born, and the establishment used this to marginalize them and their ideas as alien. Furthermore, Anglo-Saxon chauvinism and long-standing mistreatment of Italians, Irish, Germans, Russians, and Jews, all of whom figured prominently in the anarchist movement, contributed to the ease by which the anarchists were dismissed by the larger Protestant community, which considered itself authentically "American" (for the rhetoric of eugenics, see Hasian, 1996).

Debs, in contrast, was born a US citizen and he expressed a life-long admiration for US values and icons, embodying a distinctly US ethos (Salvatore, 1984, 271–72, 343–44). Debs presented himself as heir to the classic pre-Civil War Jeffersonian vision of invigorated democracy, one grounded in self-supporting, civically minded communities. With such vision, Debs forged a view of socialism compatible with traditional US values: respect for the individual's basic rights and liberties, civic commitment, working-class autonomy through self-supporting labor, tolerance for difference, virtue of character, equality, justice, and fair play (Stewart, 1973, 156). Today, Debs is widely respected for his "ethical presence" in our society, having "inspired one of the most durable and generous legends in American thought outside of George Washington and Abraham Lincoln" (Darsey, 1988, 435). In 1967, Debs's Terre Haute home was dedicated a National Historic Site.

## ✶ THE PULLMAN STRIKE AND ITS EFFECTS ✶

This section discusses Debs within the context of the Pullman Strike of 1894. The Pullman Strike, and the subsequent legal action taken to suppress the union, had a monumental effect on both Debs personally and on the contextualization of labor relations in the United States (see Papke, 1999).

The primary cause of the Pullman Strike was George Mortimer Pullman, the powerful industrialist who developed the much-celebrated Pullman car, enabling travelers to sleep in comfort during long trips and, thereby, popularizing recreational train travel among the affluent (see Leyendecker, 1994). Surrounding his industrial plant (the Pullman Palace Car Company), Pullman created what he considered to be a "model" company town in 1881, where his employees were forced to live (Leyendecker, 164; also see Buder, 1997). This community, Pullman, Illinois, was ordered and paternalistic, an experiment in industrial living, providing management with nearly complete social control over workers' lives (for a detailed description of life in Pullman, Illinois, see Lindsey, 1942, 61-89, and Dubofsky and Dulles, 1999, 158). Forbath describes the conditions of the generic company town during this era:

> The entrepreneur or corporation often owned everything from church and school to houses and stores. From a worker's perspective, life in these villages consisted of almost unbroken dependency. Receiving clothing and food for one's labor smacked of slavery. Debts to the company stores fastened workers to the mines and factories, and the stores' monopolies enabled companies to charge above market prices for the groceries and other provisions they supplied. (1985, 797)

Although the material conditions were better in Pullman than the typical company town (eg, the services of the town, which included water, power, churches, banks, libraries, theaters, cemeteries, and schools, were significant), these amenities were supported by fees drawn from the workers' paychecks, fees that were substantially higher (some 20% to 25%) than in other company towns (Leyendecker, 233). Leyendecker notes that, on occasion, "what was left of the two weeks' wages after such deductions amounted to less than one dollar" (221).

More crucially, workers grew to resent the total control that the company exerted over their lives. Pullman, for instance, used the dependency of his workers as a deterrent to dissent; thus, workers remained in the town only at the sufferance of the company. Rebellious workers stood to lose everything—they could be evicted from the town, prohibited from visiting their family and friends, and even denied access to family burial plots—if they displeased Pullman by exercising what contemporary society would consider their constitutional, civil, and human rights. The US Supreme Court generally upholds the power of private landowners to restrict the rights of people on their property.[2]

In 1893, a particularly strong recession swept the nation and business at the Pullman factory plummeted.[3] Pullman compensated by firing 4,000 of his 6,000 workers, who immediately lost their living quarters (Leyendecker, 229); the remaining workers had their wages cut by 30% (Zinn, 1980, 274). In the face of these pay cuts, there was no equivalent cut in rent for company housing or utilities (Leyendecker, 221, 229). Attempts by the workers to arbitrate the issue with Pullman were met with stern refusal: "There is nothing to arbitrate!" Pullman declared (Dubofsky and Dulles, 160).

Representatives from the Pullman workers went to the annual meeting of the ARU to enlist its support. Debs and the union had recently achieved a victory against the Great Northern railroad, and so the Pullman workers approached Debs with anticipation and hope (Leyendecker, 222). In the weeks following the Great Northern strike, "approximately 2,000 workers joined the ARU daily" (Papke, 1994, 341).

After some debate and emotional argument, the Pullman workers succeeded in receiving support from the ARU. Initially, the ARU was careful to boycott only trains carrying Pullman cars (Ruff, 1997, 69). This was a strategic and well-calculated plan, as Debs was not trying to change the entire railroad system; rather, he was trying to improve the conditions of one significant group of workers within that system. This approach reflected Debs's philosophical commitment to electoral politics, since he "disagreed strenuously" with labor organizations which repudiated "political activity" and engaged in violence and industrial sabotage (Rabban, 1994, 1065). Debs clearly comprehended that big industry—in particular, the railroads—enjoyed the political and military support of the federal government and that political counterpressure was the only effective way to initiate change.[4]

Pullman understood Debs' strategy and ordered his cars attached to a variety of different trains—particularly to those carrying the US mail—to frustrate Debs's plan (Dubofsky and Dulles, 1999, 162; Stewart, 1973, 167). This tactic forced the ARU to either give up the strike or to intensify its effect. The ARU reluctantly chose the latter, causing two thirds of the US railroads to become mired in the strike (Ruff, 1997, 69). By causing the strike to expand (and the mail to halt), Pullman successfully federalized the strike, creating a pretext for the US government to intervene, which it did—violently. The government marshaled 14,000 state and federal soldiers against the strikers, killing 35 workers (Zinn, 1980, 275). The US Supreme Court in *In re Debs* (1895) sanctioned such violence:

> The entire strength of the nation may be used to enforce in any part of the land the full and free exercise of all national powers and the security of all rights entrusted by the constitution to its care. The strong arm of the national government may be put forth to brush away all obstructions to the freedom of interstate commerce or the transportation of the mail. If the emergency arises, the army of the nation, and all of its militia, are at the service of the nation, to compel obedience to its laws. (582)

The irony is patent. Debs, in coordinating the ARU, worked hard to avoid violence (as well as violent rhetoric), and to be conscientious of federal interests. Furthermore, Debs "consistently counseled moderation and restraint" and warned the strikers to respect railroad property (Dubofsky and Dulles, 162). As with the journeymen cordwainers before him, Debs's method of effectuating social change was to withhold labor.

From the point of view of the progressive community committed to social justice advocated in this book, the government's violence in suppressing the strike was unnecessary, as the strike was essentially peaceful before the federal government interfered. Furthermore, Governor Altgeld, who had constitutional responsibility to resolve the conflict, opposed federal interference. In a letter Altgeld sent to President Grover Cleveland, he explained, "At present some of our railroads are paralyzed, not by reasons of obstruction, but because they cannot get men to operate their trains . . . As Governor of the State of Illinois, I ask the immediate withdrawal of Federal troops from active duty in this State" (Dubofsky and Dulles, 162). Along with the mayors of 50 US cities, Altgeld urged Pullman to address the concerns raised by the workers (Leyendecker, 1994, 226).[5]

Aside from the military suppression of the strike, the federal government also unleashed a series of legal assaults against the ARU. As many as 400 union members were arrested, including Debs (Dubofsky and Dulles, 1999, 164). In the tradition established by *Commonwealth v. Pullis*, the federal government charged Debs and other leaders of the union with conspiracy—in this case, conspiracy to violate the Sherman Anti-Trust Act. Although the Sherman Act was created to break up business monopolies, most Americans do not realize that the Act was enforced against labor unions years before it was enforced against business trusts (Avery, 1988, 53–54). The Bill of Indictment positioned the defendants as follows:

> In the month of May, 1894, there arose a difference or dispute between the Pullman Palace Car Company and its employees, as the result of which a considerable portion of the latter left the service of the car company; that thereafter the four officers of the railway union combined together, and with others, to compel an adjustment of such dispute, by creating a boycott against the cars of the car company; that, to make such boycott effective, the railroads running out of Chicago [were prevented] from operating their trains, and were coming to extend such boycott against Pullman sleeping cars by causing strikes among employees of all railroads attempting to haul the same. (*In re Debs*, 567)

To suppress such conspiracy, the judiciary issued an injunction precluding Debs from discussing or coordinating the strike. Debs violated this legal command and was arrested on contempt charges. The Supreme Court affirmed his subsequent conviction and gave constitutional sanction to labor injunctions as a potent weapon of class warfare. From "then on," notes Lawrence M. Friedman, "the injunction, in the hands of a strong-minded judge, was a mighty adversary that organized labor had to reckon with. The injunction was swift, and it could be murderously inclusive—broad enough in its contours to cover a total situation, outlawing every aspect of a strike and effectively crushing it" (1985, 557).

The severity of the federal reaction to this and to other strikes, including contemporary strikes, begs an inquiry into the federal interest at stake in these issues. In the following subsections, four such interests—protection of the mail, protection of commerce, protection of the wealthy from social reform, and protection of the government from political dissent—are articulated and evaluated.

## Protection of the Mail

The first federal interest discerned in the Pullman Strike is the responsibility of the government to run and to regulate the postal service. This interest is articulated by the Constitution, as noted by the Court: "Among the powers expressly given to the national government [in Article 1, section 8 of the Federal Constitution] are the control of interstate commerce and the creation and management of a post-office system for the nation" (*In re Debs*, 579). President Cleveland took this mandate so seriously that, in ordering the military suppression of the strike, he declared: "If it takes every dollar in the Treasury and every soldier in the United States to deliver a postal card in Chicago, that postal card should be delivered" (cited in Dubofsky and Dulles, 163).

Such interest, however, does not provide a morally satisfactory justification for violently repressing the Pullman Strike. Mail is an expression of community, communication, and social bonding. Only when mail fulfills these roles does the mail system attain its utility. By itself, mail—or, indeed, government—is undeserving of respect, as both gain importance only in the context of community. What matters is the health of that community and the actions of individuals to cultivate and to support that health. To respect the artifacts of community (such as its civic, political, and industrial institutions) while ignoring the substance of human life within that community, is to ignore the most essential value that underlies democratic society—equality.

Furthermore, in the context of this and other labor disputes, the community itself has broken down. The proper government response to such a situation is to reconstruct the health of the community. Consider the following analogy. If weak foundations cause a structure to collapse, the strengthening of that foundation is needed before a new structure can be erected. As in this analogy, security for a community is derived from the internal strength of the community constituting the structure, and not from the superficial reinforcement of an untenable social reality. This logic applies more generally to the social construction of property and crime. As Howard Zinn notes:

> [The] huge proportion of poor people in jail for crimes against property suggests that prisons are inevitable counterparts of banks. And so long as we have a

> system that breeds fierce and unequal competition for scarce resources . . . some steel bars will be needed to protect money, and others to confine human beings. (1997, 446)

The government's responsibility is to reduce class antagonism by encouraging mediation and compromise between industry and labor, and between the wealthy and the poor. As argued throughout this book, the construction of community involves an inclusive political vision of a society that is both just and fair. By elevating a communication form (in this case, the mail) over the living text of a people (or to elevate wealth over the text of living community), the federal government misread the source of a nation's strength: A nation is only as strong as the communities of which it is composed. A society that privileges material wealth over community strength will cease to function as a society and will decay into oligarchy, as is suggested by Zinn above.

## Protection of Commerce

The second government interest at stake concerned the government's fear that a disruption in the rail service would adversely effect the health of commerce. Similar to the constitutional authority for the government's regulation of the mail, Congress has express authorization from the Constitution to exclusively regulate interstate commerce (Article I, section 8). Given that Chicago was the choke point of the national railroad system in which twenty-four railroads converged, a major strike in that city threatened the national distribution of goods (Papke, 1994, 343). Such a strike, therefore, would constitute an unlawful usurping of powers vested in Congress, to the detriment of the entire nation. As argued by the government prosecutor:

> By reason of said unlawful combination and conspiracy and the acts and doings aforesaid thereunder, the supply of coal and fuel for consumption throughout the different states of the Union, and of grain, breadstuffs, vegetables, fruits, meats, and other necessaries of life, has been cut off, interrupted, and interfered with, and the market therefore made largely unavailable, and dealers in all of said various products and the consumers thereof have been greatly injured, and trade and commerce therein among the states has been restrained, obstructed, and largely destroyed. (*In re Debs*, 570)

This government interest is suspicious for a number of reasons. In the most general sense, the purpose of any strike is to highlight the value of labor, raise wages, and improve working conditions. The more that society recognizes that at its core is a fundamental dependence on other individuals, the more likely the intrinsic value of labor will be recognized by that society. This is a fundamental market principle: Labor is paid according to market worth. Strikes, in effect, are a way of determining the market worth of an industry. If a strike by railroad employees cripples the nation, that is an indication that these workers are undervalued. Recognizing the value of workers removes the disruption and ensures the future well-being of the system. The threat to commerce, properly speaking, is not the strike but the undervaluation of labor.[6]

More specifically, the asserted interest of the federal government is disingenuous (the Interstate Commerce Clause notwithstanding). The strike, in this instance, was focused solely on Pullman's luxury sleeping cars and did not target the federal mail, nor did the strike target produce transports or any other perishable goods. The record clearly indicates that Debs and his union did not intend to paralyze the country, destroy the economy, or overthrow the government. The strike, nevertheless, was positioned by the mass media as subversive. With hyperbole characteristic of the yellow press of the day, the *New York World* declared that the strike was "a war against the government and against society" (quoted in Dubofsky and Dulles, 160). In short, there is a strong sense that the response of the federal government was disproportionate to its interest. Although the federal government has a clear role to play in assuring social order and tranquility, this same government has an even more pressing responsibility to act on behalf of the common good of all of its citizens, not merely for the privileged few who control influential industries. Why, for instance, was Pullman, who attached his luxury cars to regular freight cars (including the mail cars), without blame? Why was Pullman not punished for refusing to negotiate with his employees or for exacerbating employee discontent to prolong the strike? Finally, why, in light of the fact that the US Attorney General who coordinated the military suppression of the strike was himself a former corporate attorney for the railroad industry and a personal friend of many railroad owners, were Pullman and his agents not culpable for their undemocratic influence that militarized the conflict and, thereby, ensured an outbreak of violence?

Satifactory answers to these questions are necessary for the US people to understand and respect the actions of their government when those actions are violent and in the interest of industrialists against the demands of the larger national community.

## Protection From Social Reform

The third government interest is more revealing of the government's motivation for crushing the striking workers and for imprisoning its leaders and hundreds of the rank-and-file members. Similar to the concern expressed in *Pullis*, and evident in hundreds of cases since, the federal government has a longstanding interest in preventing popular democratic activism—activism not controlled or contained by either of the two political parties in this country. When such activism (such as street democracy) falls outside the control of elite power, this expression of politics is declared contrary to "ordered liberty" and constitutionalism. This interest explains why social movements that attempt to expand the notion of community and political enfranchisement in the United States, no matter how patriotic and just, usually meet with substantial resistance from the establishment.

One of the more recent examples of this phenomenon occurred during the 1980s when Ronald Reagan initiated a sustained policy of harassment against the domestic resistance to US military aggression in Central America (see Gelbspam, 1991). The US Federal Bureau of Investigation (FBI) has a long history of such tactics. J. Edgar Hoover, director of the FBI from 1924 until his death in 1972, relentlessly attacked social/political deviance, including popular dissent in the United States. Starting with his persecution of suspected communists in the 1920s and 1930s, Hoover branched out to harass and repress civil rights leaders and leaders of the anti-Vietnam War movement. This harassment involved, among other things, the murder of many Black Panther leaders (see Seale, 1991). In addition, Hoover authorized the surveillance of outspoken US Americans and kept secret files on people he considered to be state enemies.

The recurrent fear, as evidenced in *Pullis*, the anarchist movement, and *In re Debs*, involves workers forming an extraconstitutional community and, thereby, weakening the power of the Republic to protect vested property interests. Although this fear may be relevant with regard to the anarchists, it is inappropriate when applied to most other expressions of the labor movement. The anarchists alone sought the overthrow of the state; all the other groups, including the later communists, sought to reinforce the republic and its institutions. The only difference between the current republic and the republic that these groups struggled to create can be found in the degree to which the larger community would be represented by the government. The traditional republic was (and largely still is) extremely exclusionary; not until the 1960s did the rights and privileges of citizenship extend meaningfully (to the extent it has) to minorities, women, and the poor. The 1960s witnessed an explosion of constitutional jurisprudence and congressional legislation directed at including greater numbers of people in the national community. However, much more needs to be done in this direction so that hunger and poverty no longer afflict generations of communities in the United States.

In upholding the power of the federal government to imprison Debs and other union members, the Supreme Court preached a "lesson" to the defendants and to the larger working community. With these remarks, the Court crystallized the establishment's fear of grassroots political change:

> It is a lesson which cannot be learned too soon or too thoroughly that under this government of and by the people the means of redress of all wrongs are through the courts and at the ballot box, and that no wrong, real or fancied, carries with it legal warrant to invite as a means of redress the co-operation of a mob, with its accompanying acts of violence. (*In re Debs*, 599)

Under this rationale, the civil rights movement, as well as most other progressive social movements in the United States, would be rendered illegitimate, as their mere existence would have been considered a "mob" threatening "democratic" processes. By rendering the "mob" undemocratic, the Court is alienating the expression of "we, the people" (the vast bulk of the US population that has never been part of the governing economic elite, and in whose interest such government seldom acts). For example, the North Carolina Agricultural & Technical State University students who demonstrated on February 1, 1960, for integration at a Woolworth's in Greensboro, North Carolina—sparking similar protests around the country—would have laughed at the Court for asserting that the redressing of social wrongs must be accomplished at the ballot box or before the judiciary (see Bowen, 1989, 88-90; Chafe, 1990). These students knew better. If struggling people in the United States were to depend on judges and voting alone to improve the conditions of their lives, this society would be vastly more impoverished. This has been the experience of labor. For decades before labor grew militant, workers petitioned both the judiciary and the legislature for relief and received little if any redress to their concerns. Therefore, there is little reason to assume that, absent the threat of mass civil disobedience, the government and the judiciary will act on behalf of the poor in the future.

## Protection From Dissent

In addition to a profound resistance to popular political organization outside of systemic constitutional channels, the government, through 1969, expressed a consistent interest in punishing speech that rejected government policy or encouraged others to critically examine government motives. This resistance can be traced, in part, to the Alien and Sedition Acts of 1801 and to the fear by the Federalist Party of domestic support for the French Revolution. Although the Alien and Sedition Acts only existed for a few years, such laws mushroomed in the United States from the Civil War period onward. Of course, prior to the Civil War, there was no First Amendment protection for slaves or anyone who spoke out against slavery. Southern legislatures frequently passed death sentences on Northern abolitionists and made possession of abolitionist literature a capital offense. David Walker, an assassinated prominent Northern abolitionist, was one such victim (Hinks, 1996).

Many of these laws against criminal syndicalism identified "anarchism" as the ideology to be outlawed. In practice, however, the statutes were intended to suppress most dissent; as other labor groups supplanted anarchism, these laws were applied to them. Throughout this period, large newspaper chains experienced little government harassment because they often parroted the views of the economic and ruling elite. On the other hand, when individuals critical of the status quo sought to express alternative views that violated the state's sense of security or threatened established interests, they were routinely silenced (Sexton, 1991, 135–136; Rabban, 1994).

Although US Americans today often take their civil liberties for granted, they fail to appreciate the historical development of these rights. Such rights are fluid; they are taken, not granted, and earned though sacrifice and hardship. In fact, prior to the twentieth century, the First Amendment was little more than a blot of ink on lifeless parchment. The Constitution itself is dead hemp; the life, vitality, vigor, and the significance of the Constitution depend on the outcomes of economic and cultural battles fought between the governing US elite and the rest of the population.

Before the United States entered the First World War, there was popular sentiment against US involvement. For example, Woodrow Wilson was elected president largely on his pledge to keep the United States out of the war. Once elected, however, Wilson had a change of heart, and he proceeded to lead the country into the conflict. Public opinion of the war turned to support Wilson, and the country succumbed to war hysteria (Clements, 1992). The US leadership grew furious when a significant portion of the population—notably, leaders associated with the labor movement—argued publicly that the war was yet another example of class warfare (Holland, 1973, 221). This perception was enhanced by, among other things, the invasion of Soviet Russia in 1918 by US, British, French, and Italian forces to depose Lenin's new government. In general, these dissenters argued that the war was caused by the petty squabbling of European nations fighting for colonial influence, as well as by the greed of the munitions and related industries. In response to criticism of the US war effort, Congress passed the Espionage Act of 1917. The Act read, in part:

> Who ever when the United States is at war, shall cause or attempt to cause insubordination, disloyalty, mutiny, or refusal of duty in the military or naval forces of the United States, or shall willfully obstruct the recruiting or enlistment services of the United States, to the injury of the service or of the United States, shall be punished by a fine of not more than $10,000 or imprisonment for not more than twenty years or both.[7]

This was the law Debs was convicted of violating, for which he received two concurrent ten-year prison sentences for delivering an antiwar speech in 1919 (*Debs v. United States*) (see Rabban, 1983). While imprisoned for this conviction, Debs campaigned for president in 1920, receiving nearly 1,000,000 votes (Debs was pardoned in 1921 by President Warren Harding). Debs had run for president in four previous elections; in 1912, for example, he received 6% of the popular vote (Zinn, 1980, 333).

Thousands of socialists, anarchists, communists and others critical of the federal government received similar—or even more stringent—prison sentences for distributing flyers, organizing meetings, or speaking in public places. The most famous of these cases involved the type of labor and political unrest discussed in this chapter. In *Abrams v. United States* (1919), *Schenck v. United States* (1919), *Masses Publishing Co. v. Patten* (1917), *Gitlow v. New York* (1925), *Whitney v. California* (1927), and *Dennis v. United States* (1951), the Court condemned and imprisoned people whose only threat were their visions of alternative political and economic orders.[8]

I locate the maturation of the First Amendment in the case of *Brandenburg v. Ohio* (1969). Prior to this decision, the US Supreme Court regularly upheld the suppression of free speech when agents of organized labor articulated, through public argument and political association, new visions of community. *Brandenburg* is an ironic case, as the defendant was not a labor representative agitating for human dignity, civil rights, and social justice; rather, defendant Brandenburg was a leader of the Ku Klux Klan and had been convicted under a state criminal syndicalism statute for advocating the use of unlawful means to accomplish an organization's political goals (see Kalvan, 1988, 119–124). In other words, this KKK leader was convicted under an anti–free speech law that had been created to control left-wing political labor radicals.

Under *Brandenburg*—which is current law—the government may only criminalize the political expression of a dissident group when a specific instance of imminent unlawful action is being advocated. Although *Brandenburg* would not have helped Debs in the context of the Pullman Strike, it would have protected him from his later conviction for sedition. Moreover, *Brandenburg* would have helped to protect thousands of other labor activists and political dissenters from the systemic political harassment they suffered for many decades.

*Brandenburg* notwithstanding, there is a recurring sentiment in the United States (particularly since September 11, 2001) that it is somehow wrong to withhold one's allegiance to the federal government. Jurisprudentially, there is no grounds for this sentiment. In holding that the First Amendment precludes the government from compelling citizens to declare their allegiance to the American flag, the US Supreme Court, in *West Virginia State Board of Education v. Barnette* (1943), determined that neither the federal or state governments have authority to compel an individual to pledge allegiance to the United States or to any government institution. Although the Supreme Court ruled that compulsory military service is not precluded by the antislavery provisions of the Thirteenth Amendment to the Federal Constitution (*Arver v. United States*, 1918) and that the government can draft a person's body for war, the government cannot draft that person's soul for any cause. In times of war, in particular, citizens maintain the moral and constitutional right to use every means of artistic persuasion to convince soldiers to put down their weapons. Indeed, in no other context is this right more important.

## Conclusion

The working class in the United States has been, and continues to be, systematically excluded from normative political representation and is allowed little opportunity to contribute to the terms and conditions of its social existence (Henwood, 1987; Moberg, 1992). Although few workers today resist such marginalization, this has not always been the case. During the formative period of US labor consciousness (from the end of the Civil War until the First World War), the political alienation of labor was routinely challenged by workers who relied extensively (and illegally) on collective self-help in their pursuit of economic justice. With this method, labor achieved many gains—including the eight-hour workday and a federally guaranteed minimal wage. These welcomed developments attest to the power of worker militancy and collective action (Zinn, 1990b, 181).

## * NOTES *

1. Eric Foner notes, "In the first fifteen years of this century, the American Socialist party appeared to rival those in Europe, except the German, in mass support and prospects for future growth" (1984, 60).

2. A well-known exception occurred half a century *after* the Pullman Strike. In *Marsh v. Alabama* (1946) the Supreme Court ruled that a Jehovah's Witness could not be prevented from distributing religious literature on the streets of a company town. This holding was limited by *Hudgens v. National Labor Relations Board* (1976), which limits the First Amendment rights of people to speak or distribute literature on any private property that does not mimic the "functions" and "activities" of a public municipality, as did the company town in *Marsh*. In a related case, *Pruneyard Shopping Center v. Robins* (1980), the Supreme Court permitted the State of California to interpret its own state constitution to grant greater free speech protection to speakers on private property than those granted by the Federal Constitution. In other words, states may grant greater First Amendment protections than is guaranteed by the federal government.

3. Deep recurring recessions were a structural part of the US economy until the Great Depression, causing much labor unrest. For example, between 1881 and 1886, there were more than 3,000 strikes and over 1,000,000 strikers (Beud, 1983, 128). Between 1881 and 1905, there were 38,303 lockouts and strikes involving 199,954 businesses and 7,444,270 employees (Stewart, 1973, 154).

4. Big industry continues to enjoy the political and military support of the federal government. See Staples (2000).

5. This is the same governor who earlier pardoned the Haymarket anarchists and was not liked by the Cleveland Administration.

6. An important assumption I make is that a well-treated and well-paid workforce would be enthusiastic about its work and supportive of the industry. It is possible for organized labor to overreach itself and demand the adoption of nonsustainable standards; such action, however, would destroy their industry, and the workers would lose their benefits. Furthermore, I do not believe that every worker collectivity currently has the common good as its goal (eg, players' unions in organized sports and the Hollywood union system come to mind). Unions work best when they work toward systemic progressive change for all workers across the occupational spectrum.

7. Stat. 217 (1917). For a case study of this statute, see Sayer (1988). As evidence of the severity of this repression, Sayer reports a cartoon from the period depicting a socialist convention: A man seeking entrance to the convention is stopped by the doorman who demands evidence of his party identification–"show me your indictment" he requests (66).

8. Although I recognize that the specific visions of these labor activists may lack contemporary appeal (as they were for forms of socialism, anarchism, and communism), their presence in US society actively advanced the cause of social justice by making the concern of the poor and the dispossessed an essential part of national politics. As these activists vocally and passionately attempted to reinvent their communities, the larger national community caught a glimpse of its own exclusionary practices, and slowly began to grow more inclusive.

# CHAPTER 12

# LAW, COMMUNITY, RACISM, AND SLAVERY

An important argument in my vision of partisan criticism is that US Americans should be critical when examining their Constitution and the world order that has flowed from its influence. As discussed below, the Constitution sanctioned slavery and allows (even encourages) other kinds of injustice, particularly economic and environmental injustice.[1] US Americans, therefore, should be suspicious of their constitutional order, even rue it when it interferes with social justice. As difficult as it is for most of us to accept, the specific things to which US Americans take most pride—freedom, justice, and equality—are often ill-served by the US government.

This and the following chapter explores the nexus between and among community, race, and the law, highlighting an important process by which social division and hierarchy are codified within legal norms. First, it engages with a lingering trait in US society, often mistakenly referred to as "racial tension," and argues that the term conceals a racist ideology, downplaying the history of white racism (and classism), as well as the responsibility for that racism in constructing and reinforcing contemporary social inequality in the United States. As part of this analysis, the chapter argues that contemporary US society is less committed to social justice and equality than what our official myths suggest.

The second half of this chapter advances with a different line of reasoning. Moving beyond a partisan critique of contemporary racial and class relationships, it prepares readers for my engagement with legal philosophy that is crucial for understanding my analysis of slavery in Chapter 13, which analyzes a series of six North Carolina slave cases that exemplify the discourse codifying slavery as a legal institution within the constitutional state. Specifically, the latter half of this chapter introduces readers to the power of judicial discourse in constructing social injustice, providing a discussion of the Nuremberg trials, and reviewing the historical debate between natural law and legal positivism and its implications for partisan criticism. This discussion of the philosophy of law and its limitations is important because, as highlighted in Chapter 13, arguments from the philosophy of law played a central role in the codification of slavery. Such arguments also illustrate weaknesses in our current conceptions of democracy.

## ✶ THE TERM "RACIAL TENSION" IS MISLEADING ✶

What people frequently refer to as racial tension has always existed in the United States. With European colonization, there arrived individuals from a variety of nations who confronted a heterogeneous indigenous population. These Europeans—themselves bitterly divided along racial, class, and religious lines—fought each other as they fought and exterminated the Native population of North America, which numbered approximately 75 million prior to the arrival of the Europeans in the fifteenth century (Marger, 1997, 151). In addition, the Europeans soon imported slaves from Africa. The first Africans appeared in Virginia in 1619, and slavery attained a formal legal status after 1660 (Jordan, 1968). The earliest statute regarding the status of slavery in North America is *The Liberties of Massachusetts Colonie in New England*, promulgated in 1641.

In short, from the sixteenth century forward, the United States has seldom experienced racial peace or social justice. Indeed, the history of North America, since Columbus, has been the history of state-sanctioned ethnic exploitation and genocide (Beaud, 1983). US Americans today are the heirs of perhaps the most egregious form of terrorism and brutality known to the modern world, Manifest Destiny. Fundamental to the United States' moral progress and to the much-needed humbling of the US character, is an acknowldgment and repudiation of this past. Even more important, however, is that, in our repudiation of the past, we repudiate that part of our culture that causes us to remain an intolerant people today. During the Vietnam War, Philip Slater remarked:

> Americans have always been a people with marked genocidal proclivities: our systematic extermination of the Indian, the casual killing of American blacks during and after slavery, and our indifference to dropping an atomic bomb on a large civilian populace—we are, after all, the *only* people ever to have used such a weapon—reflect this attitude. We

have long had a disturbing tendency to see nonwhites . . . as nonhuman, and to act accordingly. (1970, 33)

Since most US Americans refuse to acknowledge this "proclivity," we have not changed much since the Vietnam War. Moreover, since the end of the Cold War, the United States has grown increasingly bold in making life difficult for non-White people around the globe. In light of such behavior, the term racial tension is misleading, suggesting a mutuality of wrongdoing. A rope has tension when parties of near equal force pull on either end. Racial tension, therefore, implies that African Americans, as well as Anglo Americans, are equally responsible for the travesties committed against the African American. Similarly, the term racial tension implies that the Native Americans and other ethnic groups bear responsibly for the sufferings that White people have inflicted on them.

Such sentiment is insulting. African Americans, Native Americans, and others (such as the Vietnamese) were, first and foremost, victims. Few people would use the term racial tension to describe the climate of Europe in the early twentieth century, in which Jews were subjected to genocidal anti-Semitism. European Jews made an extended effort to assimilate into the larger European society and were surprised by the hatred that was directed against them prior to and during the Second World War. The Jews were not "pulling on the end of a rope," contributing to a tension in European society.

From a partisan perspective, what US Americans label as racial tension and use to describe US history is nothing more than ethnic privilege and exploitation, as well as the lingering effects of genocide. The claim that the Europeans came to the New World with the intent of slaughtering, enslaving, and plundering is undisputed; these settlers were little more than glorified (and successful) oppressors who have never been held accountable for the unfathomable suffering they created. Such an accounting is in order. As the privileged today are the heirs of such brutality, they will remain morally tainted by the actions of their ancestors until they learn to renounce their privileges and the deleterious policies that uphold them. Partisan criticism encourages all of us to examine our responsibility for the continuation of the current order, reminding us that, as US Americans, we are all responsible for the actions of our government and its policies, and it is up to us to accept agency in initiating change. If we do not work to create a more just world and simply consume without care for the cost of our consumption, we are no different from Christopher Columbus. Like him, we plunder the world and condemn our fellow humans to a life of suffering and deprivation.

The world is profoundly diseased in a variety of ways: economically, ecologically, morally, and politically. Although barbarity and suffering existed prior to Western conquest of the New World, the Europeans (and later the US Americans) made barbarity and suffering a *permanent condition* in what we now call the developing world. Thus, the Western world, in particular the United States, is to blame for many current world conditions of poverty and injustice. Moreover, the same Western forces that created our diseased world remain and prevent the world's healing process; that is, the doctor is systematically poisoning the patient. For health and balance to return to the planet, the Western nations must atone (through action) for more than 500 years of colonialism, slavery, and genocide (see Chomsky, 1993). As a result of Western conquest, the non-Western world has internalized what many partisan critics identify as the "white man's disease."

In the second half of the twentieth century, many non-Western people in the developing world have embraced some of the worst aspects of the Western colonial and racist past. Much of this is the result of inheriting the deleterious psychological and cognitive structures of Western militarism and environmental degradation. Specifically, what we now call the "developing world" was constructed by and, in the image of, its colonizers. Because of colonial and neocolonial influence, the developing world is fundamentally different from that which existed prior to colonization, in which poverty, disease, malnutrition, starvation, and mass murder were largely unknown.

Although the colonial powers have withdrawn from their former colonies, the deleterious cultural epistemes of the colonizing nations remain, embodied in neocolonial relationships that must end so that the developing world can heal. The bloodshed that followed nearly every effort of decolonization in Africa, Asia, and the Middle East was the result of epistemic residues of colonization, as well as outright manipulation by the former colonial powers. Given the success of the colonizing nations in demonstrating the effectiveness of being brutal, selfish, exploitative, and manipulative of local ethnic differences to gain economic advantage, most postcolonial governments adopted these tactics; many are scarcely more just than they were under colonial rule. Western society is wrong for blaming these societies for creating their own conditions, and a goal of partisan criticism is to make this point clear. Poverty and social injustice in places such as Africa and Asia are almost exclusively the result of Western influences (Singer, 1993, 218–246).

The Western nations, in particular, the United States, have largely refused to acknowledge that their wealth and privileges are the result of historical and contemporary theft, mass murder, and slavery. For hundreds of years, wealth in the world has flowed from the southern regions of the globe to the northern, and continues to do so (Chomsky, 1998). In the name of a greater vision of humanity, partisan critics work toward stopping this injustice by writing and teaching on these issues. In asserting the claim that the West is responsible for the condition of the developing world, I am not engaging in unbalanced representation; rather, I am simply restating an accepted historical fact. To deny this history is to curtail the possibilities of our achieving a just future. The horror of the past speaks to me as clearly as the horror of the present. Furthermore, to deny our past as a community embodying a Western perspective is demeaning to ourselves as members of a self-professed moral community. In short, the denial of our past causes Western culture to be grounded in a lie that hinders our future moral growth. Many US Americans (as well as many Europeans) believe that Western civilization is a "higher" civilization than all others. Evidence for this misconception is grounded in Western affluence and global dominance. This dominance fuels the Western ego, mystifies the past, subverts the notion of social justice, and impedes the developing world's effort to overcome its perceived sense of inferiority.

## Have US Americans Progressed?

In some respects, US society has progressed. The world in which US Americans live today is less cruel than in the past. Still, the moral faults of this nation remain pronounced. The economic and social systems of the United States systemically marginalize, povertize, and criminalize minorities, in particular African Americans (DeSena, 1994). To rectify this condition, the African American community is entitled to intervention by US society to bring them and other minorities out of poverty. In other words, we have a moral obligation as a nation to balance the social system by ensuring that African Americans have a comparable standard of living with the Anglo community. This is just one step in the larger social reorganization in the United States that social justice requires.

In a well-publicized polemic, David Horowitz (2001) argued that because many contemporary US Americans have no genealogical connection to the crimes of slavery or were themselves victims of some injustice, the United States has no responsibility for past crimes. I reject Horowitz's argument. By such reasoning, past crimes cannot be addressed, as systemic cultural crimes and injustices seldom have roots in any one particular individual and, thus, must be addressed at the societal level.[2] As the system itself unleashes and rewards cruelty and corruption, everyone who participates with that system shares in the collective guilt. Unless individuals make a conscious effort to act humanely to change the system and work toward social justice, their uncritical compliance in the system is an indictment of their moral culpability (Singer, 1993, 222).

For a brief period of time in the late 1960s, Americans seemed to grasp the truth of that sentiment and many actively worked toward social justice for the African American community as well as for other marginalized or oppressed groups. However, since the late 1970s, US Americans have witnessed the slow erosion and deinstitutionalization of essential ameliorative programs that were enacted to redress racial inequality and to create a truly inclusive society (a graphic example appears in Moran, 2000).

Two important Supreme Court cases accelerating the trend away from affirmative action are *Regents of University of California v. Bakke* (1978), holding racial quota systems in college admissions that reserve seats for minority applicants unconstitutional, and *Richmond v. J.A. Croson Co.* (1980); holding that race-based attempts to help previously disadvantaged racial minorities are subject to strict scrutiny review. Both cases represent the legal position that any race-based classification, even those clearly motivated by the worthy desire to enhance minority opportunity through affirmative action, will face a strong presumption of unconstitutionality (which is exceedingly difficult to rebut).[3] Through the 1990s, these attacks on minorities and poor people via challenges to affirmative action included frontal (and successful) assaults on the welfare state.[4] Thus, with notable irony, the United States expressed a sustained national commitment to ridding itself of centuries of ingrained racism while, at the same time, it nurtured, and continues to nurture, a sustained political backlash against important polices that played a critical role in helping to make civil and human rights an actuality for many citizens ("Court Revives Diversity Issue in Michigan," 2004).

Part of this backlash may result from the fact that a significant part of our national commitment to address racism was motivated by reasons other than social justice (Dudziak, 1988). As a result of such backlash and other state-endorsed economic policies, the income gaps, mortality rate, and life chances for African Americans lag far behind Anglo Americans and have not greatly improved since the 1960s (Wilson, 1996; Wacquant, 2001). Simply, the form of *de jure* equality (while essential) has not brought about *de facto* equality or any significant degree of unified nationality between African Americans and Anglo Americans.

The United States is a society that remains bitterly divided on race, making its normative goals of equality before the law and in the marketplace sadly unfulfilled (Cose, 1993). African Americas are not the only group to suffer from this inequality; other minority groups have also suffered significant injustice as the result of US normative legal culture. The following examples were taken from a much larger pool of heinous legal decisions in the United States:

- *Johnson v. M'Intosh* (1823)—The US Supreme Court held constitutional the forced dispossession of Native American lands by the US government.

- *State v. Rhodes* (1868)—A state Supreme Court decision constitutionalizing the husband's common law privilege to beat his wife.

- *Fong Yue Ting v. United States* (1893)—The US Supreme Court held constitutional the Chinese Exclusion Acts of 1882, calling for the incarceration and forced deportation of racial Chinese during the late nineteenth and early twentieth centuries.

- *Korematsu v. United States* (1944)—The US Supreme Court held constitutional Franklin Roosevelt's forced internment of US Americans of Japanese ancestry during the Second World War.

* *Bowers v. Hardwick* (1986)—The US Supreme Court held that state antisodomy laws did not violate the constitutional rights of homosexuals and that the right of privacy did not extend to homosexual relationships.

* *In The Matter of Allison D. v. Virginia M.* (1991)—A state appellate court decision declaring that a lesbian coparent is not a legal parent and cannot have standing to seek visitation rights with the child she coraised since birth when the two women ended their relationship.

These cases are not atypical, particularly for those decided prior to the 1960s. Their existence represents a trend in our legal system that is often overlooked by the majority of citizens in the United States who selectively celebrate US law. I realize that I am open to the charge that I selectively condemn US law. Before I attended law school, this charge might have been accurate. After studying law, however, I inductively reached the conclusion that the majority of what I studied was morally appalling: A great deal of the US legal system serves the interest of the wealthy and privileged and is hostile toward nearly everyone else. Instead of contributing to a progressive society, most US law in fact does the opposite. My point is that law is no less law for doing so, as there is no necessary connection between law and morality. For example, to assert that the US is good because it is a society "governed by laws, not men" is no more a logical or moral claim than to assert that Cuban society is bad because its leader is a communist. Consequently, no individual has any moral obligation to respect any law simply because of the law's formal status. Laws are only as good as the ends they serve. Missing from US law (and found in much Cuban law) is a compassionate and profound humanism. Law divorced from humanism and compassion is the most subtle and insidious form of tyranny. Stated differently:

> Democracy is not measured solely in the political sphere, and cannot be reduced only to the participation of the people in elections . . . it means participation by the people in political, economic, social, and cultural affairs. The more the people participate in such matters, the more democratic they will be . . . . [D]emocracy neither begins nor ends with elections. (Sandinista Liberation Front, 1986, 227)

Nor, I would add, does democracy end with the establishment of a quasipermanent congressional overclass and the legal order constructed by such a class.

## ✷ THE JUDICIARY AND THE POWER OF DISCOURSE ✷

Much has been written about the rhetoric of judicial opinions (eg, LaRue, 1995; Sarat and Kearns, 1996). An important theme in this literature involves the power of courts to enunciate "proper" responses to social and political (ie, rhetorical) exigencies.[5] An important part of this power involves the declarative tone of judicial decisions (Ferguson, 1990). Such power helps to modify the out-of-court relationships among people who internalize the moral authority of the judiciary. The declarative tone of the court contributes to moral certainty by demanding immediacy and resolution and by denying its own fallibility. By insisting on immediate resolution, judicial rhetoric "resists mystery, complexity, revelation, and even exploration" (Ferguson, 210).

Courts "sell" their judgment by forcing a language of certainties on a malleable social world, creating the illusion of truth and justice. As the law rests authoritatively on categorical reasoning and as most legal decisions are categorically correct in that they are based primarily on formal deductive reasoning (Gardner, 1993), the public is encouraged to agree with the court's conclusions because most nonlawyers lack the insight (or even a proper suspicion of the judiciary) to question how the premises that the court considers important are constructed. The basic premises of judicial reasoning are difficult to question because these premises are either previously decided statements of law (which are difficult to interrogate) or because judges create their own premises and tailor their narratives of pertinent facts and their legal interpretation to support these premises. The resulting legal "certainties"—the end product of legal reasoning—are often situated in unquestioned moral certainties in the minds of judges, which become the frames through which judges conceptualize human re-lationships.

Most people, including lawyers, have access only to the law through a fossilized text (the codification of the law in a decided case) and are not privy to the give-and-take politics of the actual legal context that created that abstract decision. Nor are the US people privy to the negotiations and debates that appellate judges engage in with litigants or other interested parties from behind closed doors as they wrestle with the difficulties of formulating public policy. In short, judicial rhetoric is as moralistic as it is constitutive, reducing the legal debate on an issue into a definitive narrative of judgment. As Ferguson notes, the product of this process, the judgment, "guides a general cultural understanding of the original event for consumption beyond the courtroom" (1990, 211). In particular:

> These acts of transference necessarily work to transpose the scene of a particular experience into an acceptable figuration of collective life. Every step of the process requires an unavoidable series of simplifications. Judgment must reduce an event to an incident and further reduce incident to a narrative about acceptable behavior. That is its mission. Everything about the enterprise, including the listener-reader of the judicial opinion, welcomes the declarative tones that make it possible. (Ferguson, 1990, 211)

In rendering a decision, judges effectively intertwine the subjectivity of the defendant with narrative, ideology, and the biases of wealth and privilege. These decisions serve to simplify the complexity of human social relations to reinforce the specific social order that both authorizes and serves as a stage for performance of that decision. In this way, legal violence and institutional prejudice become accepted because the violence and bias of the law appear to be nothing more than law itself. Put succinctly, a "primary function . . . of the law concerns the means by which command of the gun becomes ethically sanctioned" (Genovese, 1974, 25).

Reifying social injustice under the legitimacy of law makes racial and class oppression acceptable and elevates the marginalized condition of victims to a status akin to the natural order. The more natural social injustice appears, the more similar that injustice becomes to other "unquestioned" self-evident truths (such as "life," "liberty," and "property") on which the US "way of life" depends. In more rhetorical terms, as Josina Makau and David Lawrence note, judicial reasoning is important because the legal system is full of "inventional strategies [that] both reflect and help create cultural norms" (1994, 191). We should always keep in mind that such norms are reinforced by the total coercive power of the State, and that law, as currently experienced, is fundamentally situated on a field of "pain and death" (Cover, 1986, 1601).

## ✶ NATURAL LAW, POSITIVE LAW, AND SLAVERY ✶

Having argued that the judiciary speaks on behalf of a social order that they themselves have created and normalized, this section turns to a more detailed discussion of the philosophy of law. The purpose of this discussion is to help readers to understand how philosophical questions played an important role in the judicial rhetoric of slavery, which is exemplified in the preceeding chapter. For the analysis in the next chapter to be fully comprehensible, I must engage in this important prefatory discussion.

Because African slavery differed in significant ways from previous forms of Western slavery (particularly in its severity and in its caste structure) and because African slavery differed from accepted forms of indentured servitude that were practiced early in the North American colonies, an extended effort had to be made by the Southern states to define/create a new master/slave relationship. Simply, the slave identity of Africans forcefully brought to North America had to be rhetorically constructed for it to have legal significance in the law. As Thomas Ross notes, "The best of the rhetoricians [judges] constructed exquisitely horrific rhetorical structures to justify choices that society has since discredited" (1990, 7).

Slavery can be understood as involving what Eugene D. Genovese identified as the "hegemonic function of the law" (1974, 25). In Southern slave society, according to Genovese, "the law, even narrowly defined as a system of institutionalized jurisprudence, constituted a principle vehicle for the hegemony of the ruling class" (1974, 26). The law in the context of slavery was not a passive or reflective force in society; rather, the law constituted an active "partially autonomous force" (1974, 26). The effect of this hegemony was "to assure people that their particular consciences can be subordinated—indeed, morally must be subordinated—to the collective judgment of society" (27). In other words, the judiciary through its declared legal opinions played a critical role in constructing the slave persona of Africans in the United States and of effectuating systemic white control over them.

The judiciary, however, faced a significant problem as it sought to reify the hegemony of the white race. That problem was the concept of natural law. Although the concept of natural law has ancient origins in Western culture, the modern expression of natural law became politically and culturally poignant as a result of the European Enlightenment. In practical terms, natural law was an important animating ideology for both the US and French Revolutions. When the leaders of these revolutions grounded their agitation in the moral mantle of natural law, they energized an idea that has, in the words of Kathleen Jamieson, "haunted man since the inception of civilization" (1973, 235). This point is particularly true in North America, where the ideology of the US Revolution clashed fundamentally with the constitutionally codified practice of slavery. The remainder of this chapter engages this disparity to expand our understanding of the rhetoric of marginalization.

As Jamieson notes, the appeal of natural law is part of a human psychological need "to believe in a just and ordered universe" (235). As with religious appeals, people who suffer often respond to the experience of suffering or injustice by making an appeal to some idealistic force above the contingent world to mediate on their behalf. Such an appeal is an effort by humans to redescribe their powerlessness. Because human beings are at the mercy of the natural world, they have invented a God figure to make sense of and remedy their pain and suffering. Against human jurisprudence, which has historically been corruptible and self-serving of elitism (for example, *Justinian's Institutes*, 1987), the appeal to natural law petitions for relief in an "ever-just, unchangeable law above the law" (Jamieson, 237). Since natural law is argued to be unchangeable, the person who evokes such law "appeals to self-evident principles that can be known by all humans" (Frank, 1991, 263). For instance, Thomas Jefferson justified breaking colonial ties to England in *The Declaration of Independence* by appealing to the "Laws of Nature" and to "Nature's God" (*The US Constitution: And Fascinating Facts About It*, 1997, 45). These entities, argued Jefferson, "entitled" the colonies to independence. Such independence was further warranted because God granted people "unalienable Rights" to pursue life, liberty, and happiness. As Jefferson asserted, such propositions are "self-evident" (45). The role of the state is to protect and to advance these rights.

Implicit in Jefferson's argument is the assumption that there exists a necessary connection between law and morality. Law, which derives from divine order or natural rights, is moral by virtue of its *a priori* status as part of the inherent order of things. Law, in this sense, is similar to the law of gravity—it is a force whose truth is its influence. Other types of laws, such as human laws, are lesser laws. These laws can also be moral, but their moral grounding depends upon the higher order of divine or natural law. In Jefferson's narrative, state laws are only moral to the extent that they "secure these Rights" of life, liberty, and happiness (in the more pragmatic Federal Constitution, "Happiness" is replaced with "Property"). To the extent that government fails to protect the ability of individuals to seek these goods, the government betrays the "social contract" (in Rousseau's words; 1993), and becomes a nonlegal entity. Under such circumstances, people assume the right "to alter or to abolish it, and to institute new Government" (Jefferson, 45). The colonists presented the King of England with this reasoning, along with a list of grievances documenting England's transgressions of natural law, to justify their moral right to break from the authority of Britain. Such rhetoric, although an inspiring rallying cry for the Revolution, later presented practical problems for the Southern judiciary who wanted to deny black people the right to evoke natural law in an argument for emancipation.

As illustrated in the next chapter, the Southern judiciary countered the argument of natural law by evoking the argument that, within a democracy, positive law trumped natural law. The remainder of this chapter reviews the volatile debates surrounding conflicting influences of natural law and positive law, as well as reject the rhetoric of both in favor of a pragmatic critique of social injustice.[6] This pragmatic concern rejects metaphysical and positivist rationales and rests on the assumption that a socialist concern for the well-being and equality of all people is preferable to our current system in which individual interests (eg, greed and selfishness) become the basis for the social, political, and legal orders.

Major theorists in the history of natural law theory and legal positivism (ie, positive law) include St. Thomas Aquinas, John Finnis, John Austin, Jeremy Bentham, and H.L.A. Hart. Common to these theorists is the question of whether there is a necessary connection between law and morality. Natural law theorists postulate a necessary connection between law and morality for law to "really" be law.[7] "Morality" is defined as some universally true ethical position, akin to Kant's moral imperative or to a religious ethic. Natural law theorists seek to identify specific legal limitations and principles governing a legal system—such as the protection of private property against government appropriation—and to elevate this protection to the status of eternal truth. Governments that violate this law offend the natural order of society and will suffer the consequences. In short, for laws to be deemed sound, they must be traced to some higher principle that is unchanging. God, nature, or "reason" may ground such a principle. Antithetical to this reasoning are arguments from circumstance (Finnis, 1994). This reasoning parallels the "argumentative forms" articulated by Richard Weaver, as discussed in the next chapter. For natural law theorists, the important task for government is to design ontologically correct laws and to apply those laws in such a way as to render a "correct" judgment. For example, implicit in the argument that "slavery is wrong" is the assumption that no contingencies warrant a violation of some sacred freedom inherent in being a human being.

The legal positivists, on the other hand, maintain that there is no necessary connection between law and morality.[8] As stated by John Austin, "The existence of law is one thing; its merit or demerit is another. Whether it be or be not is one enquiry; either it be or be not conformable to an assumed standard, is a different inquiry" (1995, 157). Legal positivists claim that any law is law, including the law of slavery. Such law may be repulsive, but to deny its legality would be to ignore the fact that someone such as John Brown who, on October 16, 1859, led a force of eighteen men and occupied a US armory in Virginia in his attempt to inspire slave revolts in the South, could be adjudicated a criminal and executed for violating the law. Although contemporary society can honor John Brown as a hero and respect him for his crime, the fact remains to positivists that the government was not "mistaken" in condemning him. Simply, the law is no less law merely because people find it morally reprehensible. With such reasoning, legal positivists urge society to challenge unjust laws, even to break them, as they remind society that no law *per se* demands a duty of compliance other than the "duty" that can be materially coerced by fear or force.

Rather than having some grounding in a notion of "unchanging human goods," laws are considered to be the result of social conventions such as "commands," "social rules," or other norms that are not necessarily moral norms. Jeremy Bentham and Austin both argued that the law is the command of power by a sovereign and that the idea of law is content neutral.[9] Austin, for example, rejected English Jurist William Blackstone's assertion that no human law that conflicts with God's law is obligatory or binding. Austin argued that human laws do not lose their authority when they conflict with divine law (often interpreted as natural law). Such laws, in fact, exist and are continually enforced by the courts:

> Suppose an act innocuous, or positively beneficial, be prohibited by the sovereign under the penalty of death; if I commit this act, I shall be tried and condemned, and if I object to the sentence, that it is contrary to the law of God, who has commanded that the human lawgivers shall not prohibit acts which have no evil consequences, the Court of Justice will demonstrate the inconclusiveness of my reasoning by hanging me up, in pursuance of the law of which I have impugned the validity. (Austin, 158)

Between these two theories of law, legal positivism is the more persuasive legal theory for me. As critical theorists frequently argue, there is no "God's eye view" from which society can ascertain any moral truths, such as those necessary to ground an ahistorical view of morality (Rorty, 1979). Simply, there is nothing to see "correctly"; there are only shifting webs of contingency. This position does not make critical theorists moral skeptics, at least insofar as that term connotes a negative or irrational quality. As discussed below, questions of morality are extremely important in thinking about law, but they are important in ways that are different from an essentialist search for moral certainty, understanding, or philosophical clarity. Notions of certainty, understanding, and clarity are important ends for scientific research, but they are less useful or attainable in the partisan criticism advocated in this book (as well as for most humanistic endeavors). Similar to Vaclav Havel's sense of politics, such criticism derives "from a strong and utterly personal sense of responsibility for the world, a politics deriving from the awareness that none of us—as an individual—can save the world as a whole, but that each of us must behave as though it were in his power to do so" (1997, 112).

Legal positivism, however, is an incomplete system of legal philosophy. Although the issue of the separability of law and morality may be important for an academic discussion of the "nature" of law, the practice of legal criticism does not depend on theoretical orthodoxy. Pragmatic approaches to legal criticism are viable. A social critic of law can acknowledge that human morality is contingent and unconnected to legal norms, and, at the same time, recognize that humans impose moral norms. These moral norms can serve as a ground for which the morality of a law can be judged. Under this view, slavery is wrong, but not because slavery is an "unnatural" human social position or because slavery displeases God. Rather, slavery is wrong because slavery is hurtful, degrading, selfish, and repugnant, leading to militarism, heightened internal security, and to the povertization of the non-slave labor community. Slavery, in a pragmatic sense, is counterproductive to a world in which peace, prosperity, mutuality, social stability, and interdependence between all people should be considered normative values.[10]

## Pragmatic Legal Criticism: Nuremberg

The punishment of Nazi war criminals following the Second World War provided a high-profile case in which legal theorists were able to study the separability of law thesis. Natural law was central to the legal theory of the prosecution. The prosecution had to rely on natural law theory because most of the actions of the defendants were recognized as being legal under the judicial system of the Third Reich. In fact, the Nazi defendants actively evoked logical positivism in defense of their actions. This defense was rejected, and natural law theorists proclaimed a victory over logical positivism. As argued in this section, reliance on natural law to condemn the defendants was misguided. Although the Nazi leadership clearly deserved punishment, there is significant reason to doubt the motives and innocence of the governments sitting in judgment of the defendants. When contemplating the issue of justice, we should remember that the power to punish is not the same as the power to effectuate justice.

The fact that many hundreds of Nazis responsible for horrible atrocities were not punished due to their utility in fighting the Soviet Union and advancing US military science indicates that the Allies (minus the USSR) were not as disgusted with the Nazis as the public discourse surrounding the trials suggests. This, along with atrocities committed by the Allies themselves before, during, and after the war, suggests that punishing the Nazis had less to do with justice and more to do with justifying the victors' political priorities. Thus, the Nuremberg trials were disingenuous, undermining the ground on which an appeal to natural law is situated. Specifically, by cloaking their expression of power in the language of natural justice, the Allied victors created a self-serving good versus evil dichotomy. A person can be steadfastly antifascist and still argue that the Second World War was not a battle between "good" and "evil." The defeat of Fascism was necessary, but not because the Fascists were morally wrong and the Allies morally right. Rather, compared to the Allies, the Fascists were more vicious, cruel, and reprehensible. The fight against Fascism was not grounded in "justice," but in necessity. For many millions of people, living on the same planet with the Fascists was simply not possible. People who desire to attach the label of "evil" to the practices of the Nazis should be prepared to make similar arguments about their own societies. The Nazis were different only in the degree to which they practiced their cruelty and intolerance. Because people typically do not engage critically with the selfishness and crimes of their own society, their natural law discourse rings hollow.

The Allies did not need a theory of justice to punish the Nazis, as much Nazi behavior invited retribution and vengeance.[11] The problem is not that the Allies punished some Nazis but that they willfully let many others go unpunished for political reasons. The same is true for the Allied treatment of the Japanese leadership during the war. Very few of the Japanese, who were as cruel and murderous as the Nazis in their treatment of the Chinese and other Asian peoples they conquered, were punished, as most were enlisted in the new struggle against the mainland Chinese communists who emerged from the war in control of China (as well as the communists who controlled North Korea).

In short, people should offer critiques of specific laws based on standards that offend their moral imaginations, and not on some abstract moral standard or legal principle. Along with Austin, Bentham, and Hart, I urge critics to use language that people can rally behind to enact pragmatic and imaginative visions of social justice (eg, Nussbaum, 1995). These visions of social justice reject an allegiance to metaphysical or legalistic claims. The following chapter provides an example of this type of pragmatic (and partisan) social criticism and alternative legal reasoning.

## * NOTES *

1. For instance, the United States routinely rejects international efforts to improve the world (the most recent examples of which include the rejection of the Kyoto Protocol, the International Criminal Court, the Biological Weapons Convention, the United Nations' Action on the Trade in Small Arms and Light Weapons, the Convention Against Child Labor, and the withdrawal from the 1972 Anti-Ballistic Missile Treaty). Domestically, the constitutional system has helped to cause the United States to consistently rank *last* among the industrialized nations in financial parity among its citizens, educational quality, access to health care, social security protections, voter turnout rates, and environmental protections, among other things (Sklar, 1997).

2. Rather than to support reparations per se, which would benefit specific individuals and would be temporary, I support a government-sponsored commitment to eradicating poverty in the United States, which would disproportionately benefit African Americans and all minorities.

3. My analysis here is not inconsistent with *Gratz v. Bollinger* and *Grutter v. Bollinger*, a pair of surprising 2003 decisions in which the Supreme Court preserved affirmative action from what many observers thought would be its death knell. In these cases, the Court ruled in favor of the University of Michigan Law School that race can be one of many factors considered by colleges when selecting students. However, the Court also ruled that more formulaic and generic approaches such as those of the University's undergraduate admissions program (which used a point system, rating students and awarding additional points to minorities) were impermissible. The important factor for the Court is that schools provide "individualized consideration" of applicants. This means, in effect, that while the Court is willing to help minority students at the often elite upper ends of the educational hierarchy (i.e., graduate and professional school), it makes it more difficult for minority students at the front end, where they are more likely to need help entering the system.

4. Although not exclusively racial in motivation, the attacks on welfare assume a racial dimension when considering the racialization (as well as the feminization) of poverty in this country. See Claude (1986).

5. An exigence occurs when important assumptions grounding the status quo are made problematic or disrupted, destabilizing a specific community. The exigence necessitates a response from social elites who must mediate the threats and opportunities provided by the disruption to preserve or reentrench their hold on society. For a discussion of "exigency," see Bitzer (1968) and Vatz (1973).

6. Pragmatism, as I evoke it here, is "an invitation to walk away from a lot of old philosophical questions (What is the nature of human beings? What is the movement of history?) and to substitute questions about what to do next." (Rorty, 1998b, 136)

7. Early expressions of natural law theory appear in Aristotle (1998) and Aquinas (2000). Modern discussions of natural law appear in Fuller (1969), Robert P. George (1992), and Weinreb (1987).

8. The most important contemporary expositor of legal positivism is H.L.A. Hart, 1958; 1997.

9. Bentham's theory of legal positivism is articulated in several works, including "A Fragment on Government," "Of Promulgation of the Laws," "Principles of Morals and Legislation," and "Anarchical Fallacies." Many of these arguments can be found in Bentham (1996).

10. This list is not exclusive of the many other reasons why slavery (as well as class oppression, in general) should always be rejected.

11. Foucault's theory of justice is relevant here. See Foucault (1980).

# CHAPTER 13

## DEFINITIONAL ASSUMPTIONS AND DIFFERENTIAL ARGUMENTS IN THE CONSTRUCTION OF THE LAW OF SLAVERY IN NORTH CAROLINA

This chapter explores the North Carolina Supreme Court's rhetoric of definition and constitutive discourse, providing an analysis of six legal decisions, 1801–1849, that simultaneously reified slavery as the total subjection of the slave and protected slaves against specific forms of egregious treatment. Throughout these cases, the court articulated an evolving position that ranged from defining slaves as having no status to a status akin to children. These cases address an important issue existing in North Carolina during the period of slavery. Although the judiciary reasoned that slaves should be denied legal protection so as to better effectuate the "pure" state of slavery, the Court also realized that such an institution conflicted with other important social goals, such as the protection of private property, public security, and the preservation of the slave. Thus, over time, judges were pressured to modify the law of slavery and the definition of the slave persona to allow for constraints to be placed on the master and the white society that interacted with slaves.

These cases have been selected for two reasons. First, the discourse of the judges in these examples is exceedingly rich with constitutive rhetoric, inviting critical analysis. Second, the cases themselves are important in the history of slavery (Genovese, 1974; Schiller, 1992). As Reuel Schiller explains, the "conflicting obligations facing the law—and the judges who made and interpreted it—are particularly apparent in North Carolina, due to the ambiguous role slavery played in that state's economy and society" (1992, 1208). The source of the ambiguity surrounding the role of slavery in North Carolina society stemmed from the state legislature, which did not articulate clearly the social relationship between slaves and the white population. In the absence of such stipulation, the North Carolina judiciary had more responsibility than those of other state jurisdictions to define the social relationship between slaves and their white masters. Studying the legal discourse of this particular court allows access to a special forensic space that was unique and infused with a heightened symbolic, political, and constitutive significance.[1]

In what follows, this chapter reviews the politics of definition as derived from Richard Weaver. Weaver, himself a Southern apologist (although not a racist), offers a theory of rhetoric that is elitist and essentialist in ways that parallel the thinking and reasoning of the court in these cases; thus, there is a certain parallelism between Weaver's theory of definition and the practical application of the slavery argument as exemplified in the court cases. Intermingled with my discussion of Weaver's theory is a partisan critique and an explanation of his theory's ideological assumptions. Extending from Brian McGee's observation that "definition may be used to great effect by those whose cause we now find contemptible" (1999, 143), I follow my discussion of Weaver's theory with an extended analysis of judicial definitional reasoning in one jurisdiction's legal construction of slavery. The fact that slavery, as an institution, has now been discredited does not render such analysis anachronistic for partisan criticism. Rather, the repugnance of slavery to the modern psyche makes it all the more imperative that partisan critics explicate how mainstream injustices become institutionalized and normalized by judicial authority. Thus, my goal is to further an understanding of the power of constitutive discourse to marginalize groups of people and, thereby, reify an inequitable and oppressive social order (eg, Solomon, 1985). To this end, I elucidate important connections between discourse and power and highlight the need for critical, partisan analysis in such matters.

## ✶ RICHARD WEAVER AND THE POLITICS OF DEFINITION ✶

One of Weaver's most influential contributions to rhetorical theory is his argument that the manner by which an individual argues is often a better indicator of that person's values than his or her specific arguments. For example, Weaver argued that Abraham Lincoln was more conservative than the way he has been portrayed because of the argument types he utilized

(1985, 85–114). In developing this idea, Weaver postulated a typography of argument forms (genus and definition, similitude, cause and effect, and authority), each of which correlates with political and ethical norms and are hierarchically situated, with definition being the "highest" or most ethical form. As described by Weaver:

> The argument from definition . . . includes all arguments from the nature of the thing. Whether the genus is an already recognized convention, or whether it is defined at the moment by the orator, or whether it is left to be inferred from the aggregate of its species, the argument has a single postulate. The postulate is that there exist classes which are determinate and therefore predictable. In the ancient proposition of the schoolroom, "Socrates is mortal," the class of mortal beings is invoked as a predictable. Whatever is a member of the class will accordingly have the class attributes. (1985, 86)

Weaver, who assumed that political conservatives can best perceive the correct structure of the world and create policies to respect that structure, considered the argument from definition to be an expression of political conservatism.[2] In contrast, Weaver associates the argument from cause and effect with socialism and weak reasoning, because this argument form ignores the essential qualities of a thing and focuses instead on contingent fluxuations unmoored from essential (or "real") properties to which human society must conform. In a well-known passage, Weaver wrote:

> The most portentous general event of our time is the steady obliteration of those distinctions which create society. Rational society is the mirror of the logos, and this means that it has a formal structure which enables apprehension. The preservation of society is therefore directly linked with the recovery of true knowledge. For the success of our restoration it cannot be too often said that society and mass are contradictory terms and that those who seek to do things in the name of mass are the destroyers in our midst. If society is something which can be understood, it must have structure; if it has structure, it must have hierarchy; against this metaphysical truth the declamations of the Jacobins break in vain. (1984, 35)

The rhetorical and political importance of definition is grounded in Weaver's ontological view of truth; definition involves the power of the keen mind in comprehending the correct hierarchy in which any object can be described. The person using such arguments makes, in Weaver's words, the "highest order of appeal," which is to a thing's "unchanging essences or qualities" (1985, 112). In other words, definition draws its strength from an understanding of universal order, which, according to Weaver, "is a paradigm of essences, of which the phenomenology of the world is a sort of continuing approximation" (1985, 112). Thus, for Weaver, the argument from definition is ethical because, of all the argument forms, only the definitional form can capture the "permanent," the "universal," and the "essential," clearly demarcating that which is constant against that which is fleeting and ephemeral (1970, 212). For Weaver, such argument type involves a "philosophy of being" and ascribes to being the foundation of truth in a Platonic sense (1985, 87).

Although many of Weaver's arguments have appeal among modern conservatives, more liberal rhetorical theorists have taken issue with the "comprehensiveness" of the definitional argument assumed by Weaver. For example, Brian McGee argues that such comprehensiveness is nothing more than rhetorical selection, the general as transformed into immutable categories: "The act of definition isolates what might at the moment seem to be particularly important ideas or attributes of a concept, but those important ideas or attributes could be called into question in the future, when a different set of attributes seems more central to describing the term at hand" (1999, 153). Definitional arguments only appear to be truthful, as the appeal of the argument is grounded in the human propensity to assign a truth value to the defined terms encountered. This propensity is reinforced by an educational system that encourages students to "understand definitions as objectively true and right" (1999,153). Traditional education, as in the banking model, proceeds from the premise that authorities sanction knowledge; they offer definitions by which the world becomes known. Implicitly, such authority urges listeners to accept a certain factual reality "that must be taken as given and cannot be disputed" (1999, 154). Rote education and much professional training (including legal training) proceeds along this line.

Scholars are rightly suspicious of Weaver's claims. For instance, Brian McGee notes that "all definitions should be regarded as contingent and fluid categories that always are subject to revision and renegotiation" (1999, 142). Nevertheless, definitional arguments often serve a pragmatic role, a point accentuated in the work of Richard Rorty. As David Zarefsky notes, "To choose a definition is to plead a cause" (1986, 8). With this strategy, persuaders create knowledge and effectuate control over that which they describe. For Weaver, and for the North Carolina Supreme Court of 1801–1849, such control is the result of an understanding that codifies and cements social relationships. Because many white people believed that African people represented the uncontrollable passions of the primitive human, relations between them had to be carefully circumscribed and made explicit. Such positioning allowed comparison between the two races to establish categorical distinctions between them, to which a truth value then could be assigned. The tactic of definition was well suited for such delineation. As Weaver explains:

> Definition must see the thing in relation to other things, as that relation is expressible through substance, magnitude, kind, cause, effect, and other particularities. It is merely different expression to say that this is a view which transcends: perspective, detachment, and capacity to transcend are all requisites of him who would define . . . . (1985, 108)

Utilizing such tactics, the "transcendence" of the white race could be read into the text (legal, social, or otherwise) defining the two races as separate and hierarchically situated. To the extent that white people felt "brought down" or threatened by the African's presence in society, or "blood," as in the case of antimiscegenation laws (*Loving v. Virginia*, 1967), the so-called "primitive" state of the African needed discipline and control, as supplied by the institution of slavery. The more slaves in a community, the more volatile the situation for whites, and, thus, the greater the need for systemic control. For this reason, court opinions on slavery were complex rhetorical documents, having as much political as legal significance in constructing social relations between the two races.[3]

Two dimensions of the emerging law of slavery in North Carolina can be discerned in the following cases. The first involves how the law was evoked to control the type and manner of violence that could be inflicted upon slaves. When North Carolina began defining human beings as property with no legal persona, difficulties arose when the state sought to classify whites who assaulted the slaves of others and masters who brutally tortured and murdered their own slaves as criminals. This classification was problematic because, in principle, the subjection of slaves depended upon violence from slave owners and white society. In addition, the institution of slavery was threatened when masters acted barbarically, thus undermining the Southern myth of benign white paternalism. Moreover, social stability in North Carolina was threatened by the common practice of poor whites who randomly attacked slaves. Given these tensions, the court felt compelled to intervene and provide a rhetoric that delineated acceptable and unacceptable behavior.

The second dimension of African servitude involved the degree to which slaves could be held criminally responsible for protecting themselves against an unlawful or mortal assault. Here, the court faced a dilemma, related to its earlier efforts to outlaw certain assaults on slaves. If a class of corporal abuses against slaves were deemed impermissible, could a slave engage in self-protection when subjected to an unlawful assault by someone other than his or her master? Through the court's struggle over this question, three important implications can be discerned:

1) What responsibility do slaves have for protecting their master's property (ie, themselves)?

2) What are the physiological limitations of the law in suppressing the "animal nature" of slaves who attack a white person out of terror in order to preserve their lives?

3) If slaves have a legal responsibility for self-preservation in order to protect their owner's property, and if the law cannot prevent self-protection in the face of a slave's automatic responses, then what limits can be placed on the slave's right to self-protection in order to prevent slave solidarity?

Ultimately, the court's prohibition of specific cruelties and assaults against slaves was the result of fifty years of deliberation on such issues in the legal process of defining the parameters of slavery.

## ✶ DISCIPLINING WHITE VIOLENCE ✶

This section presents an analysis of *State v. Boon* (1801), *State v. Hale* (1823), and *State v. Mann* (1829). These three cases proposed that slaves had no rights and were subject to total suppression by their masters. Nevertheless, the court recognized that society had an interest in maintaining social peace. Therefore, unwarranted physical attacks against slaves by strangers were penalized on the assumption that they constituted an assault on the owner. In articulating this prohibition, the court had to advance through several layers of conceptualization. At first, the court defined the slave as being so utterly without humanity that it refused to enforce a statute criminalizing the murder of a slave by his or her master (*Boon*). The court, however, later realized that, by denying slaves any protection, the law exposed them to the predations of nonmasters, with significant economic consequences (*Hale*). By preventing such predations, however, the court cast doubt on whether the subjection of slaves was secure. The court, therefore, moved to reassert the need for total subjection (*Mann*).[4]

By tracing the evolution of the court's reasoning, this chapter encourages people to empathize with the tens of millions of African American slaves throughout the United States who were legally subjugated as a part of the constitutional order. Slavery was not an anomaly in an otherwise just society, just as inequality and poverty are not anomalies in an otherwise just economy. Although African Americans no longer suffer in precisely the same legal fashion, legal oppressions continue to exist for African Americans and for poor people everywhere.

## *State v. Boon* and the "Pure State of Slavery"

As slavery in North Carolina eventually grew subject to increased legal control and limitations, *Boon* is functional as a useful starting point for the evolution of the slave identity over the next forty years. Specifically, *Boon* advanced the rule that a master could kill his slave without cause. *Boon* is significant for two reasons. First, the court refused to enforce a state law enacted to protect slaves from murder by their masters. Second, the court confronted and distinguished the common law, which did not sanction slavery.[5] Both these actions were unusual because courts are obligated to apply legislative law unless such legislation is unconstitutional. In addition, courts, particularly during the early period of US history, generally followed the common law tradition. In rejecting these two important legal expectations, the court advanced its own vision of public policy, which viewed the slave and the slave relationship as existing outside of legal control.

Boon, a white slave owner, killed one of his slaves without cause and was indicted under a 1791 statute that had been enacted by the North Carolina legislature to prevent the wanton murdering of slaves. The court, however, would not enforce the statute and overturned Boon's murder conviction on the grounds that the statute was vague. The critical language of the 1791 statute read: "If any person shall be hereafter guilty of willfully and maliciously killing a slave, which offender shall upon the first conviction thereof be adjudged guilty of murder, and shall suffer the same punishment as if he had killed a freeman, any law, usage or custom to the contrary notwithstanding" (*State v. Boon*, 104). The court was confused by this ostensibly clear language because the legal standards for analyzing the act of homicide—when done by a white or black person or done to a white or black person—were too variant for the statute to make sense. Enforcing this law would eviscerate the minute distinctions in status, rank, and race on which the larger legal apparatus depended.

The court then dismissed the English common law (which expressly prohibited slavery), holding that it was irrelevant to issues of slavery in the newly independent state of North Carolina.[6] This rejection of the common law was unusual for a court at the beginning of the nineteenth century, because the judiciary was ideologically, conceptually, and historically grounded in the authority of the common law. To dismiss the common law's rejection of slavery, the court differentiated conditions of slavery. The court took the formally unitary concept and splintered it conceptually, arranging the pieces hierarchically. Slavery, thereafter, no longer had a singular value. Although the original value of the word remained in theory, in practice the court focused on the new meaning as being the legally relevant meaning (for an elaboration of this tactic, see Wallace, 1989, 111).

This dissociation proceeded in two steps. First, the court acknowledged the prohibition against slavery in the common law, as reflected in a well-known passage by William Blackstone, who wrote that "liberty is so deeply implanted in the English Constitution, that the moment a slave lands there, he falls under the protection of the laws, and so far becomes a free man" (quoted in *State v. Boon*, 106). Second, the court stretched the concept of slavery so as to formally respect Blackstone's rule, while reaching a contrary conclusion. The court reasoned that, if a slave were carried to England and if there were no understanding that he or she was being brought to England for the purpose of freeing him or her, the common law would not protect that slave "because a slave in a *pure* state of slavery, has no rights" (107, emphasis added). By differentiating between these two conditions of slavery—one "pure," which existed in North Carolina, and one tainted by the intervention of positive law—the court created a unique space for slavery in North Carolina existing outside legal authority. The hierarchy the court construed privileged the "pure" essence of slavery over the antecedent imposition of positive law:

> In some countries where slavery has existed, laws have been made from time to time, ameliorating its condition; the power of taking away their lives, or cruelly treating them, has sometimes been restrained: these restraints, we find, were the consequence of positive laws: they did not exist before these laws imposed them; they were unknown in a pure state of slavery. (*State v. Boon*, 107)

The slaves of North Carolina, being "pure," were thus immune from any effort by the positive law to ameliorate their condition, including laws intended to protect them from being senselessly murdered by a sadistic master. Such law, although formally existing on paper, did not affect the essence of the slave's servitude. As a result of this reasoning, the court was able to conclude that slaves "in this country possess no such rights; their condition is more abject; they are not parties to our constitution; it was not made for them" (*State v. Boon*, 108). As a categorical proposition, slaves were removed from being objects of legal protection; they existed outside of the constitutional authority of the legislature to regulate.[7] On these grounds, Boon's conviction in the lower court was unlawful.

As noted above, *Boon* stood for the proposition that masters had a special status outside of the normal legal structure and could not be held legally accountable for mistreating their slaves. This notion, however, soon created problems for society as highlighted in the subsequent cases analyzed in this chapter. This analysis illustrates how, over time, the North Carolina judiciary recognized levels of authority over slaves, as well as varying degrees of liability for specific classes of transgressors and transgressions. Likewise, the actions of slaves, as well as accountability for their actions, would not be defined monolithically but, instead, would be classified on their circumstances. Such circumstances would be measured against the defined order, wherein the wealthy, the poor, and slaves occupied a specified and immutable status. In short, the court did not mediate the social hierarchy; it merely introduced important nuances to enable the hierarchy to run more smoothly.

## *State v. Hale* and the Protection of the Master's Private Property

Hale was a white man charged with the assault of a slave he did not own. At his trial, Hale prevailed by arguing that his attack on a slave could not legally constitute an assault: "No offense has been committed, and the indictment is not sustainable, because the person assaulted [is] a slave who is not protected by the general criminal law of the State; but that, as the property of an individual, the owner may be redressed by a civil action" (*State v. Hale*, 326). The state appealed to the North Carolina Supreme Court, which held that Hale could be tried for criminal assault. The rule announced by this case was that a white person could be tried for an assault of a slave he or she did not own if the attack came without justification or attenuating circumstances. The court, however, was careful to qualify this new rule:

> A battery being committed on a *slave*, no justification or circumstances attending it being shown, is an indictable offense. But *every* battery on a slave is not indictable, because the person making it may have matter or excuse or justification, which would be no defense for committing a battery on a free person. Each case of this sort must, in a great degree, depend on its own circumstances. (*State v. Hale*, 325)

With this reasoning, a degree of legal protection emerges for the slave. However, the court made clear that it was concerned less with humanistic principles and more with protecting the privilege of private power: masters alone have dominion over their slaves. When a stranger usurps this power, the public peace is broken just as if a white person were battered:

> The instinct of a slave may be, and generally is, tamed into subservience to his master's will, and from him he receives chastisement, whether it be merited or not, with perfect submission, for he knows the extent of the dominion assumed over him, and that the law ratifies the claim. But when the same authority is wantonly usurped by a stranger, nature is disposed to assert her rights and to prompt the slave to a resistance, often momentarily successful, sometimes fatally so. (*State v. Hale*, 327)

The court found this threat to private property compelling and against the public interest. As the court argued, "A wanton injury committed on a slave is a great provocation to the owner, awakens his resentment, and has a direct tendency to a breach of the peace by inciting him to seek immediate vengeance" (327). Thus, the court adjusted public policy to protect the integrity of the master's property from the increasing threat of "degraded" members of the poor white community:

> These offenses are usually committed by men of dissolute habits, hanging loose upon society, who, being repelled from association with well disposed citizens, take refuge in the company of colored persons and slaves, whom they deprave by their example, embolden by their familiarity, and then beat, under the expectation that a slave dare not resent a blow from a white man. (*State v. Hale*, 327)

Class prejudice is evident in the court's decision, as it is evident throughout Weaver's philosophy more generally. Most white people, although of higher status than slaves, were not much wealthier than slaves. Besides the plantation owners, the only people in society at this time who could afford to own slaves were attorneys and judges, all presumed to represent the apex of Southern culture. As documented by Schiller:

> The vast majority of North Carolinians were small subsistence farmers or landless laborers. Seventy-two percent owned no slaves and sixty-nine percent worked either as owners or tenants on farms of less than one hundred acres. The state's per capita wealth was the lowest in the United States, and its rate of adult illiteracy, the highest. (1992, 1243)

Therefore, although any white person could chastise a slave for not showing proper deference, limits to this power needed to be recognized to protect the property value of the slave. As the court noted, "If such offenses may be committed with impunity the public peace will not only be rendered extremely insecure, but the value of slave property must be much impaired, for the offenders can seldom make any reparation in damages" (*State v. Hale*, 327).

*Hale*, thus, signaled the beginning of a shift in how slavery was conceptualized in North Carolina. This process, however, was not without controversy. For example, in the next case, *State v. Mann*, the court re-articulated the basic premise that the law should interfere only minimally with the master/slave relationship, as the law only interferes minimally with property relationships today. The court was worried that, by articulating legal space for the protection of slaves, slaves might assume that they had legal rights against their masters that could be enforced in court.

## *State v. Mann*, the Rejection of Natural Law, and the Perfect Submission of the Slave

In the 1829 case of *State v. Mann*, the court overtly denied the relevance of natural law to any case involving slaves. As discussed in Chapter 12, the court was forced to address the natural law issue, just as it was forced to address the common law issue. As neither natural law nor common law allowed slavery, slaves and their abolitionist supporters frequently challenged a slave's servitude on these grounds. The court, by exalting the primacy of positive law, put an end to these arguments. Specifically, the court reasoned that there was a hierarchy of law and that "positive" law (otherwise known as legislative law) was at the top of this hierarchy. By articulating this differentiation, the North Carolina judiciary was able to maintain a fidelity to positive law at the same time that they acknowledged the existence of natural law. This tactic parallels the court's reasoning in *Boon*.

The North Carolina judiciary was not the only court that argued in this fashion. In *The Antelope* case of 1825, US Supreme Court Chief Justice John Marshall had occasion to adjudicate questions regarding the international slave trade. Although the importation of slaves into the United States had by this time been prohibited, a cargo of 280 slaves reached the United States as a result of their slave ship becoming disabled. Contesting claims of ownership were immediately levied against these slaves by several parties, including foreign subjects. One claim asserted to the Court was that the slaves should be freed, as they were unlawfully transported to the United States. Marshall rejected this view and wrote,

"However abhorrent this traffic may be, it has been sanctioned, in modern times, by the laws of all nations who possess distant colonies" (recounted in Irons, 1999, 139–140).

Although Marshall continued to speak disapprovingly of slavery, arguing that he could not deny that slavery "is contrary to the law of nature," he nevertheless refused to intervene. Marshall argued that his "feelings of humanity" were legally inconsequential; of primary importance was what he called "the law of nations." As he explained, "Whatever might be the answer of a moralist to this question, a jurist must search for its legal solution." He concluded that "this traffic remains lawful to those whose governments have not forbidden it." As a result, the vast majority of the slaves were adjudicated to be the property of their Spanish and Portuguese claimants and were returned to their "rightful" owners. Of the original 280 slaves, only 16 were freed on technical grounds, which indicated that, under US law, they could not be legally held as slaves.

Judges used similar rhetorical strategies of definition and differentiation as those later championed by Weaver to counter the moral claims of abolitionists. The judges maintained that as members of the judiciary in a democratic society, they had no choice but to apply positive law (which codified slavery). In the most famous example of this rhetorical strategy, the US Supreme Court argued in *Dred Scott v. Sandford* that:

> It is not the province of the court to decide upon the justice or injustice, the policy or impolicy, of these laws [of slavery]. The decision of that question belonged to the political or law-making power; to those who formed the sovereignty and framed the Constitution. The duty of the court is to interpret the instrument they have framed, with the best lights we can obtain on the subject, and to administer it as we find it, according to its true intent and meaning when it was adopted. (1857, 404–405)

This fidelity to the "will of the people" required judges to ignore any argument from natural law about the inherent equality of all people (a point fundamental to partisan criticism). This idea assumes that popular government necessitates minority acquiescence to prevent the structure of government from collapsing. With this reasoning, the courts denied their agency in perpetuating slavery. The fallacy in the reasoning, however, is obvious: Majority rule is far from absolute—the Federal Constitution was arguably intended to provide certain checks against popular tyranny as a condition for centralized federal power. As Justice William J. Brennan has stated:

> Those whom we would banish from society or from the human community itself often speak in too faint a voice to be heard above society's demand for punishment. It is the particular role of courts to hear these voices, for the constitution declares that the majoritarian chorus may not alone dictate the conditions of social life. (*McCleskey v. Kemp*, 1987, Justice Brennan, dissent)

This claim, however admirable, remains highly contested. An influential counterargument to this position often assumes the form of "states' rights" rhetoric. Although the concept of states' rights is, constitutionally, a central legal principle in US federalism, as encapsulated in the Tenth Amendment, few critics of race and poverty issues in the United States failed to see the states' rights argument for the ugly euphemism it is. Ideographically, states' rights means the right of the white majority (or economic elites) to define as unwanted African Americans and poor people (for a discussion of ideographic argumentation, see Michael McGee, 1980). Segregation, legal discrimination, and a lack of a national "floor" guaranteeing fundamental protections are often the result of successful states' rights rhetoric,[8] which is why the civil rights movement, although incomplete, was profoundly just. Social justice demands a national commitment to both formal *and* substantive equality.

During the period of slavery, many judges embraced the positivistic view of slavery as announced in *Mann* below. Such judges may have felt that slavery was morally wrong. Nevertheless, as legislative law, slavery was an expression of democratic will, precluded by constitutional theory from judicial interference. The courts were not alone in this sentiment, as politicians and citizens often felt similarly. Recognizing this tragic bifurcation helps contemporary readers to understand the actions of leaders such as Abraham Lincoln (as well as explain, in part, the radical schizophrenia of the court in *Mann*):

> [It] must be remembered that in the eyes of the law Negro slaves were property; and Lincoln was, after all, a lawyer. Morally he believed them not to be property, but legally they were property; and the necessity of walking a line between the moral imperative and the law will explain some of his actions which seem not to agree with the popular conception of the Great Emancipator. (Weaver, 1985, 102)

The defendant in *Mann* leased a slave for one year, during which time he shot the slave in the back after she ignored his authority. The slave survived and *Mann* was charged with assault. Ultimately, *Mann* prevailed, and the *Mann* case stands for the proposition that an owner who beats his or her slave is not indictable for battery.[9] The court articulated two reasons for this holding. First, the owner's control over a slave must be absolute:

> The end [of slavery] is the profit of the master, his security and the public safety. The subject is doomed in his own person and in his posterity to life without knowledge and without the capacity to make anything his own, and to toil that another may reap the fruits. What moral conditions shall be addressed to such a being to convince him what is impossible but that the most stupid must feel and know can never be true—that he is thus to labor upon a principle of natural duty, or for the sake of his own personal happiness, such services can only be expected from one who has no will of his own; who surrenders his will in implicit obedience to that of another. Such obedience is the consequence only of uncontrolled authority over the body. There is nothing else which can operate to produce the effect. The power of the master must be absolute to render the submission of the slave perfect. (*State v. Mann*, 169)

According to this powerful, totalizing narrative, slavery was a condition of caste. Slaves were condemned because of their race, and they passed this status to their children. The enslaving power was, thus, total and penetrated to the deepest "essence" of the slave. This metaphysical condition was reinforced by a material power in which slaves were physically degraded.

Second, the court argued that, essential for slavery as an institution, slaves must understand that no authority would pass judgment on their master's treatment. Because judicial review undermined slave subservience, the master/slave relationship would be precluded from such review:

> We cannot allow the right of the master to be brought into discussion in the courts of justice. The slave, to remain a slave, must be made sensible that there is no appeal from his master; that his power is in no instance usurped; but is conferred by the laws of man at least, if not by the law of God. The danger would be great, indeed, if the tribunals of justice should be called on to graduate the punishment appropriate to every temper and every dereliction of menial duty . . . . The Court, therefore, disclaims the power of changing the relation in which these parts of our people stand to each other. (*State v. Mann*, 170)

The court's argument is crucial for understanding the rhetoric of dehumanization and the place of definitional arguments in it: Slavery was a lawless institution, wherein the humanity of the slave was defined out of existence and denied legal significance. Whatever "moral" justification for slavery could be said to have existed rested on this point. To allow a slave to be in some manner a human would undermine the rationale for slavery. Similarly, the justification for economic oppression rests on the notion that being human does not, in and of itself, entitle a person to a life of health and dignity. To acknowledge this would be to undermine the rational for neoliberalism. The poor are, thus, denied a legal significance and are dehumanized in a way that is not dissimilar to that of the slaves.

*Mann* is one of the most extreme examples of dehumanizing judicial rhetoric and is frequently cited by historians for this point. What goes unnoticed is that the *Mann* court is uncomfortable with its holding. This uneasiness (similar to that experienced by Justice Marshall) between the court's holding and the human feelings of the court deserves analysis. First, the court confessed that it "cannot but lament when such cases as present are brought into judgment" (*State v. Mann*, 168). The cause of such lament was the court's struggle between two conflicting sentiments. On the one hand, the court acknowledged that judges were human and could feel repugnance for the law that they were expounding; on the other hand, the court recognized its responsibility to society and to the law, a responsibility (or professionalism) that took precedence over the conscience of individual judges:

> It is useless, however, to complain of things inherent in our political state. And it is criminal in a Court to avoid any responsibility which the laws impose. With whatever reluctance, therefore, it is done, the Court is compelled to express an opinion upon the extent of the dominion of the master over the slave in North Carolina. (*State v. Mann*, 168)[10]

The court's discomfort grew throughout the decision, becoming absurdly uncritical, as contemporary courts often are. In what appears to be good conscience, the court denied any ability to take responsibility for the social reality reified by its actions:

> I most freely confess my sense of the harshness of this proposition; I feel it as deeply as any man can; and as a principle of moral right every person in his

> retirement must repudiate. But in the actual condition of things it must be so. There is no remedy. This discipline belongs to the state of slavery. They cannot be disunited without abrogating at once the rights of the master and absolving the slave from his subjection. It constitutes the curse of slavery to both the bond and free portion of our population. But it is inherent in the relation of master and slave. (*State v. Mann*, 170)

The court recognized that for slavery to be effective, certain social practices must be codified by the law, which is the responsibility of the court. The court's function is to give effect to the intent of the legislature, to make more perfect the institutionalization of slavery and not to intervene on behalf of the slave out of empathy or compassion:

> I repeat that I would gladly have avoided this ungrateful question. But being brought to it the Court is compelled to declare that while slavery exists among us in its present state, or until it shall seem fit to the legislature to interpose express enactments to the contrary, it will be the imperative duty of the Judges to recognize the full dominion of the owner over the slave, except where the exercise of it is forbidden by statute. And this we do upon the ground that this dominion is essential to the value of slaves as property, to the security of the master, and the public tranquility, greatly dependent upon their subordination; and, in [fact], as most effectually securing the general protection and comfort of the slaves themselves. (*State v. Mann*, 171)

The decision in *Mann* is painfully honest and callously brutal. The persona evoked by the court's decision is of an institution filled with self-doubt and moral failure. In earlier drafts, the court was even more outspoken in its condemnation of the very law it was explicating (see Schiller, 1992, 1241). The radical denial of the power of the judiciary to reconcile morality with professional practice is, to critically minded people, shocking.[11]

As an expression of an actual power relationship created and reinforced through legal and definitional norms, *Mann* lent authority to a lived experience enacted on the body of slaves and exemplifies clearly the condition of a profound human frailty that people who perpetuate social injustice often experience. The politicians who write our laws or sit on courts may believe that they act in the national interest, as the *Mann* court believed it was acting in the state's interest. This suggests that the discrepancy between our moral ideals and our material actions as US Americans involves how we define our community. In the United States, community is narrowly defined in the interest of the rich, and the law (along with economic and foreign policy) follows from that definition. How US Americans treat themselves and how they treat the rest of the world stems from this point, allowing for pervasive cruelty to exist. The sheer terror of much human cruelty has implications not only for slaves but for all humans who are victimized through a combination of physical suffering and the rhetorical justification perpetrators of injustice utilize to justify and continue that suffering. By engaging the rhetorical justifications for injustice (racial, political, or economic), partisan critics can demystify them and contribute to their obsolescence.

## ✶ DEBATING THE INTEGRITY OF THE SLAVE'S SELF ✶

Throughout most of the eighteenth century, North Carolina did not recognize any legal protection for slaves. This was followed by forty-five years in which the court, starting in *Hale*, rationalized a limited legal protection for slaves in the interest of social stability. As exemplified in *State v. Will* (1834), *State v. Hoover* (1839), and *State v. Caesar* (1849), the court struggled with the difficult conceptual problem of curtailing the types of violence that could be inflicted on slaves while not compromising the slave's subject status (as required by *Mann*). Observing such struggle exemplifies a discomforting use of the power of rhetoric.

### *State v. Will*: Even "Animals" Have Instincts

Will was a slave who had a dispute with another slave over a hoe. When Will lost his temper and angrily broke the hoe, Will was reported to the overseer, a man named Baxter. Baxter approached Will with a gun and a cowhide whip and Will fled the plantation. As Will fled, Baxter, in what the court characterized as a deliberate attempt to kill, shot Will in the back with birdshot at close range. Severely wounded and terrified, Will continued to flee. Baxter soon caught Will, and the two men wrestled. Will produced a knife and slashed Baxter's leg; Baxter bled to death. The court assumed that Will had no intent to kill.

North Carolina law divided homicide into three categories: murder, manslaughter, and simple homicide (*State v. Boon*, 1801, 14). The definition of murder included expressed or implied malice; the definition of manslaughter included sudden provocation and the absence of malice; and simple homicide was defined as being justifiable or excusable and not criminal. The court never considered Will's actions to be excusable; thus, the legal issue at stake was whether Will should be convicted of murder or manslaughter. If guilty of murder, Will had to be hanged. If Will were hanged, his owner would have no claim to compensation from the government (Schiller, 1992, 1226). Manslaughter, however, was not a capital offense. If convicted of manslaughter, Will would be sold out of state and his master would receive compensation at a price near Will's market value.

The court, in determining that Will suffered a legal provocation that mitigated his killing of a white man with authority over him, fashioned the following rule: "If a slave, in defense of his life, and under circumstances strongly calculated to excite his passion of terror and resentment, kills his overseer, the homicide is, by such circumstances, mitigated to manslaughter" (*State v. Will*, 1834, 131). The court's reasoning in reaching this counterintuitive holding is discussed below.

Recall that *Will* occurred thirty-three years after the court's decision in *Boon*, refusing to apply a 1791 statute prohibiting owners from maliciously killing their slaves. By the time of *Will*, however, the judiciary and society were more comfortable with this restriction on a master's authority—the 1791 statute was now enforceable. In light of this statutory limitation, Baxter's discipline was excessive. Therefore, Will's reaction to such excessive force lacked "malice aforethought," as the court reasoned that the slave's nature is guided—as is all life—by the instinct for self-preservation. Such instinct cannot be treated as malice:

> I am arguing no question of abstract right, but am endeavoring to prove that the natural incidents of slavery must be borne with, because they are inherent to the condition itself; and that any attempt to restrain or punish a slave for the exercise of a right, which even absolute power cannot destroy, is inhuman, and without the slightest benefit to the security of the master, or to that of society at large. The doctrine may be advanced from the bench, enacted by the Legislature, and enforced with all the varied agony of torture, and still the slave cannot believe, and will not believe, "that there is no one instance" in which the master's power is usurped. Nature, stronger than all, will discover *many* instances, and vindicate her rights at any and at every price. When such a stimulant as this urges the forbidden deed, punishment will be powerless to reclaim or to warn by example. (*State v. Will*, 1834,139)

The court's reasoning in this passage threatened the totality of the conceptual space supporting the master/slave relationship, considered so essential in *Mann*. This threat appears obvious in this passage, suggesting that the court in *Mann* overstated the sovereignty of the master. The court, perhaps sensing the danger in the principle it was articulating, carefully specified that its decision in *Will* was a refinement, not a repudiation, of *Mann* :

> The slave can only expect to learn the law of the land, as respects the power of the owner over him, from the manner in which it is generally, and almost universally, administered by the owner. If their treatment is now so mild, or becoming so, as rarely to require the interposition of any tribunal for their protection, they will soon be taught by the conduct of their masters, if not already taught, that absolute power is not the master's right; and the consequence which may be expected be that the slave will be prepared to resist its exercise, when bad men attempt to commit the cruelties allowed by it. (*State v. Will*, 140)

Noteworthy in the above passage is the further use of differentiation that the court draws between "good" and "bad" slave owners (for a study of the political uses of differentiation, see Zarefsky, Miller-Tutzauer, and Tutzauer, 1984). Distinguishing between the two was important so that slaves would better understand their duty to their master: "The interest of society demands that [this duty] should be fixed, and *permanently* fixed, that the master may know the extent of his authority, and the slave prepare himself to its accommodation" (*State v. Will*, 150).

Will had no duty to submit to Baxter's extreme discipline, the court decided, because such discipline, calculated as it was to produce death, evoked Will's instinct for survival. The law, noted the court, cannot suppress the expression of nature: "When a slave is required to bare his back to the rod, he does it, because it is usual; but when he is required to stand as a target for his master's gun, he is startled: no idea of duty sustains the requirement, and the unquelled portion of his instinct rouses his passions to resistance" (147). In thus discerning, the court defined Will's actions as resistance, not disobedience (143). As the court explained this difference:

> If the deceased had been resisted, a great degree of force might have been used, and the law would not have been scrupulous in determining the excess. If he had been chastising the prisoner, in the ordinary mode, and death had ensued, it would have been nothing more than an unfortunate accident. But the prisoner

> was neither resisting his master nor did the calamity grow out of any attempt to chastise. It is confidently contended that a master has not by the law of the land the right to kill his slave for a simple act of disobedience, however provoking may be the circumstances under which it is committed; that if the slave be required to stand, and he run off, he has not forfeited his life. (141)

Therefore, the level of Baxter's violence was unnecessary and made the court uncomfortable; Baxter had sufficient means to apply the "usual modes of correction," ie, any punishment short of death (140). The application of dangerous weapons for simple disobedience implied an intent to cause death and, itself, reflected the breakdown of order on the plantation. On the basis of this rationale, the court reasoned that it was not compromising the power of slave owners:

> I feel and acknowledge, as strongly as any man can, the inexorable necessity of keeping our slaves in a state of dependence and subservience to their masters. But when shooting becomes necessary to prevent insolence and disobedience, it only serves to show the want of proper domestic rules, but it will never supply it; and never can a punishment like this effect any other purpose but to produce open conflicts or secret assassinations. (154)

Indeed, in *State v. Hoover*, the next case, the court went further. In *Hoover*, the court argued that limitations on the slave owner—preventing owners from brutally torturing their slaves to death—was intended to protect the social stability and the institution of slavery itself. As Schiller notes, "Paternalistic laws, such as those prohibiting a master from murdering his slave or requiring a master to look after elderly or infirm slaves, might promote the hegemonic interests of the slaveholding class by making slavery appear to be a just system of labor" (1992, 1217). *Hoover* extended the reasoning of *Will* and demarked a line by which the behavior of a master could be held accountable in court.[12]

## *State v. Hoover*: The Absolute Limit on the Master's Authority

*Hoover* involved the torture and murder of the slave Mira by her owner. The murder was considered by the court to be "unjustified," in violation of the 1791 statute, because the victim was submissive, compliant, docile, and weak. She dutifully served Hoover and gave no cause for discipline, yet, for four months, including the period of time in which she delivered her child, routinely beat Mira with clubs, chains, and other deadly weapons and burned and whipped her, scarring virtually her entire body. Hoover forced Mira to work in winter weather without adequate clothing, and he refused her adequate nutrition. In addition to these privations, Hoover inflicted on this slave "other enormities too disgusting to be particularly designated" (*State v. Hoover*, 1839, 396).

The egregiousness of Hoover's actions so offended his community that Hoover was prosecuted, convicted, and hanged. His crime, explained the court, was not that he caused the death of his slave but that the death followed from "immoderate" discipline. The court contrasted "immoderate" discipline with "moderate" discipline, defined as any punishment short of death "for the purposes of the correction of the slave, or of keeping the slave in due subjection" (396). In so reasoning, the court argued that the rule of *Mann* still applied, even if its ultimate power had been attenuated.

Citing the Act of 1791, the court noted that a "master may lawfully punish his slave, and the degree must, in general, be left to his own judgment and humanity, and cannot be judicially questioned" (395). Nevertheless, "the master's authority is not altogether unlimited. He must not kill. There is, at the least, this restriction upon his power: he must stop short of taking life" (396).

By differentiating between moderate and immoderate punishment, the court, *Mann* notwithstanding, rationalized a legal imposition on the master's sovereignty. With the following argument, the court elaborated the crucial distinction between the two forms of punishment:

> If death unhappily ensues from the master's chastisement of his slave, inflicted apparently with a good intent, for reformation of example, and with no purpose to take life, or to put it in jeopardy, the law would doubtless tenderly regard every circumstance which, judging from the conduct generally of masters towards slaves, might reasonably be supposed to have hurried the party into excess. But the acts imputed to this unhappy man do not belong to a state of civilization. They are barbarities which could only be prompted by a heart in which every humane feeling had long been stifled; and indeed there can scarcely be a savage of the wilderness so ferocious as not to shudder at the recital of them. (396)

In this apologetic passage, the court told owners, slaves, and outsiders that the institution of slavery is a part of civilization and, thus, not itself barbaric. Implicitly, at least, the court recognized the potentially destabilizing effect of the public outcry against Hoover's actions, which went beyond-the "excess" enthusiasm of the "good intent" of the owner, which the court "tenderly" took into consideration. Thus, although slavery was fundamentally an institution outside of legal restraints, and although slaves were regarded as having little if any humanity, the court considered it imperative for the institution of slavery that the slave owner not appear barbaric. Such barbarism inflamed Northern antislavery sentiment, as well as upset Southern whites who viewed such atrocities—but not slavery itself (or lynching in the post–Civil War period)—as contrary to Christianity. *Hoover* illustrates that even a law that purports to be progressive can serve for the re-ification of an unjust social order. This helps to explain how partisan critics can be hostile to law, while accepting the necessity of some constitutional protections (or other laws) until the entire legal system is replaced and the social order revisioned along humanist-socialist lines.

## *State v. Caesar* and the Fear of Slave Solidarity

*Will* and *Hoover* both recognized the importance of the judiciary for mediating the most abusive expressions of the master/slave relationship. Since such mediation was expedient for the slave system of North Carolina, neither decision was particularly controversial among the members of the court. *Caesar*, however, was a different type of case. In *Caesar*, the majority of the court extended its reasoning in *Will* to protect a slave who killed a white attacker of another slave. Because *Caesar*—when combined with *Will* and *Hoover*—seriously challenged the slave persona, as articulated in *Mann*, the decision provoked a sharp dissent by Thomas Ruffin, author of the *Mann* decision.[13] The *Caesar* dissent is important because it highlights the central struggle of the court throughout the six cases discussed in this chapter. This struggle involved the court's glorification of the supremacy of master authority, on the one hand, and the need for substantial legal limitations on such authority, on the other.

At the time of the incident in *Caesar*, three slaves were violating the law by socializing away from their plantation at night. These slaves were approached by two "low" and "degraded" drunk white men, of the sort feared in *State v. Hale.* The men harassed the slaves and soon began beating one slave. This slave, however, was able to escape and the white men grew further enraged. They began brutally beating a second slave as if they intended to kill him. The third slave, a man named Caesar, picked up a fence rail and struck one white attacker, killing him. The majority declared that Caesar's actions were not murder, based on the logic of *Hale.* In its rationale, the court noted that Caesar was a "well-disposed negro" (273), and even expressed admiration for him: "Are we not forced, in spite of stern policy, to admire, even in a slave, the generosity which incurs danger to save a friend? The law requires a slave to tame down his feelings to suit his lowly condition, but it would be savage to allow him, under no circumstances, to yield to a generous impulse" (280).

For the majority, the two whites were wrong in attacking the slaves, and that was the end of the case. In so ruling, however, the court allowed to go unpunished an incident of disturbing, collective action between slaves. This became a crucial concern of the dissenter, Ruffin, who viewed the majority's holding as a repudiation of the values articulated in *Mann* :

> Shall one slave be the arbiter of the quarrels witnessed by him between another slave and the whites? It seems to be dangerous to the last degree to hold the doctrine that Negro slaves may assume to themselves the judgment as to the right or propriety of resistance, by one of his own race, to the authority taken over them by the whites, and, upon the notion of a generous sympathy with their oppressed fellow-servants, may step forward to secure them from the hands of a white man, and much less to avenge their wrongs. First denying their general subordination to the whites, it may be apprehended that they will end in denouncing the injustice of slavery itself, and, upon that pretext, band together to throw off their common bondage entirely. (296)

The dissent articulated three arguments why Caesar was guilty of murder. First, there was a temporal order of wrongdoing, with the slaves having committed the initial wrong: "They were away from home without passes from their owners, and associated in the street of a village in the middle of the night" (285). Next, the dissent moved the argument to physiological grounds. Although the white victim did, in fact, commit wrong by beating the slave, there was still no legal provocation for Caesar's retaliation. In other words, the assault on the second slave should not have caused Caesar to lose his reason:

> So it follows, as certainly as day follows night, that many things which drive a white man to madness will not have the like effect if done by a white man to a slave; and, particularly, it is true that slaves are not ordinarily moved to kill a white man for a common beating. For it is an incontestable fact that the great mass of slaves—nearly all of them—are the least turbulent of all men; that, when sober, they never attack a white man; and seldom, very seldom, exhibit any temper or sense of provocation at even gross and violent injuries from white men. (293)

For the dissent, slaves possessed "a duller sensibility to degradation," making them less subject to provocation (293).

According to the logic of *Will*, if an animal is terrified and cornered, the animal will strike out at its tormentor. However, if an animal witnesses another animal being beaten, it will run away; solidarity among animals is unexpected. Under this reasoning, Will's actions were understandable. Caesar's actions, however, were threatening: They were less those of an animal and more those of a human being. Caesar's actions undermine the central myth of slavery—the slave's animality. More practically, Caesar was acting in concert with another slave in an act of solidarity, and collusion between slaves raises the danger of rebellion, as well as undermines the perfect subordination of the slave, as considered essential in *Mann*. For the dissent, therefore, Caesar had a legal obligation to suppress his feelings of solidarity toward another slave, and should have deferred to the white victim. As the dissenting opinion argues, the court's proper function was to enforce the slave's "subordination to the white race, which alone is compatible with the contentment of the slaves with their destiny, the acknowledged superiority of the whites, and the public quiet and security" (291).

Ruffin's dissenting opinion in *Caesar* reflects the same denial of judicial power to reconcile moral critique with professional practice, as found in his *Mann* decision. Although Ruffin can imagine the immorality of slavery, he negates his own potential to condemn the practice of slavery:

> The whites forever feel and assert a superiority, and exact a humble submission from the slaves; and the latter, in all they say and do, not only profess but plainly exhibit a corresponding deep and abiding sense of legal and personal inferiority. Negroes—at least, the great mass of them—born with deference to the whitman, take the most contumelious language without answering again, and generally submit tamely to his buffets, though unlawful and unmerited. Such are the habits of the country. It is not now the question whether these things are naturally right and proper to exist. They do exist actually, legally, and inveterately. Indeed, they are inseparable from the state of slavery; and are only to be deemed wrong upon the admission that slavery is fundamentally wrong. (291)

Ruffin reiterates his condemnation of Caesar by analogizing slaves to children:

> It is found that when fathers and mothers correct those under their tutelage they are not ordinarily prone to resent by violent retaliation, much less to attempt to kill; but that, on the contrary, the younger do the elder reverence. If, then, a child under punishment slays his parent, the conclusion is that he was not moved to it by heat of blood on the sudden, but by a malignant and diabological spirit of vengeance. (292)

For Ruffin, who, incidentally, was the author of the court's *Hoover* decision, the relationship between master and slave must be unquestioned, as far as possible, by the courts. Ruffin embraced this perspective because he maintained an extreme fidelity to positive law and definitional argumentation, and, as a member of the North Carolina Supreme Court, felt obligated to perfect slavery until that time at which the legislature decided to abolish it. Thus, notwithstanding any anguish that Ruffin personally might feel (Ruffin was himself a slaveholder), he upheld the principle that any recognition of legal protection for slaves created confusion with regard to the slave persona. This persona, rhetorically constructed by political and judicial reasoning, depended on its continued reification, which careless judicial reasoning threatened to undermine.

## Conclusion

The preceding court decisions evidence a judiciary intent on solidifying their vision of the proper social order of North Carolina. Disturbingly, the court left unquestioned the more heinous aspects of an unethical division of labor and human value. Yet, through the intervening years, as the institution of slavery became more ingrained and unquestioned, improvements to the social conditions of slaves were deemed necessary for the protection of private property and the curtailment of social unrest. In spite of such improvements, there were few substantive changes to the hierarchical structure of the slave society.

On a rhetorical level, in each of the aforementioned cases, the condition and qualities deemed essential to the institution of slavery were refined through the language of the courts. Not only did the declarative tone set forth by the court allow the abridgment of rights of a particular group of slaves by an elite and unquestioned minority of wealthy slave owners, but also the operative definition of the slaves' persona was created by the rhetoric of the court. Although the justices articulated what they considered a proper response to the rhetorical exigencies of the slave culture, one that demanded the total subjugation of slaves for the security of the white population, their actions had a clear instrumental effect in the guidance of North Carolina society. Contrary to the statements of the justices, their actions influenced society in a manner similar to that of the legislature, and their pronouncements guided the culture.

Legal rhetoric has the power to substantively influence social order, and as a result, must be closely monitored by cultural critics. The rhetorical actions undertaken in the antebellum South may have their corollary in the contemporary judiciary. Without further critical inquiry into the behavioral and legislative influence of legal pronouncements, some segments of society will continue to be defined by a less than impartial court system. Such rhetorical actions must be challenged on both their axiomatic and ontological claims, lest the injustices of the past continue through the declarations of a select few whose voices are neither democratic nor just in their influence.

## ✱ NOTES ✱

1. Schiller's is the only study in the Westlaw database concerned specifically with North Carolina Supreme Court slave decisions. Schiller focuses on cases decided between 1848 and 1865 and, thus, his study begins at the period where my study ends. Whereas Schiller is interested in exploring the late antebellum period when slave laws reached their "highest level of maturity," my study explores the beginning of this institution. Between the cases of my study and Schiller's, there is almost no overlap (although Schiller refers to the earlier cases to situate his analysis). As a final note, Schiller covers a wider range of slave contexts—such as tort law and manumission. This chapter, on the other hand, focuses specifically on criminal law and criminal liability, both for slaves and for people who attack slaves in a fashion not warranted by the master/slave relationship. For an overview of constitutive rhetoric, see Charland (1987).

2. Weaver (1984) is widely considered to be a progenitor of modern conservatism in the United States.

3. I use the term "races" simply out of convenience in the context of this study; in a strict sense, I do not believe in the category of "race." See Jones (1981).

4. The three cases in the second half of this chapter reveal further social problems resulting from the court's adjudication of Boon, Hale, and Mann.

5. "Distinguished" is used in its legal sense, which means to establish essential differences between apparently similar cases or other legal standards.

6. Note how this conclusion contrasts with the decision in *Commonwealth v. Pullis* to apply English common law to suppress union activity. In both cases, it appears that the court was selectively appropriating the English common law for insidious political reasons.

7. This can be compared with modern jurisprudence in which the US Supreme Court has held that there are certain areas where the states and federal government cannot lightly intrude, such as reproductive rights and the integrity of the family. See, for example, *Skinner v. Oklahoma* (1942), *Roe v. Wade* (1973), and *Moore v. City of East Cleveland* (1977). Also see Wood (1998).

8. In writing this, I am assuming a federal government committed to providing these rights.

9. The fact that the slave was leased did not matter for the issue of criminal liability. As a result of the lease, Mann stood in the authority to the slave as did the permanent owner.

10. As in academic writing, authorial agency is often located in disciplinary as opposed to individual authority, a practice that I have been critiquing throughout this book. See Agger (1990, 145).

11. Yet even in contemporary times, the moral view I am advocating is considered controversial. See Cox (1987).

12. Hoover is an unusual case, only one of two such instances in North Carolina in which a master was executed for mistreating a slave; the second case occurred much later. See *State v. Robbins* (1855).

13. Schiller notes that "Ruffin's contemporaries viewed him as an extraordinary legal mind" and that Roscoe Pound, an influential Dean of Harvard Law School (1916–1936), "picked [Ruffin] as one of the ten greatest judges in American history" (1992, 1219).

# CHAPTER 14

# IN SEARCH OF POLITICAL TRANSCENDENCE

The opening years of the twenty-first century have witnessed the cruelties of a global neoliberalism and the heartless greed of a growing conservatism. Seldom does the hope and optimism of past periods of struggle suggest itself in modern politics. Most tragically, socialism—that great ideal of democracy and equality—has been discredited as a counterforce to elitism and hegemony. Forgotten is how the socialist struggle constituted a viable and celebrated political vision for more than 100 years, helping to restrain the excesses of Western imperialism, capitalism, and neocolonialism. Without the notion of a broadly defined socialist vision—one measuring a nation's wealth by the resources expended on uplifting its citizens—the parade of atrocities that continues to demarcate Western life will not cease. By engaging in a sustained and vigorous political critique of the United States and its policies, scholars and activists in the humanities and social sciences have the potential to publicly and collectively reinvent the humanist-socialist vision and, thus, to help change the United States for the better. As Ronald Aronson notes, "Whether it is spelled out under the old name of 'socialism' or not, victorious capitalism cannot help but generate the need for a collectively understood and democratically administered alternative" (1999, 484).

By placing selected paradigmatic experiences of the United States in their historical, social, legal, philosophical, and rhetorical contexts, this book's goal has been to advocate, in partisan terms, a reimagined US community grounded in social justice. Fundamental to this notion of social justice is a reinvigorated commitment to the democratic potential of the United States, which requires a fair and equitable distribution of power throughout society. Toward this end, this book has advocated the valuation of labor, respect and appreciation of diversity, and a critical awareness of our country's past. Above all else, it argued that meaningful change is the result of collective effort and the rejection of normative legal and political

US institutions that further injustice. In this conclusion, a solution is offered—a transcendence—by which the United States and world communities can be reimagined along the socially progressive lines.

## ✶ TRANSCENDING TO THE HUMAN COMMUNITY ✶

Critical scholars and activists have long argued that nationality, ethnicity, and religious identification are merely historical conveniences, accidents of birth. Given this, it is difficult to privilege any country, ethnic group, or religion. Instead, each nation and each community should be judged by its actions and people should align themselves with communities that practice social justice and condemn those that perpetrate social injustice. Thus, the strength of any society depends on the mutuality of respect among people of the different cultures who comprise it, as well as respect for people living in other parts of the world.

In practical terms, this means that the United States, as well as other industrialized nations, have an obligation to cease those activities that cause suffering and inequality throughout the developing world. Furthermore, we (ie, all privileged individuals) should pledge ourselves to improving the living conditions of the roughly two thirds of the human population living in utter destitution, a condition in which human beings struggle to live without adequate food, water, shelter, and health care. According to Ronald P. Cantrell, Director General of the International Rice Research Institute, there are 840 million hungry people each day, *another* 2 billion who are malnourished, and a *further* 1.3 billion who suffer in absolute poverty (ie, life at the margins of existence). Such poverty is, in the words of philosopher Peter Singer, "probably the principal cause of human misery today" (1993, 220). In addition, there are one billion people who have no access to safe drinking water and 2.4 billion without adequate sanitation.[1] By neglecting their obligation to relieve this suffering, wealthy nations reify further the politics of exclusion and deprivation that demarcated the nineteenth and twentieth centuries. Denial and inaction further the rationales that insulate us "against other people's otherness," denying them "what we would claim for ourselves" (Cameron, 1993, 27).

Fundamental to this respect for the well-being of all humans is a sustained material commitment by the US government toward abolishing the systemic alienation and impoverishment of minority and working class populations in nations where the United States has an influence. Abstract political freedoms, such as freedom of speech and religion, are worthless (and insulting) under social conditions of severe economic deprivation and political marginalization. This argument is not without precedent; the values that underlie my position are codified in the *United Nations Universal Declaration of Human Rights of 1948.* Although hortatory and not legally binding in the sense that a specific treaty between two nations would be enforceable, Article 25 of this document establishes an important *moral norm* when it states:

> Everyone has the right to a standard of living adequate for the health and well-being of himself and of his family, including food, clothing, housing and medical care and necessary social services, and the right to security in the event of unemployment, sickness, disability, widowhood, old age or other lack of livelihood in circumstances beyond his control. (Reprinted in David Harris, 1998, 634)

Article 22 reads:

> Everyone, as a member of society, has the right to social security and is entitled to realization through national effort and international co-operation and in accordance with the organization and resources of each state, of the economic, social and cultural rights indispensable for his dignity and the free development of his personality. (634)

Articles 22 and 25 are inclusive of every human being. Each person, *without exception*, is entitled to social security, a security actualized through the cooperation of the international community. The mandate for such cooperation is located in Article 2, Section 2 of the *United Nations Charter*, which requires that all members "shall fulfill in good faith the obligations assumed by them in accordance with the present Charter" (Harris, 1998, 1049).

Since the United Nations collectively guarantees to every person "dignity" and the "free development of his personality," every country is pledged, by agreement with the General Charter, to make these principles a reality and, thus, has a responsibility to provide the developing world with enough basic resources so that these nations can become contributing partners to the world community. This necessitates extending the "welfare state" to the international realm and creating a worldwide "safety net" to ensure that the poorest countries receive a fair share of the collective prosperity.[2] Although the United States has improved over time in important ways (ie, it is less overtly racist and more socially inclusive), social progress remains uneven because most people do not have a clear understanding of the issues and stakes involved in the creation of the US social structure or of the relationship between the United States and the international community. This ignorance is the result, in part, of its mass media and educational systems, which often deny or mystify US history and foreign policy, making critical evaluations difficult.

The history of a community—the evolution of its laws, politics, and morality—belongs to the members of that community; their collective memory is the nutrient by which a nation grows. Without a knowledge of its past, without a collective memory to sustain a group's self-awareness, a nation loses a sense of collective control over its destiny. Such a condition is anathema to the spirit of a democratic society. Without memory, without history, a community loses its bearings, its sense of place in time and its power of agency. Although communities require a collective memory to enact sustained communal agency, such collective politics, if narcissistic, often lead to social strife and conflict with others. Therefore, a transcendence is needed for human beings to reposition themselves as belonging to an interdependent collective family. To accomplish this, humans must reposition their allegiances from those things that separate them (eg, nationality, ethnicity, and religion). This requires that they stop competing against each other, and, instead, work together for the elevation of the species. Fundamental to such transcendence is the rejection of ethnic, national, and religious identity and the conflict that often results from these identifications.

## ✶ ETHNIC CONFLICT AND NATIONAL IDENTITY ✶

Two models often used to describe the intractable strife of the twentieth century are the Marxist and the ethnic conflict models. For the first three quarters of the twentieth century, the dominant model was some variation of the Marxist paradigm, including a generalized critique of

Western colonialism and imperialism. An alternative paradigm is the ethnic conflict model. While downplaying economic factors in ethnic conflict, this model emphasizes the symbolism of the relative power of different ethnic communities. Although these two models are quite different, they are often interdependent, as many ethnic identifications and subsequent conflicts are the direct result of European colonization and the accompanying post-colonial world pressures.

More specifically, the waning of colonial rule after the Second World War helped to accelerate ethnic identification and intergroup conflict. As the European colonial powers weakened, the question of nationality and its relationship to ethnic identity became crucial (Donald Horowitz, 2000, 4). In Malaysia, for example, large numbers of Chinese workers were imported in the nineteenth century as labor for the British colonial economy. For many decades, these Chinese were not perceived as a threat to the indigenous people of Malaysia, because they frequently returned to China after the terms of their labor were completed. Simply, the Chinese did not perceive themselves as being Malaysian; consequently, they asserted few political claims on the Malaysian government and behaved as visitors (Horowitz, 138).

This changed after the Second World War. The Chinese, active in resisting the Japanese occupation of Malaysia during the war, began to view themselves as permanent members of Malaysian society, deserving of equal rights and status. This new stance led to a crisis among the ethnic Malays, who saw the Chinese as outsiders and as a political and cultural threat (Donald Horowitz, 352; also see Silcock, 1965). The conflict, in cases such as this, often is over the symbols and perks of the state—the struggle over civil service jobs, opportunities for education, and status, the cultural capital of social existence (Horowitz, 216–226). Ethnic groups with ascriptive (birth-based) boundaries often fear being dominated in their own state by people perceived to be "other" (Connor, 1993).

Ethnic groups often fight over the question of state ownership. Central to this issue is language, as battles over national language questions often precipitate violence, as in Sri Lanka, Assam, and Malaysia (Donald-Horowitz, 216–226). In the battle over whose presence defines the state, ethnic hostility becomes acute, in part, because the presence of the "other" helps to define the "self" (see Burke, 1973). In short, the Malays became

"Malay" when contrasted with the Chinese. Thus, ethnic hostility is grounded in and reinforces symbolic currencies; group conflict, therefore, has a symbolic-political element (Horowitz, 2000, 216–226).[3] Because the colonial empires were autocratic, independence brought no tradition of power sharing or trust to the integrity of political institutions. Ethnic groups, thus, fear that the *other* will capture the state apparatus and exert a political dominance. Consequently, the relationship among schools, jobs, and the official language used in teaching and in government service becomes crucial. At root is the concept of ownership: If this is *our* state, we should not be ruled by *others*. Because of this sentiment, ethnicity (as suggested by the ethnic conflict model) often is more powerful than other kinds of identification for purposes of political mobilization (Melson, 1971).

Ethnic, national, and, in some cases, religious identifications, however, detract from the efforts of marginalized peoples to reinvent their world collectively. As social issues come to hinge on ethnicity rather than on social justice, progressive parties tend to split on ethnic lines and lose strength (Horowitz, 89–92; 334–340; Kuper, 1972). In contrast, right-wing coalitions are often more successful in crossing ethnic lines. In Malaysia, for example, a ruling coalition formed on the basis of an alliance between the Chinese capitalist class (the *Kapitan China)* and the aristocracy of the Malays (the *Raja)* (Silcock, 1965). More recently, in France, Jean-Marie Le Pen upset the French left in the initial rounds of France's presidential elections. Le Pen, who is widely perceived as xenophobic, racist, homophobic, and anti-Semitic, received support from like-minded communities that rallied under Le Pen's law-and-order banner (Trofimov, 2002).[4]

Within the ethnic conflict model, an important assumption behind the amelioration process is that terms such as *conflict resolution* (as in the Marxist model) should be avoided and terms such as *conflict management* or *conflict reduction* should be embraced. Because ethnic conflict tends to wax and wane—in other words, to remain—an important task for scholars is to formulate methods of transcendence. Rhetoricians are particularly sensitive to this goal, having learned from Burke that:

> With a few more terms in his vocabulary of motives . . . the rabid advocate of racial intolerance could become a mild one; and the mild one would not feel the need to be thus intolerant at all. And so human thought may be directed towards "the purification of war," not perhaps in the hope that war can be

> eliminated from any organism that, like man, has the motives of combat in his very essence, but in the sense that war can be refined to the point where it would be much more peaceful than the conditions we would now call peace. (1969a, 305)

Following Burke's lead, humans should aspire toward reducing the intensity of conflict, redirecting our propensity for conflict into productive channels. Possible structural strategies include proliferating the points of power, maximizing the incentives for intergroup cooperation, breaking up ethnically grouped units, encouraging alignments and identifications to form in areas other than ethnic identifications, and distributing resources so as to reduce disparities among groups (see Fearon and Laitin, 1996).

A critical scholarship is an important part of the ameliorative scheme, although such criticism is not the exclusive solution. A focus on the collective responsibilities, interests, and agencies of a community enables critics to identify cultural and individual practices harming the community in question. Opposition to these practices is strategic, taking into consideration the limitations of this approach. Specifically, I recognize that intergroup aggression is often based on an aggressor's perceived vulnerability (Donald, Horowitz, 2000, 175–184); thus, direct aggression against an aggressive group only may reinforce that group's collective fears and perpetuate cyclical violence. My point, however, is that a critical approach recognizes that antagonism among groups often is rational, not irrational; therefore, an intervention into the logic of oppression often is necessary to create conditions conducive to dialogue (see Olzak, 1992). Emma Goldman helps us to appreciate this point:

> [One] must feel intensely the indignity for our social wrongs; one's very being must throb with the pain, the sorrow, the despair millions of people are daily made to endure. Indeed, unless we have become a part of humanity, we cannot even faintly understand the just indignation that accumulates in a human soul, the burning, surging passion that makes the storm inevitable. (1969, 80)

Thus, amelioration of conflict requires individuals, first and foremost, to recognize that a condition of oppression exists. Before people can learn to describe their worlds differently, they must identify and neutralize the power conditions that limit them. In other words, the dominant norms of oppression must be confronted. Before oppressors can be "invited" to change their worldviews, their power to oppress must be taken from them.

## ✶ ELITE CONTROL AND ITS EFFECT ON THE QUALITY OF LIFE ✶

The sheer number of people in this country and in this world—and the manner in which they are organized into communities—influences the way people think, feel, and act. What people tend not to realize, however, is that social elites have had a great deal of control over how these communities are manifested. There are few sociological accidents. Poverty, pollution, deforestation, slums, unemployment, famine, and many other profound human miseries often have structural and political causes; many are anticipated and exacerbated by governments that use them as political weapons. For example, during the French colonial rule in Vietnam, the French instigated a policy of starvation in response to popular Vietnamese resistance. As a result of this policy, 2 million Vietnamese, mostly children, died (Zinn, 1980, 461).[5] Such phenomena are not incidental to civilization or industrialization; rather, they are fundamental to the current social order.[6] Most important, such phenomena are avoidable; there is little that is inevitable in the way that human society is organized. Society, in almost all of its permutations, is created rhetorically to meet certain needs and interests. When people mistake this creation for nature, they become alienated from their power to restructure the world.

An example of how the world often is created for elite interests involves the automobile. Early in the twentieth century, US policy makers made the conscious choice to promote the automobile at the expense of alternative modes of transportation (Luger, 2000). Since that time, US dependency on the automobile has been intentionally reinforced. According to Ralph Nader:

> A principal reason why the automobile has remained the only transportation vehicle to escape being called to meaningful public account is that the public has never been supplied the information nor offered the quality of competition to enable it to make effective demands through the marketplace and through government for a safe, non-polluting and efficient automobile that can be produced economically. The consumer's expectations regarding automotive innovation have been deliberately held low and mostly oriented to very gradual annual style changes. (1965, xi)

This enforced dependency is costly. The US highway system is expensive to build and to maintain, and this cost is borne by the taxpayers, not by the car manufacturers that have externalized the social cost of their product. Automobiles are costly in other ways, particularly in their environmental, ecological, and human impact. The US Department of Transportation reports that in the United States "injuries resulting from motor vehicle crashes are the leading cause of death for persons of every age from 6 to 27 years old."[7] According to the Department of Transportation, 30,000 to 40,000 people lose their lives annually in automobile accidents, and hundreds of thousands are injured or crippled. The economic cost of these accidents is more than $150 billion a year. In addition, millions of people suffer from asthma and other respiratory disease because of the air pollution caused by automobiles.

I am not a Luddite; nothing in this book should be construed to suggest that I am against technological advancement. However, even though I recognize the value of technology for the improvement of the human condition, I argue that the quality of human life is more important than the quantity of material production and that citizens of the United States must rethink their basic notions of property, community, and economy: Social justice is the only wealth worth celebrating. The conditions of the material world must follow from the condition of social justice. As Goldman argued, "Real wealth consists in things of utility and beauty, in things that help to create strong, beautiful bodies and surroundings inspiring to live in" (1969, 55). Goldman's point is becoming increasingly important as competition for limited natural resources will tend, over the coming years, to make necessities more expensive, to lower the quality of human life, and to threaten delicate and crucial eco-systems on which the prosperity of the human species depends (Bueler, 1997).

With increased population comes increased social responsibility for providing food, shelter, water, safety, health care, and education. The question is not merely one of physical space. Rather, the important question is: How well do we treat the people already here? In other words, how judiciously have world resources been allocated? Most of the poverty and hunger in the world is not due to the lack of food or resources, but to distribution breakdowns, political conflicts, and a lack of commitment on the part of the industrial world to better the lives of people in the developing world (Singer, 1993, 220).

Poverty, overpopulation, and political instability in the developing world are increasingly major threats to world security. Prior to the September 11 attacks on the United States, the United States spent billions of dollars each year to reinforce the inequitable status quo of the developing world; since 9/11, this amount has substantially increased. The US commitment toward policing the developing world will continue well into the future because this influence of the United States does not address, as our own domestic policing does not address, the systemic causes of unrest and insecurity throughout the world. The police are quick to put people in jail, but they (and we) do not ask the more difficult question of why conditions are such that the United States has an incarceration rate of 481 per 100,000 people, whereas Japan, in comparison, has an incarceration rate of 40 per 100,000 people (Murphy, 2001).

In the current global community, US citizens cannot tend to their own gardens and not care about what happens to people in other parts of the world. Ignoring the plight of these people will not cause their conditions to improve, nor will it keep US Americans safe from the retaliations of oppressed people in the developing world. Humanistic solutions to the problems of the developing world cannot be forever prevented through military intervention by the United States.[8] Although governments can be destroyed and movements squashed, the spirit animating threats to US power will continue to reemerge in different forms. Therefore, the prudent action is to address the world's problems through compassion, which necessitates a sustained and genuine commitment to resolving issues of hunger, poverty, and widespread illness.[9]

By far, the twentieth century was the most strife-ridden, bloody, and destructive century in human history. By the end of that century, however, after hundreds of millions of lives had been lost and countless trillions of dollars wasted, the power imbalances, the distributions of wealth, and, indeed, the class and property systems that existed at the beginning of the twentieth century remained firmly entrenched. More crucially, the same antiprogressive dogmatism that denied the possibility of thinking differently that characterized the twentieth century is still practiced today. But now, in the twenty-first century, human technology and weapons have increased so rapidly in their destructive powers that society has been unable to develop a moral balance to temper its destructive capabilities. Technological advances in the late twentieth century have given the rich more military and police powers to suppress those who seek to initiate change. External and internal "security" now appear as a permanent addition to our society and as an extension of the will of the elites to make permanent their privilege. In many ways, the twenty-first century threatens to be an extension of, rather than a repudiation or an overcoming of, the conflicts of the twentieth century.

The twentieth century was the "century of labor," an era of self-determination and nationhood for the formerly colonized nations, as well as a period that nurtured an ecological consciousness. For all of its threats and poisons, the twentieth century had the potential to bring the human community together in ways that were unthinkable in previous centuries, but, unfortunately, this potential was not realized. Currently, the dignity and organization of labor is in ruins. The former colonized nations, although experiencing *de jure* freedom and independence, are nevertheless locked into an economic neocolonization, giving the former colonizing nations a *de facto* control over their old colonies. All the while, the environment continues to be destroyed at a rate in which its regeneration seems improbable. Social elites do not seem to care. In Peter Berger's terms, "As the physicists are busy engineering the world's annihilation, the social scientists can be entrusted with the smaller mission of engineering the world's consent" (1963, 152).

## ✶ THE KROPOTKIN SOLUTION ✶

The paragraphs above articulate a narrative of the world's condition. Although this vision is dour, there are encouraging signs. One hopeful trend originated with Peter Kropotkin, a nineteenth-century Russian geographer, evolutionist, and political philosopher who anticipated many of the concerns facing contemporary life. Kropotkin's critique remains viable because many contemporary problems originate from the way society thinks, and the way society currently thinks is largely the product of his century.

Popular in Kropotkin's day was the doctrine of social evolution (ie, "survival of the fittest"), as articulated by Herbert Spencer. Spencer's thought was used by social elites in England and the United States to justify the predatory economic systems of the late nineteenth and early twentieth centuries. Unlike Charles Darwin, Spencer argued that individual humans were pitted against each other in a brutal competition, and Spencer downplayed other important human values, such as solidarity, compassion, and mutual aid (see Gould, 1977, 34–40). The most dominant image of this concept comes from Thomas Huxley, a social biologist. Huxley argued that, in nature, animals fight "tooth and claw," and they vindicate their species in the fight for survival with blood and torn flesh. Spencer and Huxley's views of human nature leads, among other things, to the state worship of military might, as well as to internal police measures that mirror aggressive military views on how the state should impose law and order.

Kropotkin had second thoughts about characterizing evolution as a battle between the stronger and the weaker, and he questioned the practice of defining our political commitments based on this reading of human nature (see Gould, 1992). Kropotkin rejected the competition model for organizing human relationships, suggesting that *mutual aid* was the more important law of nature:

> Life in societies enables the feeblest animals to resist and to protect themselves from the most terrible birds and beasts of prey . . . . Therefore, while fully admitting that force, swiftness, protective colors, cunning, and endurance to hunger and cold . . . are so many qualities making the individual, or the species, the fittest under certain circumstances, we maintain that, under *any* circumstance, sociability is the great advantage in the struggle for life. Those species who willingly or unwillingly abandon it are doomed to decay; while those animals which know best how to combine have the greatest chance of survival and of further evolution, although they may be inferior to others [in strength, endurance, etc.]. (1989, 57)

In other words, we do not act out of love for another when we rush to help a stranger in need; rather, we act out of "a far wider, even through more vague, feeling or instinct of human solidarity and sociability" (1989, xli). This feeling constitutes "an instinct that has been slowly developed among animals and men in the course of an extremely long evolution, and which has taught animals and men alike the force they can borrow from the practice of mutual aid and support, and the joys they can find in social life" (57). Kropotkin argues further that human beings have a consciousness for solidarity, a knowledge "of the close dependency of every one's happiness upon the happiness of all; and of the sense of justice, or equity, which brings the individual to consider the rights of every other individual as equal to his own" (1989, xlii).

When considering population and urbanization and the effects they have on community life, the wisdom of Kropotkin's sentiments becomes apparent. There is no question that, as a species, human beings must struggle for survival. For example, mosquitoes spread diseases such as malaria, the largest single cause of human death worldwide. The more successful mosquitoes are in breeding, the more danger they pose to human beings. Thus, humans may ethically implement policies designed to disrupt the breeding habits and survival of mosquitoes. Darwin, however, never suggested that humans must struggle against each other; nevertheless, this is precisely the claim that social Darwinists advance, and they continue to have political influence (Midgley, 2001, 193–198).

To the extent that competition stimulates innovation, a degree of competition is necessary, but competition can be crushing, as when people are forced to succeed or fail in areas of life that are inappropriate to this model (eg, health care). Furthermore, competition rewards only those who have strengths in limited economic areas, denying most other areas of human experience (consider the low cultural status of the typical artist). When competition becomes the dominant model for social reward, only a few can succeed, whereas the rest grow embittered.

This bitterness becomes accentuated when an individual's noneconomic skills become wasted because there is no forum available for their expression. For instance, a career in classical music is available to only a few privileged individuals; most people do not have the leisure to devote their lives to mastering the musical arts. Furthermore, as the market is so small for classical musicians, only a handful of people who have succeeded in mastering these skills can earn their living with this occupation. Thus, if a person born into a poor family has a predilection to excel as a classical musician, the chances are slim that he or she will be encouraged to develop the necessary skills. As a practical matter, this person would have to support him or herself by competing in the ordinary labor market. In such a market, this person may be disadvantaged because, owing to his or her musical or artistic strengths, he or she may be less adept in a mainstream working environment. Under this scenario, the world loses its next Mozart and gains another Wal-Mart cashier.

The larger human community is more important than the artificial and limited communities constructed on nationalist, ethnic, and religious lines. An appreciation of this importance allows people to see beyond the provincialities of these institutions to grasp a more fundamental specieswide identification. Nature does not distinguish among nations, ethnicities, or religions; these are ideas that humans bring to the world and impose on each other. Humans will live or die as a species, not as Muslims or Christians, Chinese or English, or as bankers or bricklayers. Something more essential than passports and holy texts connects humans with the mass of human suffering (or human achievement).

Critical scholarship can nurture this type of transcendence. Using social, critical, legal, and rhetorical criticism, scholars and activists work to explain how systemic factors work against the vision of community celebrated through generations of struggle. With such analysis, we can nurture a cultural desire among US citizens to resist elitism, privilege, and aristocracy. By questioning the construction of their communities, people will be able to translate their rhetorical and normative commitments to freedom, justice, and equality into substantive action. Positive social change occurs when an inspiring vision of the good is combined with agitation and practical political organization. With the union of words and deeds, citizens can resist the social control systemic in US society.

## ✱ NOTES ✱

1. See International Rice Research Institute web page at http://www.irri.org/.

2. Singer (1993, 246) suggests revising the ancient custom of tithing and applying it to the global community.

3. On the political, systemic, and ritualistic uses of ethnic violence, see Brass (1997).

4. Le Pen was subsequently unsuccessful in capturing the French presidency.

5. Karnow (1991) attributes the famine to Japanese policies during the Second World War. Both Karnow and Zinn recognize the same number; either way, these 2 million people perished as the result of the political use of famine.

6. On the politics of famine, see McCaughan (2001). McCaughan calls famine "the most common form of violence in today's world" (40).

7. Public Information Fact Sheet on Motor Vehicle and Traffic Safety, published by the National Highway Traffic Safety Administration's National Center for Statistics and Analysis, online at http://www.nhtsa.dot.gov/people/ncsa/ovrfacts.html.

8. Few US Americans ask the sensitive question of why the United States needs to police the world. Rather than confronting themselves with an embarrassing past, as well as an inhumane present, US Americans reduce international political problems to military solutions.

9. The United States, although committed rhetorically toward peace, often frustrates the United Nations in its efforts to improve the condition of life in the developing world. See Chomsky (2000) and Chomsky, Sahulka, and Ruggerio (1999).

# BIBLIOGRAPHY


*A Dictionary of American History*. Oxford: Blackwell Reference, 1995.

Agger, Ben. *The Decline of Discourse: Reading, Writing, and Resistance in Postmodern Capitalism*. New York: The Falmer Press, 1990.

Allen, Brenda J., Mark P. Orbe, and Margarita Refugia Olivas. "The Complexity of Our Tears: Dis/enchantment and (In)Difference in the Academy." *Communication Theory* 9 (1999): 402–429.

Anderson, Perry. *A Zone of Engagement*. London: Verso, 1992.

Angelou, Maya. *The Complete Poems of Maya Angelou*. New York: Random House, 1994.

Aquinas, Thomas. *Treatise on Law*, trans., Richard Regan. Indianapolis, IN: Hackett Publishing, 2000.

Aristotle. *The Nicomachean Ethics*, trans., David Ross. New York: Oxford University Press, 1998.

Aronson, Ronald. "Hope After Hope." *Social Research* 66 (1999): 471–494.

Artz, Lee. "Critical Ethnography for Communication Studies: Dialogue and Social Justice in Service-Learning." *Southern Communication Journal* 66 (2001): 239–250.

Artz, Lee and Bren O.A. Murphy. *Cultural Hegemony in the United States*. Thousand Oaks, CA: Sage, 2000.

Austin, John. *The Province of Jurisprudence Determined*. Cambridge: Cambridge University Press, 1995.

Avery, Dianne. "Images of Violence in Labor Jurisprudence: The Regulation of Picketing and Boycotts, 1894–1921." *Buffalo Law Review* 37 (1988): 1–117.

Avrich, Paul. *The Haymarket Tragedy*. Princeton, NJ: Princeton University Press, 1984.

Ayto, John. *Dictionary of Word Origins*. New York: Arcade Publishing, 1990.

Bach, Tullen, Carole Blair, William Nothstine, and Anne Pym. "How to Read 'How to Get Published.'" *Communication Quarterly* 44 (1996): 399–422.

Bain, David. *Empire Express: Building the First Transcontinental Railroad.* New York: Viking Press, 1999.

Bakunin, Michael. *God and the State.* New York: Dover Press, 1970.

Barthes, Roland. *Mythologies.* New York: The Noonday Press, 1957.

Bartlett, Katharine and Angela Harris. *Gender and Law: Theory, Doctrine, and Commentary* 2nd ed. New York: Aspen Law & Business, 1998.

Bavis, Craig D. "*Vriend v. Alberta, Law v. Canada, Ontario v. M and H:* The Latest Steps on the Winding Path to Substantive Equality." *The Alberta Law Review* 37 (1999): 683–714.

Beaud, Michel. *A History of Capitalism: 1500–1980.* New York: Monthly Review Press, 1983.

Beevor, Antony. *The Spanish Civil War.* New York: Penguin, 2001.

Bender, Leslie. "From Gender Difference to Feminist Solidarity: Using Carol Gilligan and an Ethic of Care in Law." *Vermont Law Review* 15 (1990): 1–48.

—"A Lawyer's Primer on Feminist Theory and Tort." *Journal of Legal Education* 38 (1988): 3–37.

Bentham, Jeremy. *An Introduction to the Principles of Morals and Legislation,* ed., H.L.A. Hart. New York: Oxford University. Press, 1996.

Berger, Peter. *Invitation to Sociology: A Humanistic Perspective.* Garden City, N.Y.: Doubleday & Company, 1963.

Bitzer, Lloyd. "The Rhetorical Situation." *Philosophy and Rhetoric* 1(1968): 1–14.

Black, Edwin. *Rhetorical Criticism: A Study in Method.* Madison: University of Wisconsin Press, 1978.

—"The Second Persona." *Quarterly Journal of Speech* 56 (1970): 109–119.

Blair, Carole, Leslie A. Baxter, and Julie R. Brown. "Disciplining the Feminine." *Quarterly Journal of Speech* 80 (1994): 383–409.

Bologh, Roslyn Wallace. "Learning From Feminism: Social Theory and Intellectual Vitality." In *Intellectuals and Politics: Social Theory in a Changing World,* edited by Charles Lemert, 31–43. Newbury Park, CA: Sage, 1991.

Bonaparte, Charles J. "Lynch Law and Its Remedy." *Yale Law Journal* 8 (1899): 335–343.

Bonnie, Richard J., Anne M. Coughlin, John C. Jeffries, Jr., and Peter W. Low. *Criminal Law.* Westbury, NY: Foundation Press, 1997.

Bookchin, Murray. *The Spanish Anarchists: The Heroic Years: 1868–1936.* New York: Free Life Editions, 1977.

Bowen, James S. "Law, Legitimacy and Black Revolution." *The Yale Journal of Law and Liberation* 1 (1989): 83–99.

Boyd, Richard. "Compromising Positions: Or, the Unhappy Transformtions of a 'Transformative Intellectual.'" *Communication Theory* 9 (1999): 377–401.

Boyle, James. "Introduction." *Critical Legal Studies.* New York: New York University Press, 1992, xiii–liii.

Brass, Paul. *Theft of an Idol: Text and Context in the Representation of Collective Violence.* Princeton, NJ: Princeton University Press, 1997.

Broad, Dave. "New World Order Versus Just World Order." *Social Justice* 25 (1998): 6–16.

Bromwich, David. "Anti–Intellectualism." *Raritan* 16 (1996): 18–27.

Bruce, Robert V. *1877: Year of Violence.* Chicago: Ivan R. Dee Publisher, 1989.

Brummett, Barry. "Rhetorical Theory as Heuristic and Moral: A Pedagogical Justification." *Communication Education* 33 (1984): 97–107.

Bruner, M. Lane. "Global Constitutionalism and the Arguments Over Free Trade." *Communication Studies* 53 (2002): 25–39.

Buder, Stanley. *Pullman: An Experiment in Industrial Order and Community Planning, 1880–1930.* New York: Oxford University Press, 1997.

Bueler, William M. *An Agenda for Sustainability: Fairness in a World of Limits.* Notre Dame, IN: Cross Cultural Publications, 1997.

Burgoon, Michael. "Instruction About Communication: On Divorcing Dame Speech." *Communication Education* 38 (1989): 303–308.

Burke, Kenneth. *Permanence and Change.* Berkeley, CA: University of California Press, 1984.

—"Realisms, Occidental Style." In *Asian and Western Writers in Dialogue: New Cultural Identities*, edited by Guy Amirthanayagam, 26–47. London: Macmillan Press, 1982.

—*The Philosophy of Literary Form: Studies in Symbolic Action.* Berkeley, CA: University of California Press, 1973.

—*The Rhetoric of Religion: Studies in Logology.* Berkeley: University of California Press, 1970.

—*A Grammar of Motives.* Berkeley: University of California Press, 1969a.

—*A Rhetoric of Motives.* Berkeley: University of California Press, 1969b.

—"Revolutionary Symbolism in America." In *American Writers' Congress*, ed., Henry Hart, 87-94. New York: International Publishers, 1935.

Cameron, Edwin. "Human Rights, Racism, and AIDS: The New Discrimination." *South African Journal on Human Rights* 9 (1993): 22-29.

Campbell, Karlyn Kohrs. "Criticism: Ephemeral and Enduring." *Speech Teacher* 23 (1974): 9-14.

—"The Ontological Foundations of Rhetorical Theory." *Philosophy and Rhetoric* 3 (1970): 97-108.

Camus, Albert. *Resistance, Rebellion, and Death.* New York: Vintage, 1960.

Carbone, Michael. "Empowering the Liberal Arts: Analysis and Paradigms From Critical Theory." *Quarterly Journal of Ideology* 12 (1988):1-14.

Cardozo, Benjamin. *The Nature of the Judicial Process.* New Haven: Yale University Press, 1921.

Chafe, William Henry. *Civilities and Civil Rights: Greensboro, N.C. and the Struggle for Freedom.* New York: Oxford University Press, 1990.

Chaliand, Gerard. *Terrorism: From Popular Struggle to Media Spectacle.* London: Saqi Books, 1985.

Charland, Maurice. "Constitutive Rhetoric: The Case of the *Peuple Quebecois.*" *Quarterly Journal of Speech* 73 (1987): 133-150.

Chase, Anthony. "Historical Reconstruction in Popular Legal and Political Culture." *Seton Hall Law Review* 24 (1994): 1969-2029.

Chemerinsky, Erwin. *Federal Jurisdiction* 3rd ed. New York: Aspen, 1999.

—"History, Tradition, the Supreme Court, and the First Amendment." *Hastings Law Journal* (1993): 901-919.

Chomsky, Noam. *Rogue States: The Rule of Force in World Affairs.* Boston: South End Press, 2000.

—*Profit Over People: Neoliberalism & Global Order.* New York: Seven Stories Press, 1998.

—"'Consent Without Consent': Reflections on the Theory and Practice of Democracy." *Cleveland State Law Review* 44 (1996): 431–432.

—*Year 501: The Conquest Continues.* Boston: South End Press, 1993.

—*Necessary Illusions: Thought Control in Democratic Society.* Boston: South End Press, 1989.

—*Problems of Knowledge and Freedom*. New York: Pantheon Books, 1971.

—, Stuart Sahulka, and Greg Ruggerio, editors. *The Umbrella of Power: The Universal Declaration of Human Rights and the Contradictions of US Policy*. New York: Seven Stories, 1999.

Chowaniec, Michael. (From a town committee defining "partisan"). 1998. http://www.burlingtongop.org/defining.htm.

Claude, Judy. "Poverty Patterns for Black Men and Women." *The Black Scholar* 17 (1986): 20–23.

Clements, Kenrick A. *The Presidency of Woodrow Wilson*. Lawrence, KS: University Press of Kansas, 1992.

Cloud, Dana. "The Materiality of Discourse as Oxymoron: A Challenge to Critical Rhetoric." *Western Journal of Communication* 58 (1994): 141-163.

Cochran, Bert. "The Achievement of Debs." In *American Radicals: Some Problems and Personalities*, edited by Harvey Goldberg, 163–178. New York: Modern Reader Paperbacks, 1969.

Condit, Celeste Michelle. "The Critic as Empath: Moving Away From Totalizing Theory." *Western Journal of Communication* 57 (1993): 178–190.

Connor, Walker. "Beyond Reason: The Nature of the Ethnonational Bond." *Ethnic and Racial Studies* 16 (1993): 373–389.

Cooley, Thomas. *A Treatise on the Constitutional Limitations Which Rest Upon the Legislative Powers of the States of the American Union*. Boston: Little, Brown and Company, 1871.

Cooper, Jerry. *The Army and Civil Disorder: Federal Military Intervention in Labor Disputes, 1877–1900*. Westport, CT: Greenwood Publishing Group, 1980.

Corey, Frederick and Thomas Nakayama. "Nextext." *Journal of Homosexuality* 45 (2003): 319–334.

—"Sextext." *Text and Performance Quarterly* 17 (1997): 58–68.

Cose, Ellis. *The Rage of a Privileged Class: Why are Middle-Class Blacks Angry? Why Should America Care?* New York: HarperCollins, 1993.

"Court Revives Diversity Issue in Michigan." *The New York Times* (June 14, 2004): A11.

Cover, Robert. "Violence and the Word." *Yale Law Journal* 95 (1986): 1601–1629.

Cox, Archibald. "The Role of the Supreme Court: Judicial Activism or Self–Restraint." *Maryland Law Review* 47 (1987): 118–138.

—, Derek Curtis Bok, Robert A. Gorman, and Matthew W. Finkin. *Labor Law: Cases and Materials* 11th ed. New York: The Foundation Press, 1991.

Cushman, Ellen. "The Rhetorician as an Agent of Social Change." *College Composition and Communication* 47 (1996): 211–233.

Dalton, Harlon. *Racial Healing: Confronting the Fear Between Blacks and Whites.* New York: Anchor Books, 1996.

Darsey, James. "Must We All Be Rhetorical Theorists?: An Anti-democratic Inquiry." *Western Journal of Communication* 58 (1994): 164–181.

—"The Legend of Eugene Debs: Prophetic Ethos as Radical Argument." *Quarterly Journal of Speech* 74 (1988): 434–452.

David, Henry. *The History of the Haymarket Affair.* New York: Collier-Books, 1963.

Deetz, Stanley A. and Linda L. Putnam. "Thinking About the Future of Communication Studies." In *Communication Yearbook* 24, edited by William B. Gudykunst, 1–14. Thousand Oaks, CA: Sage, 2001.

Dervin, Brenda. "The Potential Contribution of Feminist Scholarship to the Field of Communication." *Journal of Communication* 37 (1987): 107–120.

DeSena, Judith N. "Local Gate Keeping Practices and Residential Segregation." *Sociological Inquiry* 64 (1994): 307–321.

Dewey, John. *The Quest for Certainty.* New York: G.P. Putnam, 1929.

Dorfman, Ariel. "Ideology, Exile, Language: An Interview With Ariel Dorfman." *Salmagundi* 82–83 (1989): 142–163.

Drinnon, Richard. *Rebel in Paradise.* Chicago: University of Chicago Press, 1982.

Du Bois, W.E.B. *Against Racism: Unpublished Essays, Papers, Addresses, 1887–1961.* Ed. Herbert Aptheker. Amherst: The University of Massachusetts Press, 1985.

Dubofsky, Melvyn and Foster Rhea Dulles. *Labor in America: A History* 6th ed. Wheeling, IL: Harlan Davison, Inc., 1999.

Dudziak, Mary. "Desegregation as a Cold War Imperative." *Stanford Law Review* 41 (1988): 61–120.

Dukeminier, Jesse and James Krier. *Property* 4th ed. New York: Aspen, 1998.

Dunn, Richard S. and Gary B. Nash. *Sugar and Slaves: The Rise of the Planter Class in the English West Indies,* 1624–1713. Chapel Hill, NC: University of North Carolina Press, 2000.

Easterbrook, Gregg. "Run–On Sentencing." *The New Republic* (April 26 and May 3, 1999), 57 and 60.

Edelman, Murray. "The Political Language of the Helping Professions." In *Selected Issues in Logic and Communication*, edited by Trudy Govier, 111–124. Belmount, CA: Wadsworth, 1988.

Ehrenreich, Barbara. *Nickel and Dimed: On (Not) Getting By in America.* New York: Metropolitan Books, 2001.

Eisenberg, Eric. "Flirting With Meaning." *Journal of Language and Social Psychology* 17 (1998): 97–109.

Ellickson, Robert C., Carol M. Rose, and Bruce A. Ackerman, editors. *Perspectives on Property Law* 2nd ed. Aspen Publishers, 1995.

Engen, David. E. "The Communicative Imagination and Its Cultivation." *Communication Quarterly* 50 (2002): 41–57.

Entine, Jon. "Rain–Forest *Chic.*" In *Business Ethics: Readings and Cases in Corporate Morality,* edited by W. Michael Hoffman, Robert E. Frederick, and Mark S. Schwartz, 590–598. New York: McGraw–Hill, 2001.

Farrell, Thomas. "On the Disappearance of the Rhetorical Aura." *Western Journal of Communication* 57 (1993): 147–158.

Fearon James and David Laitin. "Explaining Interethnic Cooperation." *American Political Science Review* 90 (1996), 715–733.

Feldstein, Martin. "Reducing Poverty, Not Inequality." *The Public Interest* 137 (1999): 33–41.

Ferguson, Robert A. "The Judicial Opinion as Literary Genre." *Yale Journal of Law & the Humanities* 2 (1990): 201–219.

Filippatos, Parisis. "The Doctrine of *Stare Decisis* and the Protection of Civil Rights Liberties in the Rehnquist Court." *Boston College Third World Law Journal* 11 (1991): 335–377.

Finnis, John. *Natural Law and Natural Rights.* New York: Oxford University Press, 1994.

Fish, Stanley. *Doing What Comes Naturally: Change, Rhetoric, and the Practice of Theory in Literary and Legal Studies.* Durham, NC: Duke University Press, 1989.

Flacks, Dick. "Making History and Making Theory: Notes on How Intellectuals Seek Relevance." In *Intellectuals and Politics: Social Theory in a Changing World*, edited by Charles Lemert, 3–18. Newbury Park, CA: Sage, 1991.

Foner, Eric. "Why Is There No Socialism in the United States?" *History Workshop Journal* 17 (1984): 57–80.

Foner, Philip. *May Day: A Short History of the International Workers' Holiday, 1886–1986.* New York: International Publishers, 1986.

—*The Great Labor Uprising of 1877.* New York: Monad Press, 1977.

Forbath, William E. *Law and the Shaping of the American Labor Movement.* Cambridge, MA: Harvard University Press, 1991.

—"The Ambiguities of Free Labor: Labor and the Law in the Guilded Age." *Wisconsin Law Review* 4 (1985): 767–817.

Fornek, Scott. "You're with us or against us, Bush says," http://www. sun times.com /terror/stories/cst–nws–main21.html. [2001]

Foss, Karen A., Sonja K. Foss, and Cindy L. Griffin. *Feminist Rhetorical Theories.* Thousand Oaks, CA: Sage, 1999.

Foss, Sonja K. and Cindy L. Griffin. "Beyond Persuasion: A Proposal for an Invitational Rhetoric." *Communication Monographs* 62 (1995): 2–18.

— Cindy L. Griffin, and Karen A. Foss. "Transforming Rhetoric Through Feminist Reconstruction: A Response to the Gender Diversity Perspective." *Woman's Studies in Communication* 20 (1997): 117–135.

— and Karen A. Foss. *Inviting Transformation: Presentational Speaking for a Changing World.* Prospect Heights, IL: Waveland Press, 2003.

Foucault, Michel. "On Popular Justice: A Discussion With Maoists." In *Power/Knowledge: Selected Interviews & Other Writings*, edited by Colin Gordon, 1–36. New York: Pantheon, 1980.

—*Discipline & Punish.* New York: Vintage, 1979.

Frank, Robert L. "Reason and Religion in *Rerum Novarum.*" *Southern Communication Journal* 56 (1991): 257–268.

Fraser, David. "If I Had a Rocket Launcher: Critical Legal Studies as Moral Terrorism." *Hastings Law Journal* 41 (1990): 777–804.

Fraser, Nancy. "What's Critical About Critical Theory? The Case of Habermas and Gender." *New German Critique* 35 (1985): 97–131.

Freeman, Sally, Stephen Littlejohn, and W. Barnett Pearce. "Communication and Moral Conflict." *Western Journal of Communication* 56 (1992): 311–329.

Frey, Lawrence R., W. Barnett Pearce, Mark A. Pollock, Lee Artz, and Bren A. O. Murphy. "Looking for Justice in all the Wrong Places: On a Communication Approach to Social Justice." *Communication Studies* 47 (1996): 110–127.

Friedland, Lewis A. "Communication, Community, and Democracy: Toward a Theory of the Communicatively Integrated Community." *Communication Research* 28 (2001): 358–391.

Friedman, Lawrence M. *A History of American Law* 2nd ed. New York: Simon & Schuster, 1985.

Frug, Gerald E. "The City as a Legal Concept." *Harvard Law Review* 93 (1980): 1059–1154.

Fuller, Lon L. *The Morality of Law.* New Haven: Yale University Press, 1969.

Fuoss, Kirk W. "'Community' Contested, Imagined, and Performed: Cultural Performance, Contestation, and Community in an Organized–Labor Social Drama." *Text and Performance Quarterly* 15 (1995): 79–98.

Gabel, Peter. "Reification in Legal Reasoning." *Research in Law and Sociology* 3 (1980): 25–51.

—rev. of *Taking Rights Seriously,* by Ronald Dworkin. *Harvard Law Review* 91 (1977): 302–315.

Gandhi, Mahatma. *Gandhi on Non–Violence.* New York: New Directions Publishing, 1965.

Gardner, James A. *Legal Argument: The Structure and Language of Effective Advocacy.* Charlottesville, VA: The Michie Company, 1993.

Gearhart, Sally Miller. "The Womanization of Rhetoric." *Women's Studies International Quarterly* 2 (1979): 195–201.

Gelbspam, Ross. *Break–Ins, Death Threats, and the FBI: The Covert War Against the Central America Movement.* Boston: South End Press, 1991.

Genovese, Eugene D. *Roll, Jordan, Roll: The World the Slaves Made.* New York: Pantheon Books, 1974.

George, Robley E. *Socioeconomic Democracy: An Advanced Socioeconomic System.* Westport: Pager, 2002.

Gibney, Mark. "United States' Responsibly for Gross Levels of Human Rights Violations in Guatemala from 1954 to 1996." *Journal of Transnational Law and Society* 7 (1997): 77–95.

Gilligan, Carol. *In a Different Voice.* Cambridge, MA: Harvard University Press, 1982.

Giroux, Henry A. "Public Pedagogy and the Responsibility of Intellectuals: Youth, Littleton, and the Loss of Innocence." *Journal of Advanced Composition* 20 (2000): 9–42.

—*Schooling and the Struggle for Public Life: Critical Pedagogy in the Modern Age.* Minneapolis: University of Minnesota Press, 1988.

Goldberg, Arthur J. "Klaus Barbie and the United States Government." *Harvard Civil Rights–Civil Liberties Law Review* 19 (1984): 1–14.

Goldhagen, Daniel. *Hitler's Willing Executioners: Ordinary Germans and the Holocaust.* New York: Vintage, 1997.

Goldman, Emma. *My Disillusionment in Russia.* Reprint Services Corp., 1991.

—*Living My Life.* New York: Dover Publications, 1970.

—*Anarchism and Other Essays.* New York: Dover Publications, 1969.

Goodrich, Peter. "Sleeping With the Enemy: An Essay on the Politics of Critical Legal Studies in America." *New York University Law Review* (1993), 389–425.

Gould, Stephen J. "Kropotkin Was No Crackpot." In *Bully For Brontosaurus,* 325–349. New York: W.W. Norton & Company, 1992.

—*Ever Since Darwin: Reflections in Natural History.* New York: Norton, 1977.

Graham, Hugh Davis and Ted Robert Gurr, editors. *Violence in America.* Beverly Hills, CA: Sage, 1979.

Griffin, Leland. "A Dramatistic Theory of the Rhetoric of Movements." In *Critical Responses to Kenneth Burke,* edited by William H. Rueckert, 456–478. Minneapolis: University of Minnesota Press, 1969.

Guattari, Felix and Antonio Negri. *Communists Like Us.* New York: Semiotext(e), 1990.

Guerin, Daniel. *Anarchism.* New York: Monthly Review Press, 1970.

Hansen, Mogens Herman. *The Athenian Democracy in the Age of Demosthenes.* Oxford, UK: Blackwell, 1991.

Hardt, Michael and Antonio Negri. *Empire.* Cambridge, MA: Harvard University Press, 2001.

Hariman, Robert. "The Rhetoric of Inquiry and the Professional Scholar." In *Rhetoric in the Human Sciences,* edited by Herbert Simons, 211–232. Newbury Park, CA: Sage, 1989.

Harris, David. *Cases and Materials on International Law* 5th ed. London: Sweet & Maxwell, 1998.

Hart, H.L.A. *The Concept of Law* 2nd ed. New York: Oxford University Press, 1997.

—"Positivism and the Separation of Law and Morals." *Harvard Law Review* 71 (1958): 593–629.

Hart, Roderick P. "Why Communication? Why Education? Toward A Politics of Teaching." *Communication Education* 42 (1993): 97–105.

—"The Functions of Human Communication in the Maintenance of Public Values." In *Handbook of Rhetorical and Communication Theory,* edited by Carroll C. Arnold and John Waite Bowers, 749–791. Boston: Allyn and Bacon, 1984.

Hasian, Marouf A. *The Rhetoric of Eugenics in Anglo-American Thought.* Athens: University of Georgia Press, 1996.

Havel, Vaclav. *The Art of the Impossible.* New York: Alfred A. Knopf, 1997.

Henwood, Doug. "Talking About Work." *Monthly Review* 49 (1987): 18–30.

Herman, Edward. "The United States Versus Human Rights in the Third World." *Harvard Human Rights Journal* 4 (1991): 85–104.

Hinks, Peter P. *To Awaken My Afflicted Brethren: David Walker and the Problem of Antebellum Slave Resistance.* College Park, PA: The Pennsylvania State University Press, 1996.

Hoffer, Eric. *The True Believer: Thoughts on the Nature of Mass Movements.* New York: HarperPerrenial, 1989.

Holland, Dewitte. "Socialism: Path to Economic Justice, 1890–1912." In *America in Controversy: History of American Public Address,* edited by DeWitte Holland, 205–222. Dubuque, IA: Wm. C. Brown Company Publishers, 1973.

Hollihan, Thomas. "Evidencing Moral Claims: The Activist Rhetorical Critic's First Task." *Western Journal of Communication* 58 (1994): 229–234.

Holt, Wythe. "Labour Conspiracy Cases in the United States, 1805–1842: Bias and Legitimation in Common Law Adjudication." *Osgoode Hall Law Journal* 22 (1984): 591–663.

Holtzman, Elizabeth. "United States Involvement With Nazi War Crimes." *New York Law School Journal of International and Comparative Law* 11 (1990): 337–345.

Hong, Nathaniel. "Constructing the Anarchist Beast in American Periodical Literature, 1880–1903." *Critical Studies in Mass Communication* 9 (1992): 110–130.

hooks, bell. *Killing Rage: Ending Racism.* New York: Henry Holt, 1995.

Horowitz, David. "Ten Reasons Why Reparations for Blacks Is a Bad Idea For Blacks—and Racist Too." *Front Page Magazine.com* (January 3, 2001).

Horowitz, Donald. *Ethnic Groups in Conflict* 2nd ed. Berkeley: University of California Press, 2000.

Hovenkamp, Herbert. "Regulatory Conflict in the Gilded Age: Federalism and the Railroad Problem." *Yale Law Journal* 97 (1988): 1017–1072.

Hunt, Everett Lee. "Plato and Aristotle on Rhetoric and Rhetoricians." In *Historical Studies of Rhetoric and Rhetoricians*, edited by Raymond F. Howes, 19–70. Ithaca, NY: Cornell University Press, 1961.

Ikenberry, G. John. "American Grand Strategy in the Age of Terror." *Survival* 43 (2001): 19–34.

Ingram, Jason. "Hegemony and Globalism: Kenneth Burke and Paradoxes of Representation." *Communication Studies* 53 (2002): 4–39.

Irons, Peter. *A People's History of the Supreme Court: The Men and Women Whose Cases and Decisions Have Shaped Our Constitution.* New York: Viking, 1999.

Ishitsuka, Shoji. "The Fall of Real Socialism and the Crisis in the Human Sciences, With Implications for Social Justice." *Social Justice* 21 (1994), 25–34.

Ivie, Robert. "Images of Savagery in American Justifications for War." *Communication Monographs* 47 (1980): 279–294.

Jacoby, Russell. "The Decline of American Intellectuals." In *Cultural Politics in Contemporary America*, edited by Ian Angus and Shut Jhally, 271–281. New York; Routledge, 1989a.

—"The Responsibility of Intellectuals?" *Grand Street* 8 (1989b): 185–195.

Jamieson, Kathleen. "Natural Law as Warrant." *Philosophy & Rhetoric* 6 (1973), 235–246.

Jennings, Marianne M. and Jon Entine. "Business With a Soul: A Reexamination of What Counts in Business Ethics." *Hamline Journal of Public Law and Policy* 20 (1999): 1–88.

Johnson, Sonia. "The Bears and Anarchy." In *The Ship That Sailed Into the Living Room: Sex and Intimacy Reconsidered*, 263–277. Estancia, NM: Wildfire Books, 1991.

Jones, J.S. "How Different are Human Races?" *Nature* 293 (1981), 188–190.

Jordan, Winthrop. *White Over Black*. Chapel Hill: University of North Carolina Press, 1968.

*Justinian's Institutes*. Trans. Peter Birks and Grant McLeod. Ithaca, NY: Cornell University Press, 1987.

Kalven, Harry, Jr. *A Worthy Tradition: Freedom of Speech in America*. New York: Harper & Row, 1988.

Karnow, Stanley. *Vietnam: A History*. New York: Penguin Press, 1991.

Katz, Stanley N. "Choosing Justice Over Excellence." *Chronicle of Higher Education* (May 17, 2002): B7.

Kellett, Peter M. and H.L. Goodall, Jr. "The Death of Discourse in Our Own (Chat) Room: 'Sextext,' Skillful Discussion, and Virtual Communities." In *Soundbite Culture: The Death of Discourse in a Wired World*, edited by David Slayden and Rita Whillock, 155–189. Thousand Oaks, CA: Sage, 1999.

Kennedy, Donald. *Academic Duty*. Cambridge, MA: Harvard University Press, 1997.

Kennedy, Duncan. *Legal Education and the Reproduction of Hierarchy: A Polemic Against the System*. Cambridge, MA: Afar, 1983.

Kennedy, Robert. "Is One Person's Terrorist Another's Freedom Fighter? Western and Islamic Approaches to 'Just War' Compared." *Terrorism and Political Violence* 11 (1999): 1–21.

Kidwell, Erin Rahne. "The Paths of the Law: Historical Consciousness, Creative Democracy, and Judicial Review." *Albany Law Review* (1998): 91–146.

King, Andrew. *Power & Communication.* Prospect Heights, IL: Waveland Press, 1987.

King, Jr., Martin Luther. *The Trumpet of Conscience.* New York: HarperCollins, 1987.

—*Stride Toward Freedom.* New York: HarperCollins, 1986.

Klehr, Harvey and John Earl Haynes. *The American Communist Movement.* New York: Twayne Publishers, 1992.

Klumpp, Jim and Thomas Hollihan. "Rhetorical Criticism as Moral Action." *Quarterly Journal of Speech* 75 (1989): 84–97.

Kolko, Gabriel. *The Politics of War: The World and United States Foreign Policy, 1943–1945.* New York: Pantheon Books, 1990.

Kornblum, William. *Sociology in a Changing World* 5th ed. New York: Harcourt Brace, 2000.

Kropotkin, Peter. *Evolution and Environment.* New York: Black Rose Books, 1995.

—*Mutual Aid: A Factor of Evolution.* New York: Black Rose Books, 1989.

Kuhn, Thomas S. *The Structure of Scientific Revolutions* 2nd ed. Chicago: University of Chicago Press, 1970.

Kuper, Leo. "Race, Class and Power: Some Comments on Revolutionary Change." *Comparative Studies in Society and History* 14 (1972): 400–421.

Lang, Bert. "Language and Genocide." In *Echoes From the Holocaust,* edited by Alan Rosenberg and Gerald E. Myers, 341–361. Philadelphia, PA: Temple University Press, 1988.

LaRue, L.H. *Constitutional Law as Fiction: Narrative in the Rhetoric of Authority.* University Park, PA: The Pennsylvania University Press, 1995.

Law, Carolyn Leste. "Introduction." In *This Fine Place So Far From Home: Voices of Academics From the Working Class.* Edited by C.L. Barney Dews and Carolyn Leste Law, 1–12. Philadelphia: Temple University Press, 1995.

Lawson, Don. *The Abraham Lincoln Brigade: Americans Fighting Fascism in the Spanish Civil War.* New York: Harper Collins: 1989.

Lee, WenShu. "Social Scientists as Ideological Critics." *Western Journal of Communication* 57 (1993): 221–232.

Lentricchia, Frank. *Criticism and Social Change.* Illinois: University of Chicago Press, 1985.

Levy, Leonard W. *The Law of the Commonwealth and Chief Justice Shaw: The Evolution of American Law, 1830–1860.* New York: Harper & Row, 1957.

Lewis, Justin. "Reproducing Political Hegemony in the United States." *Critical Studies in Mass Communication* 16 (1999): 251–267.

Leyendecker, Liston Edgington. *Palace Car Prince: A Biography of George Mortimer Pullman.* Niwot, CO: University Press of Colorado, 1994.

Licht, Walter. *Working for the Railroad: The Organization of Work in the Nineteenth Century.* Princeton, NJ: Princeton University Press, 1990.

Lindsey, Almont. *The Pullman Strike.* Chicago: University of Chicago Press, 1942.

Luger, Stan. *Corporate Power, American Democracy, and the Automobile Industry.* New York: Cambridge University Press, 2000.

Lum, Dyer D. *The Great Trial of the Chicago Anarchists.* New York: Arno Press, 1969.

Macke, Frank. "Communication Left Speechless: A Critical Examination of the Evolution of Speech as an Academic Discipline." *Communication Education* 40 (1991): 125–143.

MacKinnon, Catharine A. *Feminism Unmodified: Discourses on Life and Law.* Cambridge, MA: Harvard University Press, 1987.

—*Toward a Feminist Theory of the State.* Cambridge, MA: Harvard University Press, 1989.

Madriz, Esther. "Terrorism and Structural Violence." *Social Justice* 28 (2001): 45–47.

Makau, Josina and David Lawrence. "Administrative Judicial Rhetoric: The Supreme Court's New Thesis of Political Morality." *Argumentation and Advocacy* 30 (1994), 191–205.

Manicas, Peter T. "John Dewey: Anarchism and the Political State." *Transactions of the Charles S. Pierce Society* 18 (1982): 133–158.

Maresca, John J. "A New Concept of Business." *The Washington Quarterly* (Spring, 2000): 155–163.

Marger, Martin N. *Race and Ethnic Relations: American and Global Perspectives* 4th ed. Belmont, CA: Wadsworth, 1997.

Marx, Karl. *Early Writings*. New York: McGraw–Hill, 1964.

—*Selected Writings in Sociology & Social Philosophy*. New York: McGraw Hill, 1956.

McCaughan, Edward J. "Violence, Inequality, and the 'Civilized' World." *Social Justice* 28 (2001): 39–41.

McChesney, Robert. *Rich Media, Poor Democracy: Communication Politics in Dubious Times*. New York: New Press, 2000.

McGee, Brian. "The Argument From Definition Revisited: Race and Definition in the Progressive Era." *Argumentation and Advocacy* 35 (1999), 141–158.

McGee, Michael McGee. "The 'Ideograph': A Link Between Rhetoric and Ideology." *Quarterly Journal of Speech* 66 (1980), 1–16.

McKerrow, Raymie. "Critical Rhetoric: Theory and Praxis." *Communication Monographs* 56 (1989): 91–111.

Meehan, Eileen R. "Working Hard for a Living: Labor and Media." *Journal of Communication* 47 (1997): 165–169.

Melson, Robert. "Ideology and Inconsistency: The 'Cross–Pressured' Nigerian Worker." *American Political Science Review* 65 (1971): 161–171.

Messer–Davidow, Ellen. *Disciplining Feminism*. Durham, NC: Duke University Press, 2002.

Midgley, Mary. *Science and Poetry*. New York: Routledge, 2001.

Miliband, Ralph. "The New World Order and the Left." *Social Justice* 23 (1996): 14–21.

Mills, C. Wright. "The Social Role of the Intellectual." In *Power, Politics, and People: The Collected Essays of C. Wright Mills*, 292–304. New York: Ballatine Books, 1963.

—*The Sociological Imagination*. New York: Oxford University Press, 1959.

Moberg, David. "Union Busting, Past and Present: Charting an Old American Tradition." *Dissent* (Winter, 1992): 73–80.

Moran, Rachel F. "Diversity and its Discontents: The End of Affirmative Action at Boalt Hall." *California Law Review* 88 (2000), 2241–2353.

Murphy, Cait. "Crime and Punishment." *Fortune* (April 30, 2001): 126–132.

Murphy, Rhoads. *East Asia: A New History*. New York: Longman Publishing Group, 1997.

Nader, Ralph. *Unsafe at Any Speed: The Designed-In Dangers of the American Automobile.* New York: Gossman Publishers, 1965.

Nelles, Walter. "*Commonwealth v. Hunt.*" *Columbia Law Review* 32 (1932): 1166–1169.

—"The First American Labor Case." *Yale Law Journal* 41 (1931): 165–200.

Nielsen, Kai. "A Moral Case for Socialism." *Critical Review* 3 (1989): 542–553.

Nietzsche, Friedrich. *Daybreak: Thoughts on the Prejudices of Morality.* New York: Cambridge University Press, 1997.

—*The Birth of Tragedy & The Genealogy of Morals.* New York: Doubleday, 1956.

Nothstine, William, Carole Blair, and Gary A. Copeland. "Professionalization and the Eclipse of Critical Invention." In *Critical Questions: Invention, Creativity, and the Criticism of Discourse and Media*, edited by William Nothstine, Carole Blair, and Gary A. Copeland, 15–70. New York: St. Martin's Press, 1994.

Nothstine, William and Gary A. Copeland. "Against the Bureaucratization of Criticism." *Pennsylvania Speech Communication Annual* 45 (1989): 19–28.

Nussbaum, Martha C. "Compassion and Terror." *Daedalus* (Winter 2003): 10–26.

—*Poetic Justice: The Literary Imagination and Public Life.* Boston: Beacon, 1995.

Olzak, Susan. *The Dynamics of Ethnic Competition and Conflict.* Stanford, CA: Stanford University Press, 1992.

Ono, Kent A. "A Letter/Essay I've Been Longing to Write in My Personal/Academic Voice." *Western Journal of Communication* 61 (1997): 114–125.

Orwell, George. *Homage to Barcelona.* New York: Harcourt Brace & Company, 1952.

Owen, Susan and Peter Ehrenhaus. "Animating a Critical Rhetoric: On the Feeding Habits of American Empire." *Western Journal of Communication* 57 (1993): 169–177.

*Oxford American Dictionary of Current English.* New York: Oxford University Press, 1999.

Packer, George. "America's Age of Empire: For Liberals Who Oppose Bush's Imperial Strategy, It's Time to Come Up with a Foreign Policy Vision of Their Own." *Mother Jones* (Jan.–Feb.), 2003, 34.

Palley, Claire. *Constitutional Law and Minorities.* London: Minority Rights Group Report No. 36, 1978.

Palmeri, Anthony J. "On Cultural Studies and Radical Politics: Movements, Critique of Capitalism, and Rhetoric." *Journal of Communication Inquiry* 21 (1997): 35–44.

Papke, David Ray. *The Pullman Case: The Clash of Labor and Capital in Industrial America.* Lawrence, KS: University Press of Kansas, 1999.

—"Eugene Debs as Legal Heretic: The Law–Related Conversion, Catechism, and Evangelism of an American Socialist." *University of Cincinnati Law Review* 63 (1994): 339–375.

— *Framing the Criminal: Crime, Cultural Work, and the Loss of Critical Perspective, 1830–1900.* Hamden, CT: Archon Books, 1987.

Parenti, Christian. "Crime As Social Control." *Social Justice* 27 (2000): 43–49.

Parenti, Michael. *Blackshirts & Reds: Rational Fascism & the Overthrow of Communism.* San Francisco: City Lights, 1997.

— *The Anti–Communist Impulse.* New York: Random House, 1969.

Payne, Stanley G. *Fascism in Spain.* Madison: University of Wisconsin Press, 1999.

Phillips, Edward. *The New World of English Words.* Menston, England: The Scholar Press Limited, 1658/1969.

Phillips, Kevin. *Wealth and Democracy: A Political History of the American Rich.* New York: Broadway Books, 2002.

Pinkerton, Edward C. *Word for Word.* Detroit, MI: Verbatim, 1982.

Plato. *Gorgias*, trans. W.C. Helmbold. Indianapolis: The Bobbs–Merrill Co., 1952.

Platt, Anthony M. "Social Insecurity: The Transformation of American Criminal Justice, 1965–2000." *Social Justice* 28 (2001): 138–156.

Rabban, David M. "The IWW Free Speech Fights and Popular Conceptions of Free Expression Before World War I." *Virginia Law Review* 80 (1994): 1055–1158.

— "The Emergence of Modern First Amendment Doctrine." *University of Chicago Law Review* 50 (1983): 1247–1265.

*Racial Equality: Public Policies for the Twenty-First Century.* New York: The American Assembly, 2001.

Rawlins, William. "Teaching as Mode of Friendship." *Communication Theory* 10 (2000): 5–26.

Readings, Bill. *The University in Ruins.* Cambridge, MA: Harvard University Press, 1997.

Redding, W. Charles. "Rocking Boats, Blowing Whistles, and Teaching Speech Communication." *Communication Education* 34 (1985): 245–258.

Ricks, Thomas E. "Empire or Not? A Quiet Debate Over US Role." *The Washington Post* (August 21, 2001): A01.

Riley, Susan. "Productivity, Private Wealth and Public Squalour." *The Ottawa Citizen* (1999, Jan. 15), A–13.

Robinson, William I. and Jerry Harris. "Towards a Global Ruling Class? Globalization and the Transnational Capitalist Class." *Science & Society* 64 (2000): 11–54.

Rodden, John G. "Field of Dreams." *Western Journal of Communication* 57 (1993): 111–138.

Rodriguez, Amardo. *On Matters of Liberation (1): The Case Against Hierarchy.* Cresskill, NJ: Hampton Press, 2001.

Rorty, Richard. "Humiliation or Solidarity?" *Dissent* (Fall 2003): 23–26.

— *Against Bosses, Against Oligarchies.* Chicago: Prickly Paradigm Press, 2002.

—*Philosophy and Social Hope.* New York: Penguin, 1999.

—*Achieving our Country,* Cambridge, MA: Harvard University Press, 1998a

— "Marxists, Straussians, and Pragmatists." *Raritan* 18 (1998b): 128–137.

—"What's Wrong With 'Rights.'" *Harpers* (June 1996): 15–19.

—"The Professor and the Prophet." *Transition* 52 (1991): 70–78.

— *Contingency, Irony, and Solidarity.* New York: Oxford University Press, 1989a.

—"Education Without Dogma." *Dissent* (Spring, 1989b): 198–205.

—"The Humanistic Intellectual: Eleven Theses." *ACLS Occasional Papers* 11 (1989c): 9–12.

—"What Are Philosophers For?" *The Center Magazine* (Sep./Oct. 1983): 40–44.

—*Philosophy and the Mirror of Nature.* Princeton, NJ: Princeton University Press, 1979.

Ross, Thomas. "The Rhetorical Tapestry of Race: White Innocence and Black Abstraction." *William and Mary Law Review* 32 (1990), 1–40.

Rousseau, Jean-Jacques. *The Social Contract and the Discourses*, trans. G.D. Cole. New York: Everyman's Library, 1993.

Ruff, Allen. "We Called each Other Comrade": Charles H. Kerr & Company, Radical Publishers. Urbana: University of Illinois Press, 1997.

Said, Edward. "Gods That Always Fail." *Raritan* 13 (1994): 1–14.

Salvatore, Nick. *Eugene V. Debs: Citizen and Socialist.* Urbana: University of Illinois Press, 1984.

Sanders, Marion. *The Professional Radical: Conversations With Saul Alinsky.* New York: Harper & Row, 1970.

Sandinista Liberation Front. In *Central American Crises Reader*, edited by Robert Leiken and Barry Rubin. New York: Summit Books, 1986.

Sarat, Austin and Thomas R. Kearns, editors. *The Rhetoric of Law.* Ann Arbor: The University of Michigan Press, 1996.

Sayer, John. "Art and Politics, Dissent and Repression: The Masses Magazine Versus the Government, 1917–1918." *The American Journal of Legal History* 32 (1988): 42–78.

Schiappa, Edward. "Intellectuals and the Place of Cultural Critique." In *Rhetoric, Cultural Studies, and Literacy*, edited by Fred Reynolds, 21–18. Hillsdale, NJ: Lawrence Erlbaum, 1995.

Schiller, Reuel E. "Conflicting Obligations: Slave Law and the Late Antebellum North Carolina Supreme Court." *Virginia Law Review* 78 (1992): 1207–1251.

Schmitz, David F. *United States and Fascist Italy, 1922–1940.* Chapel Hill: University of North Carolina, 1988.

Schultz, Bud and Ruth Schultz. *It Did Happen Here: Recollections of Political Repression in America.* Berkeley: University of California Press, 1990.

Sciffrin, Andre, editor. *The Cold War & The University: Toward An Intellectual History of the Postwar Years.* New York: The New Press, 1997.

Scott, Robert L. and Donald K. Smith. "The Rhetoric of Confrontation." *Quarterly Journal of Speech* 55 (1969): 1–8.

Seale, Bobby. *Seize the Time: The Story of the Black Panther Party and Huey P. Newton.* Baltimore: Black Classics Press, 1991.

Sexton, Patricia Cayo. *The War on Labor and the Left.* Boulder, CO: Westview Press, 1991.

Shapiro, Svi. "Clinton and Education: Policies Without Meaning." *Tikkun* (May–June, 1994): 17–20.

Sharma, Sohan and Surinder Kumar. "Debt Relief—Indentured Servitude for the Third World." *Race & Class* (2002): 45–56.

Shlapentokh, Dmitry. "The New Anti-Americanism: America as an Orwellian Society." *Partisan Review* 69 (2002): 263–273.

Silcock, T.H. "The Effects of Industrialization on Race Relations in Malaya." In *Industrialization and Race Relations: A Symposium*, edited by Guy Hunter, 177–199. Oxford University Press, 1965.

Simon, Steven and Daniel Benjamin. "The Terror." *Survival* 43 (2001): 5–18.

Simpson, John. and Edmund S. Weiner. *The Oxford English Dictionary* 2nd ed. v. 11 Oxford: Clarendon Press, 1989.

Sinclair, Upton. *The Jungle.* Cutchogue, NY: Buccaneer Books, 1996.

Singer, Peter. *Practical Ethics* 2nd ed. Cambridge, UK: Cambridge University Press, 1993.

Sklar, Holly. "Imagine a Country." *Z Magazine* (July/August, 1997). http://www. thirdworldtraveler.com /Society/ImagineZ.html.

Slater, Philip. *The Pursuit of Loneliness: American Culture at the Breaking Point.* Boston: Beacon Press, 1970.

Slaughter, Thomas P. *The Whisky Rebellion: Frontier Epilogue to the American Revolution.* New York: Oxford University Press, 1988.

Sloan, John. H. "American Imperialism." In *America in Controversy: History of American Public Address*, edited by DeWitte Holland, 123–134. Dubuque, IA: Wm. C. Brown Company Publishers, 1973.

Smith, Christopher E. and Avis Alexandria Jones. "The Rehnquist Court's Activism and Risk of Injustice." *Connecticut Law Review* 26 (1993): 53–77.

Smith, Tony. *The Pattern of Imperialism: The United States, Great Britain, and the Late-Industrializing World Since 1815.* New York: Cambridge University Press, 1981.

Solomon, Martha. "The Rhetoric of Dehumanization: An Analysis of Medical Reports of the Tuskegee Syphilis Project." *Western Journal of Speech Communication* 49 (1985), 233–247.

Sontag, Susan. "America." *Partisan Review* (1967): 51–58.

Spitzack, Carole and Kathryn Carter. "Research on Women's Communication: The Politics of Theory and Method." In *Doing Research on Woman's Communication: Perspective on Theory and Method*, edited by Kathryn Carter and Carole Spitzack, 11–39. Norwood, HN: Ablex Publishing, 1989.

Staples, Steven. "The Relationship Between Globalization and Militarism." *Social Justice* 27 (2000): 18–22.

Stewart, Charles. "Labor Agitation in America: 1865–1915." In *America in Controversy: History of American Public Address*, edited by DeWitte Holland, 153–169. Dubuque, IA: Wm. C. Brown Company Publishers, 1973.

—, Craig Allen Smith, and Robert Denton, Jr., *Persuasion and Social Movements* 2nd ed. Prospects Heights, IL: Waveland Press, 1989.

Stowell, David O. *Streets, Railroads, and the Great Strike of 1877.* Chicago: University of Chicago Press, 1999.

Strate, Lance. "Community, Citizen, Cyberspace, and Communication," presented at the University of Denver to the Rocky Mountain Communication Association, February 16, 2002.

Swartz, Omar. *Socialism and Communication: Reflections on Language and Left Politics.* Aldershot, UK: Ashgate Press, 1999.

— *Conducting Socially Responsible Research: Critical Theory, Neo-Pragmatism, and Rhetorical Inquiry.* Thousand Oaks, CA: Sage, 1997a.

—"Disciplining the 'Other': Engaging Blair, Brown, and Baxter." *Southern Communication Journal* 62 (1997b): 253–256.

Taylor, Alan. *Liberty Men and Great Proprietors: The Revolutionary Settlement on the Maine Frontier, 1760–1820.* Chapel Hill: University of North Carolina Press, 1990.

Thayer, Lee. "On 'Doing' Research and 'Explaining' Things." *Journal of Communication* 33 (1983): 81–91.

*The US Constitution: And Fascinating Facts About It* 6th ed. Naperville, IL: Oak Hill Publishing, 1997.

Thomas, Francis–Noel and Mark Turner. *Clear and Simple As The Truth.* Princeton, NJ: Princeton University Press, 1994.

Thoreau, Henry David. *A Plea For Captain John Brown.* Boston: D.R. Godline, 1969.

—— "Civil Disobedience." In *Walden and Civil Disobedience*, 222–240. The New American Library, 1960.

Trent, Judith S. "Prospects for the Future: The Communication Scholar as Citizen." *Communication Studies* 51 (2000): 189–194.

Trofimov, Yaroslav. "Voters Fed up With Petty Crime Give Le Pen Boost." *Wall Street Journal* (April 29, 2002, Section A; Page 1, Column 1).

Tucker, Robert. "The Purposes of American Power." *Foreign Affairs* (Winter, 1980): 241–274.

Tyson, Ann Scott. "Where Antiterror Doctrine Leads: Bush Lays Groundwork for Striking First at Nations With Weapons of Mass Destruction." *The Christian Science Monitor* (February 7, 2002), http://www.csmoni tor. com/2002/0207/ p01s03–usmi.html.

Unger, Roberto Mangabeira. *Critical Legal Studies Movement*. Cambridge, MA: Harvard University Press, 1986.

Van Alstyne, William W. *First Amendment: Cases and Materials* 2nd ed. Weston, NY. The Foundation Press, 1995.

Vatz, Richard. "The Myth of the Rhetorical Situation." *Philosophy and Rhetoric* 6 (1973): 154–157.

Veblen, Thorstein B. *The Theory of the Leisure Class*. Amherst, NY: Prometheus Books, 1998.

Voltaire. *The Portable Voltaire*. Ed. Ben Ray Redman. New York: Penguin Books, 1977.

Voos, Paula B. "Progressive Perspectives on Union Renewal." *Work and Occupations* 27 (2000): 244–253.

Voss, Kim. *The Making of American Exceptionalism: The Knights of Labor and Class Formation in the Nineteenth Century*. Ithaca, NY: Cornell University Press, 1994.

Wacquant, Loic. "Deadly Symbiosis: When Ghetto and Prison Meet and Mesh." *Punishment and Society* 3 (2001): 95–134.

Wallace, Karl R. "Topoi and the Problem of Invention." In *The New Rhetoric of Chaim Perelman*, edited by Ray D. Dearin, 107–120. Lanham, MD: University Press of America, 1989.

Wallis, Victor. "A Radical Approach to Justice for 9/11." *Socialism and Democracy* 16 (2002): 156–160.

Wander, Philip C. "Freeing a Leafhopper: A Note on Rhetorical Contextualization and Cultures." In *Communication: Views From the Helm For the twenty-first Century*, edited by Judith S. Trent, Boston, 404–417. Boston: Allyn Bacon, 1998.

—"Commentary." In *Critical Questions: Invention, Creativity, and the Criticism of Discourse and Media*, edited by William L. Nothstine, Carole Blair, and Gary A. Copeland, 383–388. New York: St. Martin's Press, 1994.

—"Introduction: Special Issue on Ideology." *Western Journal of Communication* 57 (1993): 105–110.

—"The Politics of Despair." *Communication* 11 (1990): 277–290.

—"The Rhetoric of American Foreign Policy." *Quarterly Journal of Speech* 70 (1984a): 339–361.

—"The Third Persona: An Ideological Turn in Rhetorical Theory." *Central States Speech Journal* 35 (1984b): 197–216.

—"The Ideological Turn in Modern Criticism." *Central States Speech Journal* 34 (1983): 1–18.

—and Steven Jenkins. "Rhetoric, Society, and the Critical Response." *Quarterly Journal of Speech* 58 (1972): 441–450.

Ward, Tony and Penny Green. "Legitimacy, Civil Society, and State Crime." *Social Justice* 27 (2000): 76–94.

Weaver, Richard. *The Ethics of Rhetoric*. Davis, CA: Hermagoras Press, 1985.

—*Ideas Have Consequences*. Chicago: University of Chicago Press, 1984.

—*Language is Sermonic: Richard M. Weaver and the Nature of Rhetoric*. Editors Richard L. Johannesen, Rennard Strickland, and Ralph T. Eubanks. Baton Rouge: Louisiana State University Press, 1970.

Webster, Noah. *An American Dictionary of the English Language* v. 2. New York: Johnson Reprint Corporation, 1828/1970.

Weinreb, Lloyd. *Natural Law and Justice*. Cambridge, MA: Harvard University Press, 1987.

White, James Boyd. *When Words Lose Their Meaning: Constitutions and Reconstitutions of Language, Character, and Community*. Illinois: University of Chicago Press, 1984.

Wilkinson, James D. "Truth and Delusion: European Intellectuals in Search of the Spanish Civil War." *Salmagundi* (Fall 1987–Winter 1988): 3–52.

Willis, Paul E. *Learning to Labour: How Working Class Kids Get Working Class Jobs.* New York: Columbia University Press, 1981.

Wilson, Carter. *Racism: From Slavery to Advanced Capitalism.* Thousand Oaks, CA: Sage, 1996.

Wood, Julia T. "Ethics, Justice, and the 'Private Sphere.'" *Women's Studies in Communication* 21 (1998): 127–149.

Wright, R.S. *The Law of Criminal Conspiracies and Agreements.* Philadelphia, PA: The Blackstone Publishing Company, 1887.

Zarefsky, David. *President Johnson's War on Poverty: Rhetoric and History.* Tuscaloosa: University of Alabama Press, 1986.

—, Carol Miller–Tutzauer, and Frank E. Tutzauer. "Reagan's Safety Net for the Truly Needy: The Rhetorical Uses of Definition." *Central States Speech Journal* 35 (1984): 113–119.

Zinn, Howard. *The Politics of History* 2nd ed. Urbana: University of Illinois Press, 1990a.

—"Economic Justice: The American Class System." In *Declarations of Independence: Cross–Examining American Ideology,* 147–181. New York: HarperPerennial, 1990b.

—*A People's History of the United States.* New York: HarperPerrenial, 1980).

—*Disobedience and Democracy: Nine Fallacies on Law and Order.* New York: Vintage Books, 1968.

## ✶ CASES CITED ✶

*Abood v. Detroit Board of Education,* 431 US 209 (1977).

*Abrams v. United States,* 250 US 616 (1919).

*Arver v. United States,* 245 US 366 (1918).

*Bottoms v. Bottoms,* 457 S.Ed.2d 102 (Va. 1995).

*Bowers v. Hardwick,* 478 US 186 (1986).

*Brown v. Board of Education of Topeka,* 349 US 294 (1955).

*Brandenburg v. Ohio,* 395 US 444 (1969).

*Commonwealth v. Hunt,* 4 Metc, 111 (1842).

*Commonwealth v. Pullis,* Mayor's Court of Philadelphia, 1806. Reprinted in Commons, Phillips, Gilmore, Sumner, and Andrews, *A Documentary History of American Industrial Society,* 59-248.

*Debs v. United States*, 249 US 211 (1919).

*Dennis v. United States*, 341 US 494 (1951).

*Dred Scott v. Sandford*, 60 US (19 How.) 393 (1857).

*Ex parte Milligan*, 71 US 2 (4 Wall.) (1866).

*FDA vs. Brown & Williamson Tobacco Corp*, 529 US 120 (2000).

*Fong Yue Ting v. United States*, 149 US 698 (1893).

*Gitlow v. New York*, 268 US 652 (1925).

*Gratz v. Bollinger*, 539 US 244 (2003).

*Grutter v. Bollinger*, 539 US 306 (2003).

*Hudgens v. National Labor Relations Board*, 424 US 507 (1976).

*In The Matter of Allison D. v. Virginia M.*, N.Y. Ct. of App., 77 N.Y.2d 651 (1991).

*In re Debs*, 158 US 564 (1895).

*In re Jacobs*, 98 N.Y. 98 (1885).

*Johnson v. M'Intosh*, 21 US (8 Wheat.) 543 (1823).

*Korematsu v. United States*, 323 US 214 (1944).

*Lochner v. New York*, 198 US 45 (1905).

*Loving v. Virginia*, 388 US 1 (1967).

*Marsh v. Alabama*, 26 US 501 (1946).

*Masses Publishing Co. v. Patten*, 244 Fed. 535 (S.D.N.Y. 1917).

*McCleskey v. Kemp*, 481 US 279 (1987).

*Moore v. City of East Cleveland*, 431 US 494 (1977).

*Muller v. Oregon*, 208 US 412 (1908).

*Nebbia v. New York*, 291 US 502 (1934).

*Nollan v. California Coastal Commission*, 483 US 825 (1987).

*Painter v. Bannister*, 140 N.W.2d 152 (1966).

*Palmore v. Sidoti*, 466 US 429 (1984).

*Personnel Administrator of Massachusetts v. Feeney*, 442 US 256 (1979).

*Plessy v. Ferguson*, 163 US 537 (1896).

*Pruneyard Shipping Center v. Robins*, 447 US 74 (1980).

*Reed v. Reed*, 404 US 71 (1971).

*Regents of University of California v. Bakke*, 438 US 265 (1978).

*Rex v. Journeymen Tailors of Cambridge*, 8 Modern 10 (K.B., 1721).

*Richmond v. J.A. Croson Co.*, 448 US 555 (1980).

*Roe v. Roe*, 324 S.E.2d 691 (Va. 1985).

*Roe v. Wade*, 410 US 113 (1973).

*San Antonio Independent School District v. Rodriguez*, 411 US 1 (1973).

*Schenck v. United States*, 249 US 47 (1919).
*Skinner v. Oklahoma*, 316 US 535 (1942).
*Slaughter-House Cases*, 83 US 36, (1872).
*State v. Boon*, Taylor's (N.C.) Reps. 246 (1801).
*State v. Caesar*, 9 Iredell (N.C.) 391 (1849).
*State v. Hale*, 2 Hawks (N.C.) 582 (1823).
*State v. Hoover*, 4 Devereux and Battle's Law Reps. (N.C.) 365 (1839).
*State v. Mann*, 2 Devereux and Battle's Law Reps. (N.C.) 263 (1829).
*State v. Rhodes*, N.C. Sup. Ct., 61 N.C. 453 (1868).
*State v. Robbins*, 48 N.C. (3 Jones) 249 (1855).
*State v. Will*, 1 Devereux and Battle's Law Reps. (N.C.) 121 (1834).
*Tahoe-Sierra Preservation Council, Inc. v. Tahoe Regional Planning Agency*, 216 F.3d 764 (2002).
*The Antelope*, 23 US 66 (1825).
*United States v. Mitchell*, 26 F.Cas.1277 (1795).
*Vegelahn v. Guntner*, 167 Mass. 92, (1886).
*West Virginia State Board of Education v. Barnette*, 319 US 624 (1943).
*Whitney v. California*, 274 US 357 (1927).
*Yania v. Bigan*, 155 A.2d 343 (1959).

# INDEX


Ackerman, Bruce A., 126
Agger, Ben, 2, 71, 95, 130, 242
Allen, Brenda J., 99, 110
Anderson, Perry, 109
Angelou, Maya, 14
Aquinas, Thomas, 207, 212
Aristotle, 5, 69, 212
Aronson, Ronald, 127, 128, 245
Artz, Lee, 2, 12, 19, 63, 64, 129
Austin, John, 207, 208, 209, 211
Avery, Dianne, 141, 142, 161, 178, 184
Avrich, Paul, 159, 169
Ayto, John, 3
Bach, Tullen, 93
Bain, David, 158
Bakunin, Michael, 128, 160, 173
Barthes, Roland, 77
Bartlett, Katharine, 105
Bavis, Craig D., 105
Baxter, Leslie A., 86, 93, 94
Beaud, Michel, 140, 196
Beevor, Antony, 164
Bender, Leslie, 67
Benjamin, Daniel, 43, 56, 118
Bentham, Jeremy, 207, 209, 211, 213
Berger, Peter, 255
Bitzer, Lloyd, 212
Black, Edwin, 25, 118
Blair, Carole, 86, 93, 94, 118
Bologh, Roslyn Wallace, 130
Bonaparte, Charles J, 170
Bonnie, Richard J., 145
Bookchin, Murray, 162
Bowen, James S., 190
Box, Derek Curtis, 155
Boyd, Richard, 8, 13, 106, 136
Boyle, James, 21, 38
Brass, Paul, 259
Broad, Dave, 41
Brown, Julie R., 86, 93, 94
Bruce, Robert V., 141
Brummett, Barry, 129
Bruner, M. Lane, 125, 127, 175
Buder, Stanley, 181
Bueler, William M., 253
Burgoon, Michael, 35
Burke, Kenneth, xv, xvi, xvii, 7, 10, 29, 71, 91, 99, 114, 124, 128, 162, 249, 250, 251
Cameron, Edwin, 246
Campbell, Karlyn Kohrs, 97
Camus, Albert, 7, 91, 117
Carbone, Michael, 70, 87
Cardozo, Benjamin, 43, 56
Carter, Kathryn, 8, 90
Chafe, William Henry, 190
Chaliand, Gerard, 165
Charland, Maurice, 242
Chase, Anthony, 64
Chemerinsky, Erwin, 43
Chomsky, Noam, 7, 41, 59, 119, 134, 160, 198, 199, 259
Chowaniec, Michael, 3
Claude, Judy, 212
Clements, Kenrick A., 191
Cloud, Dana, 109, 110
Cochran, Bert, 177
Connor, Walker, 249
Cooley, Thomas, 41
Cooper, Jerry, 161
Copeland, Gary A., 86, 118
Corey, Frederick, 82, 84
Cose, Ellis, 201
Coughlin, Anne M., 145
Cover, Robert, 205
Cox, Archibald, 155, 242
Cushman, Ellen, 132
Dalton, Harlon, 136
Darsey, James, 97, 180
David, Henry, 140, 169
Deetz, Stanley A., 31
Dervin, Brenda, 90

DeSena, Judith N., 199
Dewey, John, 27, 175
Dorfman, Ariel, 122
Drinnon, Richard, 160
Du Bois, W.E.B., 133
Dubofsky, Melvyn, 174, 181, 182, 183, 184, 185, 187
Dudziak, Mary, 201
Dukeminier, Jesse, 69
Dunn, Richard S., 125
Easterbrook, Gregg, 171
Edelman, Murray, 99
Ehrenhaus, Peter, 69, 70, 72
Ehrenreich, Barbara, 130
Eisenberg, Eric, 123
Ellickson, Robert C., 126
Engen, David. E, 19
Entine, Jon, 52
Farrell, Thomas, 110
Fearon James, 251
Feldstein, Martin, 124
Ferguson, Robert A., 203, 204
Filippatos, Parisis, 43
Finkin, Matthew W., 155
Finnis, John, 207, 208
Fish, Stanley, 90
Flacks, Dick, 86
Foner, Eric, 178, 194
Foner, Mark, 174
Foner, Philip, 141, 168, 169, 171
Forbath, William, 40, 43, 140, 152, 178, 181
Fornek, Scott, 59
Foss, Karen A., 98, 101, 154
Foss, Sonja K., 22, 98, 101, 104, 154
Foucault, Michel, 7, 91, 113, 117, 157, 213
Frank, Robert L., 206
Fraser, David, 25, 110
Frederick, Robert E., 82, 91
Freeman, Sally, 102
Frey, Lawrence R., xiii, 2, 19, 63
Friedman, Lawrence M., 184
Frug, Gerald E., 27
Fuller, Lon L., 212
Fuoss, Kirk W., 21, 153
Gabel, Peter, 20, 21, 28, 29
Gandhi, Mahatma, 14, 76, 108, 162, 171
Gardner, James A., 203
Gearhart, Sally Miller, 102, 115
Gelbspam, Ross, 188
Genovese, Eugene D., 204, 205, 215
George, Robley E., 132
Gibney, Mark, 116
Gilligan, Carol, 65
Giroux, Henry A., 68
Goldberg, Arthur J., 164
Goldhagen, Daniel, 10
Goldman, Emma, 7, 126, 159, 160, 161, 175, 251, 253
Goodall, Jr, H.L., 83
Goodrich, Peter, 91
Gorman, Robert A., 155
Gould, Stephen J., 256
Graham, Hugh Davis, 166
Green, Penny, 58
Griffin, Cindy L., 98, 101, 154
Griffin, Leland, 112
Guattari, Felix, 120, 121
Guerin, Daniel, 160, 178
Gurr, Ted Robert, 166
Hamilton, Charles V., 52
Hansen, Mogens Herman, 158
Hardt, Michael, 70, 71
Hariman, Robert, 84, 98
Harris, David, 247
Hart, H.L.A., 68, 211, 207
Hart, Roderick P., 167
Hasian, Marouf A., 180
Havel, Vaclav, 44, 45, 209
Haynes, John Earl, 178
Henwood, Doug, 24, 119, 193
Herman, Edward, 116
Hinks, Peter P., 190
Hoffer, Eric, 127, 128
Holland, Dewitte, 191
Hollihan, Thomas, 95, 96
Holt, Wythe, 143, 147
Holtzman, Elizabeth, 164
Hong, Nathaniel, 159
hooks, bell, 13
Horowitz, David, 200
Horowitz, Donald, 249, 250
Hovenkamp, Herbert, 158
Hunt, Everett Lee, 15, 158
Ikenberry, G. John, 15

Ingram, Jason, 41, 115
Irons, Peter, 43, 46, 48, 227
Ishitsuka, Shoji, 179
Ivie, Robert, 12
Jacoby, Russell, 7, 98, 99, 171
Jamieson, Kathleen, 206
Jeffries, Jr., John C., 145
Jenkins, Steven, 89, 110
Jennings, Marianne M., 52
Johnson, Sonia, 160
Jones, Avis Alexandria, 43
Jordan, Winthrop, 196
Karnow, Stanley, 44, 259
Katz, Stanley N., 35, 132
Kearns, Thomas R., 203
Kellett, Peter M., 83
Kennedy, Donald, 99
Kennedy, Duncan, 121
Kidwell, Erin Rahne, 41
King, Andrew, 73, 75, 130, 159
King, Jr., Martin Luther, 7, 14, 56, 76, 108, 129, 171, 179
Klehr, Harvey, 178
Klumpp, Jim, 96
Kolko, Gabriel, 133
Kornblum, William, 129, 131
Krier, James, 69
Kropotkin, Peter, xvii, 119, 123, 160, 179, 255, 256, 257
Kuhn, Thomas S, 34
Kumar, Surinder, 126
Kuper, Leo, 250
Laitin, David, 251
Lang, Bert, 111
LaRue, L.H, 203
Law, Carolyn Leste, 120
Lawrence, David, 204
Lawson, Don, 163
Lee, WenShu, 94, 95
Lentricchia, Frank, 132
Levy, Leonard W., 158
Lewis, Justin, 38, 134
Leyendecker, Liston Edgington, 181, 182, 183
Lindsey, Almont, 181
Littlejohn, Stephen, 102
Low, Peter W., 145
Luger, Stan, 252
Lum, Dyer D., 169, 171, 172, 173, 175
Macke, Frank, 29
MacKinnon, Catharine A., 68, 105
Madriz, Esther, 107, 136
Makau, Josina, 204
Manicas, Peter T., 175
Maresca, John J., 124
Marger, Martin N., 56, 196
Marx, Karl, 7, 83, 117, 126, 129, 131
McCaughan, Edward J., 109, 115, 259
McGee, Brian, 216, 218
McGee, Michael, 97, 228
McKerrow, Raymie, 34
Meehan, Eileen R., 121
Melson, Robert, 250
Messer-Davidow, Ellen, 35
Midgley, Mary, 67, 257
Miliband, Ralph, 59
Miller-Tutzauer, Carol, 234
Mills, C. Wright, 21, 167
Moberg, David, 119, 193
Moran, Rachel F, 200
Murphy, Cait, 254
Murphy, Bren A.O. , 2, 19, 63
Nader, Ralph, 252
Nakayama, Thomas, 82, 84
Nash, Gary B., 125
Negri, Antonio, 70, 120
Nelles, Walter, 143, 144, 158
Nielsen, Kai, 109
Nietzsche, Friedrich, 4, 7, 74, 75, 76, 91, 117
Nothstine, William, 86, 93, 118
Nussbaum, Martha C., 9, 211
Olivas, Margarita Refugia, 99, 110
Olzak, Susan, 251
Ono, Kent A., 7, 14
Orbe, Mark P., 99, 110
Orwell, George, 163
Owen, Susan, 69, 70, 72
Packer, George, 72
Palley, Claire, 65
Palmeri, Anthony J., 84
Papke, David Ray, 164, 177, 181, 182, 186
Parenti, Christian, 131
Parenti, Michael, 7, 113

Payne, Stanley G., 164
Pearce, W. Barnett, 2, 19, 63, 102
Phillips, Edward., 3, 119
Phillips, Kevin, 119
Pinkerton, Edward C., 3
Plato, 156
Platt, Anthony M., 6, 24, 105
Pollock, Mark A., 2, 19, 63
Putnam, Linda L., 31
Pym, Anne, 93
Rabban, David M., 182, 190, 191
Readings, Bill, 35
Redding, W. Charles, 12
Ricks, Thomas E., 72
Robinson, William I., 10
Rodden, John G., 90, 91, 92, 93
Rodriguez, Amardo, 7, 77, 123
Rorty, Richard, x, xv, 4, 5, 7, 21, 30, 31, 32, 33, 35, 46, 59, 61, 84, 111, 113, 114, 115, 117, 125, 209, 212, 218
Rose, Carol M., 126
Ross, Thomas, 205
Rousseau, Jean-Jacques, 207
Ruff, Allen, 182, 183
Said, Edward, 11, 120
Salvatore, Nick, 180
Sanders, Marion, 88
Sandinista Liberation Front, 202
Sarat, Austin, 203
Sayer, John, 194
Schiappa, Edward, 88
Schiller, Reuel E, 215, 225, 231, 233, 235, 242, 243
Schmitz, David F., 164
Sciffrin, Andre, 7
Scott, Robert L., 8, 46, 48, 77, 227
Seale, Bobby, 188
Sexton, Patricia Cayo, 190
Shapiro, Svi, 29
Sharma, Sohan, 126
Shlapentokh, Dmitry, 15
Silcock, T.H., 249, 250
Simon, Steven, 91, 118
Simpson, John, 3
Singer, Peter, 199, 200, 246, 253, 259
Sklar, Holly, 212
Slater, Philip, 6, 196
Slaughter, Thomas P., 41, 158
Sloan, John. H., 73
Smith, Christopher E., 43
Smith, Donald K., 8
Solomon, Martha, 25, 216
Sontag, Susan, 14
Spitzack, Carole, 8, 90
Staples, Steven, 11, 116, 175, 194
Stewart, Charles, 106, 178, 180, 183, 194
Stowell, David O., 141
Strate, Lance, 55
Swartz, Omar, v, xv, xvi, xvii, 94, 118
Taylor, Alan, 158
Thayer, Lee, 85, 86, 88
Thomas, Francis-Noel, 81
Thoreau, Henry David, 133, 166
Trent, Judith S., 12
Trofimov, Yaroslav, 250
Tucker, Robert, 59
Turner, Mark, 81
Tutzauer, Frank E., 234
Tyson, Ann Scott, 57
Unger, Roberto Mangabeira, 66, 68
Van Alstyne, William W., 39
Vatz, Richard, 212
Veblen, Thorstein B., 124
Voltaire, 61
Voos, Paula B., 139
Voss, Kim, 141
Wacquant, Loic, 201
Wallace, Karl R., 222
Wallis, Victor, 51
Wander, Philip C., xiii, 13, 14, 24, 25, 87, 88, 89, 90, 92, 110, 118
Ward, Tony, 58
Weaver, Richard, xi, 208, 216, 217, 218, 219, 225, 227, 228, 242
Webster, Noah, 3
Weiner, Edmund S., 3
Weinreb, Lloyd, 212
White, James Boyd, xi, 37, 197
Wilkinson, James D., 164
Willis, Paul E., 130
Wilson, Carter, 191, 201
Wood, Julia T., 242
Wright, R.S., 22, 144, 167
Zarefsky, David., 218, 234
Zinn, Howard., 7, 44, 50, 119, 133, 140, 141, 157, 174, 175, 182, 183, 185, 186, 191, 193, 252, 259

# FRONTIERS IN POLITICAL COMMUNICATION

*General Editors*
*Lynda Lee Kaid and Bruce Gronbeck*

At the heart of how citizens, governments, and the media interact is the communication process, a process that is undergoing tremendous changes as we embrace a new millennium. Never has there been a time when confronting the complexity of these evolving relationships been so important to the maintenance of civil society. This series seeks books that advance the understanding of this process from multiple perspectives and as it occurs in both institutionalized and non-institutionalized political settings. While works that provide new perspectives on traditional political communication questions are welcome, the series also encourages the submission of manuscripts that take an innovative approach to political communication, which seek to broaden the frontiers of study to incorporate critical and cultural dimensions of study as well as scientific and theoretical frontiers.

For more information or to submit material for consideration, contact:

BRUCE E. GRONBECK
Obermann Center for Advanced Studies
N134 OH
The University of Iowa
Iowa City, IA 52242-5000

LYNDA LEE KAID
Political Communication Center
Department of Communication
University of Oklahoma
Norman, OK 73109

To order other books in this series, please contact our Customer Service Department:

(800) 770-LANG (within the U.S.)
(212) 647-7706 (outside the U.S.)
(212) 647-7707 FAX

Or browse online by series:

WWW.PETERLANGUSA.COM